Examining Court Delay

The Pace of Litigation in 26 Urban Trial Courts, 1987

by
John Goerdt

with
Chris Lomvardias
Geoff Gallas
Barry Mahoney

National Center for State Courts

Final report of a research project conducted pursuant to a grant to the National Center for State Courts from the Bureau of Justice Assistance, U.S. Department of Justice.

©1989 National Center for State Courts
Printed in the United States of America
NCSC R-112

Library of Congress Cataloging-in-Publication Data
Goerdt, John.
　Examining court delay: the pace of litigation in 26 urban trial courts, 1987 / by John Goerdt, with Chris Lomvardias, Geoff Gallas, Barry Mahoney.
　　p. cm.
　Includes bibliographical references.
　ISBN 0-09656-094-5
　1. Court congestion and delay—United States. 2. Court administration—United States. I. Lomvardias, Chris. II. Gallas, Geoff. III. Mahoney, Barry. IV. Title.
　KF8727.G64　1989
　347.73′013—dc20
　[347.30713]　　　　　　　　　　　　　　　　　　　89-13271
　　　　　　　　　　　　　　　　　　　　　　　　　　　　CIP

Final report of a research project conducted pursuant to a grant to the National Center for State Courts from the Bureau of Justice Assistance, United States Department of Justice.

This project was supported by Grant Number 87-DD-CX-0002 awarded by the Bureau of Justice Assistance (BJA), Office of Justice Programs, U.S. Department of Justice. BJA provided $1,600,000 for phase I of the Large Court Capacity (LCC) Increase Program. The pace of litigation study, which was part of the LCC Program, cost $187,000. These funds amounted to 100 percent of the costs of the project. The Assistant Attorney General, Office of Justice Programs, coordinates the activities of the following program offices and bureaus: the Bureau of Justice Assistance, the Bureau of Justice Statistics, the National Institute of Justice, the Office of Juvenile Justice and Delinquency Prevention, and the Office for Victims of Crime. Points of view or opinions in this document are those of the author and do not necessarily represent the official position or policies of the U.S. Department of Justice.

Table of Contents

	Page
List of Figures	v
List of Tables	vii
Acknowledgments	ix
Foreword	xi
Summary of Findings	xiii

The Pace of Litigation in 26 Urban Trial Courts, 1987 3
    Notes.. 9

The Pace of Civil Case Litigation, 1987 11
    Civil Case Processing Time in 25 Urban Trial Courts 11
    The ABA Civil Case Disposition Time Standards 15
    Civil Caseload Mix 17
    Jury Trial Rates and Disposition Times 23
    Court Size and Court Resources 26
    Caseflow Management Procedures 30
        Calendar Type and Judicial Assignments 30
        Early Control, Trial Backup Systems, and
            Firm Trial Dates 32
        Disposition Time Goals 35
    Civil Case Backlog Index 36
    Summary of Factors Related to the Pace of
        Civil Case Litigation 38
    Perceived Causes of Civil Case Delay 41
    Trends in the Pace of Civil Case Litigation: 1976–1987...... 43
    Summary: The Pace of Civil Case Litigation, 1987 48
    Notes.. 50

The Pace of Felony Case Litigation, 1987 53
   Felony Case Processing Times in 26 Urban Trial Courts 53
   The ABA Criminal Case Disposition Time Standards 57
   Felony Caseload Mix 59
   Jury Trial Rates and Disposition Times 66
   Bench Warrant Rates 69
   Court Size: Population and Number of Filings and Judges 71
   Court Resources: Felony Caseload per Judge 73
   Charging and Caseflow Management Procedures 75
     Charging, Calendar, and Judicial Assignment Systems ... 75
     Disposition Time Goals and Caseflow Information 78
     Early Resolution of Pretrial Motions and
       Firm Trial Dates 80
   Backlog Index 83
   Jail Crowding 84
   Summary of Factors Related to the Pace of
     Felony Case Litigation 86
   Perceived Causes of Felony Case Delay 90
   Trends in the Pace of Felony Case Litigation: 1976-1987 92
   Trends in Drug-Related Cases and the Pace of Litigation 97
   The Relationship Between Civil and
     Felony Caseflow Management 99
   Summary: The Pace of Felony Case Litigation, 1987 101
   Implications for Court Management and Future Research 103
     Implications for Court Management 103
     Implications for Future Research 106
   Notes 109

Appendices 113

Bibliography 139

List of Figures

		Page
1.	Courts in the NCSC Pace of Litigation Study, 1987 by Region of the United States	6
2.	Median Civil Case Processing Times for Large Urban Trial Courts–1987	12
3.	All Civil Cases, Filing to Disposition–1987	13
4.	All Civil Cases with a Trial Readiness Document Filed, Filing to Disposition–1987	14
5.	Percent of All Civil Cases over ABA Standards–1987	16
6.	Average Civil Caseload Mix, 23 Large Urban Trial Courts–1987	17
7.	Civil Case Mix–1987	18
8.	Tort Cases, Filing to Disposition–1987	20
9.	Contract Cases, Filing to Disposition–1987	22
10.	Tort vs. Contract Cases, Filing to Disposition–1987	23
11.	Jury Trials vs. All Civil Cases, Filing to Disposition–1987 ...	25
12.	Civil Caseload per FTE Civil Judge–1987	28
13.	Civil Case Mix and Caseload per FTE Judge–1987	29

14. Summary: Bivariate Correlations Related to
    Civil Case Processing Time–1987 38

15. Summary: Multivariate Analysis of Factors Related to
    Civil Case Processing Time–1987 40

16. Median Felony Case Processing Times for
    Large Urban Trial Courts–1987 54

17. Felony Case Processing Time, Arrest to Disposition–1987 ... 55

18. Felony Case Processing Time, Indictment/Information to
    Disposition–1987 56

19. Percent of All Felony Cases Over ABA Standards–1987 58

20. Average Felony Caseload Mix, 23 Large
    Urban Trial Courts–1987 59

21. Felony Caseload Mix–1987 60

22. Drug Sale vs. Most Serious Cases, Indictment/Information
    to Disposition–1987 65

23. Drug Sale vs. Less Serious Cases, Indictment/Information
    to Disposition–1987 66

24. Jury Trial Cases vs. All Felony Cases, Indictment/
    Information to Disposition–1987 67

25. Felony Cases Filed per FTE Felony Judge–1987 74

26. Summary: Bivariate Correlations Related to
    Felony Case Processing Time–1987 87

27. Summary: Multivariate Analysis of Factors Related to
    Felony Case Processing Times–1987 89

List of Tables

		Page
1.	Jury Trial Rate and All Civil Case Processing Time–1987	24
2.	Court Size, Filings per Judge, and Tort Case Processing Time–1987	27
3.	Calendar, Judicial Assignment, and Tort Case Processing Time–1987	31
4.	Elements of Caseflow Control and Tort Case Processing Time–1987	34
5.	Civil Case Backlog Index and Tort Case Processing Time–1987	37
6.	Rating Problems Affecting Civil Case Delay–1987	42
7.	Tort Case Processing Time Trends, Filing to Disposition, 1976–1987	44
8.	Trends in Civil Case Filings per FTE Civil Judge, 1976–1987	45
9.	Median Felony Case Processing Times by Case Types–1987	64
10.	Jury Trial Rate and Felony Case Processing Time–1987	68

11. Percent Bench Warrants, Cases Over ABA Standards, and Felony Case Processing Time–1987. 70

12. Court Size, Filings per Judge, and Felony Case Processing Time–1987 72

13. Charging Procedure and Felony Case Processing Time–1987 76

14. Calendar Type, Judicial Assignment, and Felony Case Processing Time–1987 77

15. Elements of Caseflow Control and Felony Case Processing Time–1987 80

16. Backlog Index and Felony Case Processing Time–1987 83

17. Jail Crowding and Information Received about Jail Population 85

18. Rating Problems Affecting Felony Case Delay–1987 91

19. Felony Case Processing Time Trends, Indictment/ Information to Disposition, 1976–1987. 93

20. Trends in Filings per FTE Felony Judge, 1976–1987 95

21. Percentage of Drug-Related Cases and Case Processing Times, 1983–1987 98

22. Rankings on Civil and Felony Case Processing Times–1987 100

Acknowledgments

The National Center for State Courts (NCSC) is grateful to the Bureau of Justice Assistance (BJA) for its support of this research project. Special thanks go to Jay Marshall, BJA Chief, Courts Branch; Dr. Charles Smith, Director of the Bureau of Justice Assistance; James Swain, BJA Director of Discretionary Grants; and Linda McKay, BJA program manager. The NCSC is also indebted to all the presiding judges, court administrators, clerks, and other court staff in each court that provided assistance in data collection and comments on the report. Others who provided important review and comments include David Rottman, Victor Flango, Roger Hanson, Thomas Henderson, David Steelman, Alex Aikman, Harvey Solomon, Ingo Keilitz, and Joy Chapper. JoAnn Adkins and Kelly Smith made substantial contributions through editing, typing, and data entry. Finally, several coders and research assistants, especially Leah Hardenbergh, Charles Powers, and Mary Jo Allen, were invaluable. Their efforts made this a highly accurate report.

Foreword

With data from 26 urban trial courts, this report presents the most broadly based empirical evidence ever collected regarding the extent and nature of court delay. The study shows that several courts provide a relatively expeditious pace of litigation and are within 10 percent of meeting the American Bar Association (ABA) disposition time standards. Many courts, however, continue to experience varying degrees of court delay and must improve considerably in order to approach compliance with the ABA or other nationally recognized time standards. But substantial reduction in court delay is clearly achievable. Those courts that instituted delay reduction programs in the 1980s have shown considerable improvement in their pace of litigation.

Unlike most earlier studies of case processing time, *Examining Court Delay: The Pace of Litigation in 26 Urban Trial Courts, 1987* provides some clear policy directions for reducing delay. In both civil and felony cases, early court control and firm trial dates were characteristics shared by faster courts. While these factors require coordination among courts, the private bar, prosecutors, law enforcement agencies, and others, the achievement of early control, early resolution of motions, and firmer scheduling of trials are within the court's control.

Another important contribution of this study is its analysis of the impact of drug-related cases on court delay. This report and future articles derived from the data on drug cases provide a good empirical basis for assessing the impact on the courts of the "war on drugs."

The Bureau of Justice Assistance (BJA) is pleased to have sponsored this important research project by the National Center for State Courts (NCSC). The BJA and NCSC are very grateful to the judges, administrators, clerks and court staff in the 26 courts who make the data collection on which this project rests possible. We believe that as a result of this work and others in progress the efficiency of court management and the quality of justice in the United States is being advanced.

>CHARLES P. SMITH
>*Director*
>Bureau of Justice Assistance
>
>JAY MARSHALL
>*Chief, Courts Branch*
>Bureau of Justice Assistance

Summary of Findings

This report is the product of the most recent and largest national study ever performed regarding the pace of litigation in urban trial courts. Although the findings provide some basis for optimism about reducing court delay, there is considerable evidence that much work remains.

The good news is that 7 of the 26 large urban trial courts were close (i.e., within 5 percent) to meeting the ABA disposition time standard that all felony cases be disposed within one year after arrest. Fourteen had 10 percent or less of their cases over one year old at disposition. None of the 26 courts, however, were close (i.e., within 5 percent) to meeting the ABA standard that 98 percent of felony cases be disposed within 180 days after arrest.

Data from civil cases in 25 urban trial courts are not as encouraging as data from felony cases. Only two courts were close (within 5 percent) to meeting the ABA disposition time standard that all civil cases be disposed within two years after the complaint is filed. Seven others had 10 percent or less of their cases over two years old at disposition. Furthermore, the ABA standards suggest that 90 percent of all civil cases be disposed within one year after filing. None of the 25 courts met this goal, and only one was within 10 percent of the standard.

A substantial association was found between the rankings of the courts on felony case processing times and their rankings on civil case processing times. Courts that were relatively fast on felony cases tended to be fast on civil cases; courts slow on one tended to be slow on the other. This suggests that delay reduction efforts, whether for felony or civil cases, should involve effective resource and caseflow management across all cases within a court's jurisdiction.

Several factors related to the pace of civil and criminal case processing were examined. Correlation coefficients suggest complex relationships among the indicators of court size, case mix, caseload per judge, case management characteristics, and case processing times. A more sophisticated multivariate analysys leads to the identification of the most important factors producing relatively expeditious case processing. This analysis revealed that for civil cases, early court control over the scheduling of case events was the most important predictor of shorter case processing times. Case processing time goals were also important, especially in reducing the age of the oldest cases. In addition case mix (i.e., a larger percentage of tort cases) was related to longer case processing times, but only for cases in which a trial readiness document had been filed. Consistent with past research, filings per judge were not related to civil case processing times. In general, court size, filings per judge, calendar type, and jury trial rate were not significant predictors of civil case processing times when other factors were controlled through statistical analysis.

Analysis of felony case data, using the same statistical techniques, revealed similar findings. A firm trial date policy (i.e., a high percentage of jury trial cases starting on the first scheduled trial date) was the best predictor of faster case processing times. Courts that resolved pretrial motions earlier were more likely to have firm trial dates. Together, early resolution of pretrial motions and firm trial dates indicate that the faster courts tended to feature early and continuous control over their cases and caseflow. However, higher percentages of most serious (murder, rape, and robbery) and drug sale cases and a higher percentage of cases with a bench warrant were also related to longer disposition times. The size of the court and caseload per judge were not related to the pace of felony case litigation.

In general, these findings should be encouraging to judges and administrators. The most salient factor related to faster disposition times in civil and felony cases is early and continuous court control. Unlike court size, case mix, or caseload per judge, the timing and degree of control over caseflow is largely within the control of the court.

Perceptions of judges and court administrators about the causes of court delay were also examined. Judges and administrators from both fast and slow courts rated the increase in drug-related cases as a serious problem. In addition, judges and administrators from the six courts with the slowest civil case processing times rated "insufficient number of judges" as a "serious" problem. Judges and administrators from the six fastest civil courts rated "insufficient number of judges" as a "minor" problem. Interestingly, there was little difference between the faster and slower courts in the number of cases filed per judge. Ratings from the slower courts probably reflect the traditional view that a relative lack of judicial resources slows the pace of litigation. This view is not supported by the data reported here. However, nonjudicial resources (e.g., the number of prosecutors, public defenders, or court staff), which were not examined in this study, could play an important role in determining the pace of felony case litigation.

Of course, one interpretation of the finding that none of the 26 courts met the ABA case processing standards is that none or few of these state trial courts had sufficient judicial resources. There is a point when the caseload per judge becomes so large that even effectively managed courts produce slower case processing times. Data on pace of litigation trends since 1976 suggest that a caseload/case processing saturation point was reached in five courts (three civil and two felony). The five courts shared these characteristics: (1) relatively fast case processing times in 1983 or 1985; (2) comparatively large caseloads per judge; and (3) a substantial increase in filings per judge from 1985 to 1987. Despite relatively fast case processing times in previous years, increased caseload in these five courts from 1985 to 1987 resulted in longer case processing times in 1987 as compared to 1985. Thus, an efficient court reaches a point where significant caseload increases must be matched with additional judges.

Effective caseflow and resource management are clearly related to a faster pace of litigation. Several findings support this conclusion. First, early and continuous control over case events was the best predictor of faster case processing times. Second, caseload per judge was not related to the pace of litigation. Third, the percentage of bench warrant cases was moderately to strongly associated with the percentage of all felony cases (including bench warrant cases) over the ABA disposition time standards, but a higher percentage of bench warrant cases was also related to a higher percentage of nonbench warrant cases over the ABA time standards. Thus, efficient criminal caseflow management appeared to be associated with effectiveness in pretrial screening and monitoring of defendants released on recognizance or bail.

Finally, analysis of case processing time trends from 1976 to 1987 shows that more progress was made in felony than in civil case processing. Only 5 of 18 courts reduced median tort disposition times since 1976, while 8 of 17 courts reduced median upper court processing times in felony cases since 1976. Each of the courts that reduced civil case processing times by 10 percent or more since 1976 had changed case management procedures to reduce civil case delay. Court delay can be reduced substantially where there is a commitment to do so. But given the overall findings in this report, it is clear that much work remains before these and other courts meet the ABA case processing time standards.

Examining Court Delay

*The Pace of Litigation
in 26 Urban Trial Courts, 1987*

The Pace of Litigation in 26 Urban Trial Courts, 1987

Delay haunts the administration of justice. It postpones the rectification of wrong and the vindication of the unjustly accused. It crowds the dockets of the courts, increasing the costs for all litigants, pressuring judges to take shortcuts, interfering with the prompt and deliberate disposition of those causes in which all parties are diligent and prepared for trial, and overhanging the entire process with the pall of disorganization and insolubility. But even these are not the worst of what delay does. The most erratic gear in the justice machinery is at the place of fact finding, and possibilities for error multiply rapidly as time elapses between the original fact and its judicial determination. If the facts are not fully and accurately determined, then the wisest judge cannot distinguish between merit and demerit. If we do not get the facts right, there is little chance for the judgment to be right.
—*Southern Pacific Transportation Co. v. Stoot*, 530 S.W.2d 930 (1975).

This report will present the findings from the largest national database ever compiled to examine the pace of litigation in urban America. Data were collected from 26 large urban trial courts regarding how caseload charactcristics, judicial resources, and case management procedures are related to case processing time. But why another study of the pace of litigation? Literally hundreds of articles have been written since the early part of this century that directly or indirectly address court delay.[1] Most writers, naturally, decry the evils of delay. This does not mean, however, that there is a consensus about the nature, extent, or, especially, the remedies for court delay. Sarat, for instance, suggests we must at least consider the possibility that "slow justice is more certain justice."[2] Others question whether a slower pace of litigation entails serious evils.[3] Most delay, after all, is simply "waiting" time rather than processing time. In an earlier era, Zeisel also argued that delay was not a problem as long as the court was prepared to take the next case awaiting disposition.[4] This work begins from the premise that case processing time beyond the time necessary for a fair resolution of a case has a negative effect on the quality of justice. Memories fade, witnesses move or die, plaintiffs may be deterred from seeking legal vindication of a claim, and undue delay may favor one litigant over another. Furthermore, delay could ultimately set criminals free.[5] It is also clear that the American public considers court delay a serious national problem.[6]

Concern about the negative effect of court delay is long-standing. Few of the early articles or books, however, were grounded with empirical research. But since 1976 at least eight national projects[7] and a number of smaller studies[8] have focused on the pace of litigation. These studies advanced our understanding of the extent and nature of case processing times in urban trial courts. Most importantly, they resulted in a reassessment of the "old conventional wisdom" about the causes of court delay. For instance, earlier National Center for State Courts (NCSC) studies by Church et al. (1978a) and Mahoney et al. (1985, 1988) found that conventional explanations for court delay, including court size, caseload per judge, the percentage of violent felonies in the caseload, and the type of criminal case calendaring system, were generally unrelated to case processing times. According to the "new conventional wisdom," efforts to reduce court delay should concentrate on such factors as more effective court leadership, commitment to achievement of disposition time goals, early and continuous court control over caseflow, and increased judicial accountability for case processing.[9]

One outgrowth of the movement toward greater court control over caseflow has been the adoption of disposition time standards by the American Bar Association (ABA), the Conference of Chief Justices (CCJ), and the Conference of State Court Administrators (COSCA). Adoption of disposition time standards by these organizations was an important milestone in judicial administration. The standards provide goals for courts, which before had little guidance regarding a measurable definition of delay. This and earlier studies make clear that much work needs to be done in most urban trial courts before they achieve these standards. For example, none of the 18 courts in the Mahoney et al. (1988) study of 1985 case processing times achieved the ABA time standards. Therefore, despite the wealth of research and writing in the area of court delay, the pace of litigation in American courts continues to warrant concern and attention.

This report adds to our understanding of delay in urban trial courts by providing the most current barometer of case processing times among the largest number of courts ever included in a national pace of litigation study.

The 1987 study alone includes approximately 31,000 cases from the 26 courts, whose jurisdictions include approximately 12 percent of the United States population. Second, the report reexamines hypotheses regarding the relationships among court size, case mix, caseload per judge, case management procedures, and case processing time. Finally, by building upon earlier research performed by the NCSC and others,[10] this study provides a look at trends in the pace of litigation among 17 urban trial courts since 1976.[11]

METHODOLOGY AND REPORT ORGANIZATION

Figure 1 displays the list of sites included in this study. Each court, identified by the city in which it resides, includes the general jurisdiction state court for the county in which the city is located. Figure 1 reports whether earlier studies of case processing time existed for each court, the population served by each of the study courts, the total number of judges in the court, and the court's jurisdiction. Courts were selected with the goal of being able to look at change in case processing times over a period of years. Of the 26 sites in this study, 17 were selected because they were included in the NCSC study by Mahoney and others of civil and felony case processing times from 1983 through 1985. Nineteen sites were part of the landmark NCSC study by Church and others of the pace of litigation during 1976 in 21 courts.[12] The remaining 7 courts were added to expand the sample and to increase the representation of courts from various regions of the country. The sample provides good representation from the various regions of the United States and maximizes our ability to look at the pace of litigation over time. But the nonrandom sample of courts does limit the ability to generalize findings to large urban trial courts as a whole.

It is essential to note that sampling and coding procedures used by Church et al. (1978a) and Mahoney et al. (1985, 1988) were followed as closely as possible in this study. By remaining consistent with these earlier studies, comparisons over time can be made with a higher degree of confidence.

Criminal cases in the sample included only felony cases in which an indictment or information was filed in the general jurisdiction court[13] and in which a disposition (guilty plea, dismissal, deferred adjudication, diversion, or trial judgment) was entered during 1987. Civil cases in the sample included all cases (excluding probate, domestic relations, small claims, appeals from a lower court, and injunctions) in which a disposition (settlement, dismissal, summary or default judgment, or trial verdict) was entered during 1987.[14] Cases were randomly selected from lists of cases that were disposed during 1987 in each court. An additional random sample of 100 cases that were disposed by trial was obtained from most courts to increase the number of trials for purposes of data analysis.

Approximately 500 civil and 500 felony cases were randomly sampled (excluding the additional trial samples) from each site. Approximately 370 randomly sampled cases are sufficient in most courts to assure that the

Figure 1

Courts in the NCSC Pace of Litigation Study, 1987 by Region of the United States

	1986 Population[a]	Total # of Judges	Jurisdiction[b]
Northeast			
Boston, MA (Suffolk Co. Superior Court)*†	661,000	16	C/F
Bronx, NY (Bronx Co. Supreme Court)*†	1,194,000	37	C/F/D
Jersey City, NJ (Hudson Co. Superior Court)*	553,000	25	C/F/S/D/P/H/J
Newark, NJ (Essex Co. Superior Court)*†	842,000	50	C/F/S/D/P/H/J
Pittsburgh, PA (Allegheny Co. Common Pleas Court)*†	1,374,000	41	C/F/M/D/P/H/J
Providence, RI (Superior Court)*	582,000	9	C/F/M
Southeast			
Atlanta, GA (Fulton Co. Superior Court)*†	623,000	15	C/F/M/D/J/O
District of Columbia (Superior Court)	626,000	51	ALL TYPES
Fairfax, VA (Fairfax Co. Circuit Court)	710,000	11	C/F/M/D/O
Miami, FL (Dade Co. Circuit Court)*†	1,769,000	60	C/F/M/D/P/J
New Orleans, LA (Orleans Parish District Court)*†	554,000	36	C/F/M/D/P/J/O
Norfolk, VA (Norfolk Cir. Court)	275,000	9	C/F/M/D/P/O
Midwest			
Cleveland, OH (Cuyahoga Co. Common Pleas Court)*†	1,445,000	37	C/F/D/P/J
Dayton, OH (Montgomery Co. Common Pleas Court)*	566,000	12	C/F/D/P/J
Detroit, MI (Wayne Co. Circuit/Recorder's Courts)*†	2,164,000	69	C/F/D
Minneapolis, MN (Hennepin Co. District Court)*†	988,000	59	ALL TYPES
St. Paul, MN (Ramsey Co. District Court)*†	474,000	32	ALL TYPES
Wichita, KS (Sedgwick Co. District Court)*	391,000	22	ALL TYPES
Western			
Colorado Springs, CO (El Paso Co. District Court)	380,000	20	C/F/D/P/J
Denver (Denver Co. District Court)	505,000	20	C/F/D
Oakland, CA (Alameda Co. Superior Court)*†	1,209,000	33	C/F/D/P/J
Phoenix, AZ (Maricopa Co. Superior Court)*†	1,900,000	56	C/F/M/D/P/J
Portland, OR (Multnomah Co. Circuit Court)*†	567,000	34	C/F/D/P/H/J
Salinas, CA (Monterey Co. Superior Court)	340,000	8	C/F/D/P/J
San Diego, CA (San Diego Co. Superior Court)*†	2,201,000	52	C/F/D/P/J
Tucson, AZ (Pima Co. Superior Court)	602,000	20	C/F/M/D/P/J

* In Mahoney et al. (1985 & 1988); data from 1983–1985.
† In Church et al. (1978a); data from 1976.
a From *County and City Data Book, 1988*, U.S. Bureau of the Census.
b Jurisdiction: C = Civil (includes tort, contract and real property); F = Felony; M = Misdemeanor; S = Small Claims; D = Domestic Relations; P = Probate and Estate; H = Mental Health; J = Juvenile; O = Ordinance Violation/Traffic.

statistics derived from the sample are within plus or minus 5 percent of the actual case processing times in the respective courts.[15]

The case processing time statistics reported in this study are in the form of percentiles. The median (i.e., 50th percentile) is the midpoint along the range of case processing times; half the cases took more time and half took less time to disposition.[16] A 90th percentile of 550 days means 90 percent of the cases were less than 550 days old at disposition and 10 percent were more than 550 days old. Pearson's correlation coefficient (r) is used to measure the degree of association between various factors and measures of case processing time. A correlation coefficient, which ranges from -1.0 to 1.0, indicates the strength of a relationship between two variables. A correlation is stronger as it approaches 1.0 or –1.0. A positive correlation indicates that one variable (e.g., case processing time) increases as the other variable (e.g., percent tort cases) increases. A negative correlation indicates that one variable (e.g., case processing time) increases as the other (e.g., filings per judge) decreases. Although there is no consensus on how to describe the strength of correlations, the following criteria and terminology will be used to interpret the correlation coefficients:

+/– 0 to .19 = no relationship;
+/– .20 to .39 = weak relationship;
+/– .40 to .59 = moderate relationship;
+/– .60 or higher = strong relationship.

This report will focus primarily on factors that display at least moderate and statistically significant correlations with case processing times.[17]

It should be noted that 26 courts constitute a relatively small sample for correlation analysis. Correlations can change with a small sample if one or two courts are excluded due to missing or noncomparable data. Thus, correlations should be viewed as a form of evidence, not as definitive proof, of the strength of a relationship between factors.[18]

At the end of the sections on the pace of civil case litigation and felony case litigation a summary subsection is included. In each summary, the findings from the preceding bivariate correlation analysis are refined through a more sophisticated statistical technique.[19] The analysis clarifies which factors are most important in explaining differences in the pace of litigation.

The report is organized in the following manner. First, the findings regarding civil case processing are presented, followed by the findings regarding the pace of felony litigation. Each of the sections (civil and felony) begins with an overview of the pace of litigation among the courts. Court performance is examined in light of the ABA disposition time standards. Then, through the presentation of charts and bivariate correlation statistics, various factors are examined to determine their relationship to the pace of litigation. These factors include court size, case mix, caseload per judge, jury trial rates, caseflow management procedures, and backlog. In the section on felony case processing, the relationship of jail crowding to case processing time is also examined. After the factors related to case processing time are examined, findings are summarized and refined through multivariate analysis. Ratings of problems related to case processing, as provided by the court administrators or presiding judges, are then reviewed. At the end of each section, trends in the pace of litigation are examined, followed by a summary of the major findings in the previous sections. The report then addresses the relationship between felony and civil case processing times and concludes with an examination of the implications of this study for court management and future research.

Notes

1. Some of the prominent works on the issue of court delay are: Church et al. (1978a); Church (1982, 1986); Friesen et al. (1978); Neubauer et al. (1981); Grossman et al. (1981); Mahoney et al. (1985, 1988); Flanders (1977, 1980); Solomon (1973); Solomon and Somerlot (1987); Katz et al. (1972); Gillespie (1977); Zeisel et al. (1959). For comprehensive bibliographies on court delay, see Church (1978b) and Otto (1985).
2. Sarat (1978) p. 324.
3. See Grossman et al. (1981).
4. Zeisel et al. (1959).
5. Recently, a murder suspect was freed in Montgomery County, Maryland, when the prosecutor failed to get a case to trial within the 180-day time limit. See Hall (1986), *Washington Post*, p. A1.
6. See Yankelovich et al. (1978).
7. See Flanders (1977); Church et al. (1978a); Friesen (1978); Grossman et al. (1981); Neubauer et al. (1981); Chapper et al. (1984); Mahoney et al. (1985, 1988).
8. See, e.g., Boyum (1979); Gillespie (1977); Nimmer (1976); Luskin and Luskin (1986); Flemming et al. (1987).
9. See Mahoney et al. (1988) pp. 197-205; Church (1982) pp. 404-06.
10. Church et al. (1978a); Mahoney et al. (1985, 1988); Neubauer (1981, 1983).
11. The data from two of the courts are from 1979; the data from one court are from 1978.
12. Church et al. (1978a).
13. A felony case included all charges against one defendant in one indictment or information. California courts and the Bronx allow guilty pleas to felony charges in lower courts so that some cases from these sites do not have indictments or informations filed in the upper (general jurisdiction) court. Guilty pleas to felony charges filed by means of an information in the lower court were included in this report in the analysis of upper court time (from filing an information or indictment to disposition).
14. Domestic relations and probate cases are excluded for two reasons. First, they were excluded from earlier pace of litigation studies (e.g., Church et al. (1978a); Mahoney et al. (1988)), and it was desirable to maintain comparability. Second, probate and domestic cases are very different from tort and contract cases and deserve separate attention. To study all these case types in one study would require much larger sample sizes in order to analyze the case types separately.
15. Approximately 370 cases also provide confidence that the statistics derived from the samples will be reliable within plus or minus five percentage points in 95 out of 100 samples. See Arkin and Colton (1963) p. 145. Because they are based on smaller sample sizes, case processing times for specific case types (e.g., torts, drug cases) have a range of error greater than plus or minus 5 percent. For the total number of valid cases included in the various case processing time measures for each court, see Appendices P and Q.
16. The median was used rather than the mean (the sum of all disposition times divided by the number of cases in the calculation) for two reasons. Church et al. (1978a) and Mahoney et al. (1985, 1988) reported medians and comparisons with earlier years are a key component of this report. Also, unlike the mean, the median is not skewed upward by unusually long cases. The mean is usually somewhat longer than the median.

17. The strength of a correlation could be moderate but lack statistical significance. A measure of statistical significance indicates the probability (p) that the correlation was due to chance. In this report, a correlation with a probability of .05 or lower (e.g., .01 or .001) is considered statistically significant. This means that the relationship would be likely to occur by chance in only 5 out of 100 samples.

18. Courts with noncomparable data are generally excluded from correlation analyses in this study. Data from a minimum of 12 courts are used for reporting correlations. This is a very small sample size for correlation analysis. The authors recognize the volatility of correlations obtained with small sample sizes. Larger sample sizes are clearly preferable.

19. Through a form of regression analysis, the effects of two explanatory factors (e.g., calendar system and case mix) are examined simultaneously to determine whether neither, one, or both factors display a statistically significant relationship with the dependent variable (case processing time) when both explanatory factors are considered. See also Appendix A.

The Pace of Civil Case Litigation, 1987

Civil Case Processing Time in 25 Urban Trial Courts

The pace of litigation for *all civil* and *trial list* cases in the 25[20] courts is examined first in this report. *All civil* cases is the most inclusive category examined in this study. It includes the case processing times (from filing of a complaint to disposition) for all the civil case types in the court, except probate, domestic relations, and small claims, regardless of the type of disposition (e.g., trial verdict, dismissal, or settlement). Because some courts do not take an active role in moving a case to disposition until the parties request a trial date, the disposition times in *trial list* cases (those in which a trial readiness document had been filed) will also be examined. *Trial list* cases include all case types in which the parties requested a trial. The most inclusive categories of civil cases are examined first, because nationally recognized disposition time standards, which are examined in the next section, apply to all civil cases.

Figure 2 shows the aggregate median, 75th, and 90th percentile case processing times for all civil, tort, contract, trial list, and jury trial cases for all the courts in this study. The median disposition time for all civil cases among all the courts in this study was approximately 11 months (333 days). In other words, half the cases were disposed in 11 months or less, but half the cases took longer. It took 19 months (576 days) for the courts to dispose of 75 percent of their civil cases, and approximately 27 months (819 days) to dispose of 90 percent of their cases. Ten percent of the cases in these courts required more than 27 months from filing of a complaint to disposition. The typical (median) trial list case required 558 days from filing to disposition, 225 days more than the median disposition time for all cases combined. The 90th percentile trial list cases required almost three years (1,079 days). Although tort, contract, and jury trial cases will be examined later, it is worth noting now that the median processing time in tort cases (441) was more than five months longer than in contract cases (286). Finally, as one would expect, cases disposed by jury trial showed the longest median (661 days, over 22 months) and 90th percentile time (1,223 days, just under 3.5 years).

Median case processing times in Figure 2 can be used as a basis for comparison with the performance of courts in this study and for monitoring the overall progress of urban trial courts in the area of court delay. Although the sample of courts was not randomly selected, it provides the broadest available base of knowledge about the pace of civil case litigation.

Obviously, aggregating case processing times obscures the substantial differences in the pace of litigation among the individual courts. **Figure 3** displays the median, 75th, and 90th percentile case processing times for all civil cases for 24 of the 25 courts in the study, and ranks them according to their median time to disposition Median times ranged from 177 days in Dayton to 1,105 days in Boston.[21] Thirteen courts had median times of less than one year; three courts had median times that were longer than two years.

At the 90th percentile, courts ranged from 457 days in Wichita to 2,154 days in Boston. In fact, Wichita disposed of 90 percent of its cases in the time it took the slowest five courts to dispose of 50 percent of their cases.

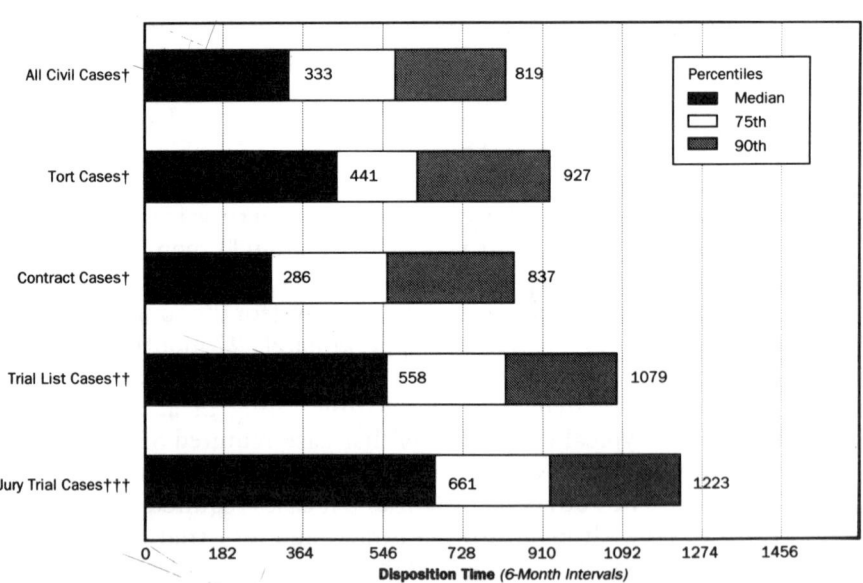

Figure 2
Median Civil Case Processing Times for Large Urban Trial Courts—1987

† Median of the medians from 23 courts.
†† Median from cases in which a trial readiness document was filed (16 courts).
††† Median of the medians from 18 courts.

Some courts with long median times, including Newark and Jersey City, got to their 90th percentile case in a relatively short time compared to other courts with comparable medians. On the other hand, Norfolk, the District of Columbia, and Salinas had relatively long 90th percentile times compared to courts with comparable medians.

The 90th percentile is important because it represents the time required to dispose of those cases that were probably most complex. However, it also reflects the extent to which the court actively monitored the status of cases to assure that settled or inactive cases were recorded as

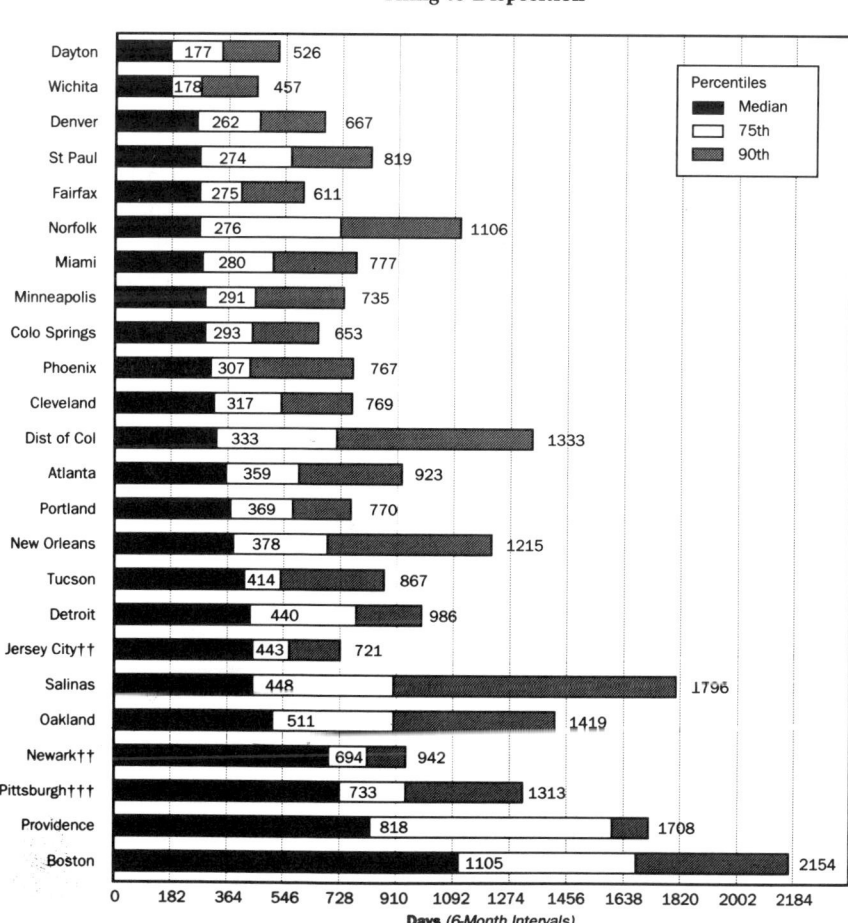

Figure 3
All Civil Cases –1987†
Filing to Disposition

† Excludes probate and domestic relations. San Diego not included; data include only cases in which a trial readiness document was filed.
†† Civil cases include only those in which an answer was filed.
††† Pittsburgh does not include cases disposed by arbitration.

disposed. Some courts have the authority to dismiss cases on their own motion for lack of prosecution after two years (e.g., Fairfax and Norfolk). Other courts are prohibited from dismissing such cases until five years after the complaint is filed (e.g., California courts). Courts that are granted the authority to clear inactive cases from the docket after two years have a greater ability to shorten their overall disposition times. Courts that must wait five years to dismiss cases on their own motion (e.g., Salinas) are disadvantaged compared to courts (e.g., Fairfax and Norfolk) that may dismiss cases after two years.

Trial list cases moved more slowly overall than all other case categories (excluding cases disposed by jury trial, see Figure 2) because trial list cases include only those that reached the stage of setting a trial date. A substantial proportion of cases are settled or dismissed before the stage when a trial date is set in most courts. Median times in trial list cases ranged from 181 days in Wichita to 1,407 days in Providence (see **Figure 4**). There was also considerable disparity in how long it took courts to get to their 90th percentile cases. New Orleans and Salinas had disproportionately long 90th percentile times compared to courts with similar medians.[22] Providence, which was the slowest court among those that used a trial

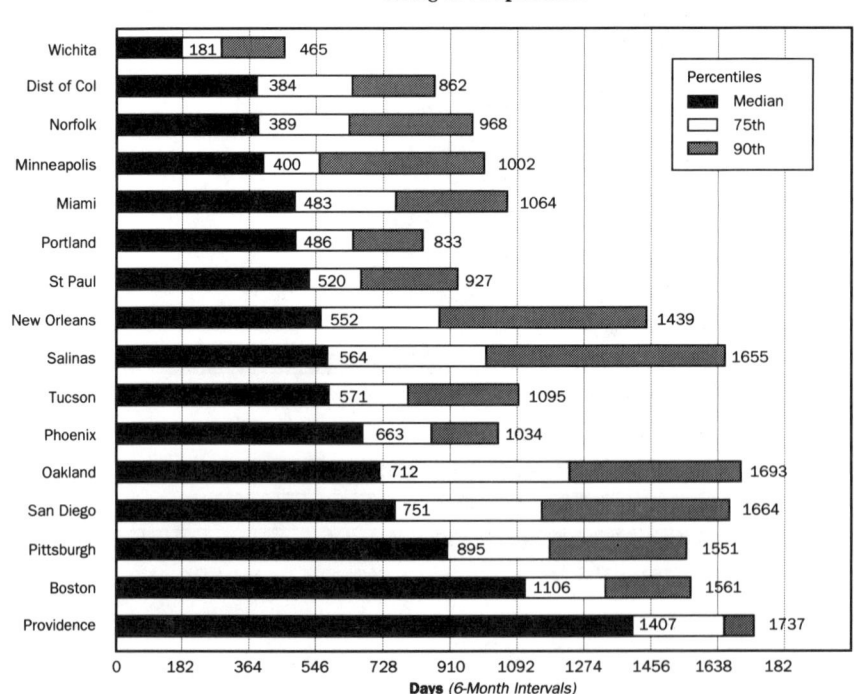

Figure 4
All Civil Cases with a Trial Readiness Document Filed–1987
Filing to Disposition

readiness document, required 1,407 days to dispose of 50 percent of its trial list cases but got to the 90th percentile case 330 days later (1,737 days total). Providence simply had a problem getting cases to trial readiness.[23]

The preceding discussion highlights the variations and patterns within and among courts on case processing times for all civil and trial list cases. However, the statistics presented thus far do not answer an important question: Is there some basis for determining the extent of unnecessary delay in case processing in these courts? The following discussion attempts to address this issue.

The ABA Civil Case Disposition Time Standards

Without some standard that has achieved considerable acceptance in the legal community, among those who know the limitations and the potential of judges and court staff, it is difficult to draw conclusions from the foregoing data regarding the extent of unnecessary delay among the courts in this study. In 1984 the American Bar Association (ABA) adopted the case processing time standards, which had been developed by its National Conference of State Trial Judges. The Conference of State Court Administrators (COSCA) adopted similar time standards in 1983. The COSCA Standards were endorsed by the Conference of Chief Justices (CCJ) in 1984. The standards were passed by each professional organization after considerable study and discussion. It is reasonable, then, to use the standards adopted by these organizations as a basis for estimating the extent of court delay in American trial courts.

The ABA and COSCA/CCJ time standards are listed below. The ABA standards will be referred to throughout this report because they are more clearly stated and, therefore, somewhat more useful.[24]

COSCA/CCJ and ABA Civil Case Disposition Time Standards

	COSCA/CCJ	ABA
Jury Cases	18 months	90% in 12 months
Non-Jury Cases	12 months	98% in 18 months
General Civil		100% in 24 months
Summary Civil (landlord-tenant, small claims, etc.)		30 days

Figure 5 illustrates how the courts performed in 1987 in relation to the ABA time standards. According to the ABA standards, no more than 10 percent of a court's civil cases should be over one year old and no cases should be more than two years old at disposition. Figure 5 suggests that no courts in this study met the ABA standards for all civil cases at either the

one- or two-year marks. At the one-year mark, Wichita came closest to the ABA standard with 18 percent of its cases more than one year old at disposition, eight percentage points over the standard. Dayton was second with 23 percent of its cases more than one year old. The courts ranged up to 96 percent of their cases over one year old at disposition.[25] At the two-year mark, several courts were close to meeting the ABA standard, but none of the courts actually achieved the goal. Wichita was closest to the ABA standard with only 3 percent of its cases over two years old; Dayton had only 5 percent over two years old. On the other hand, three courts had more than 50 percent of their general civil cases over two years old at disposition. Overall, the 23 courts had an average of approximately 20 percent of their civil cases over two years old at disposition.[26]

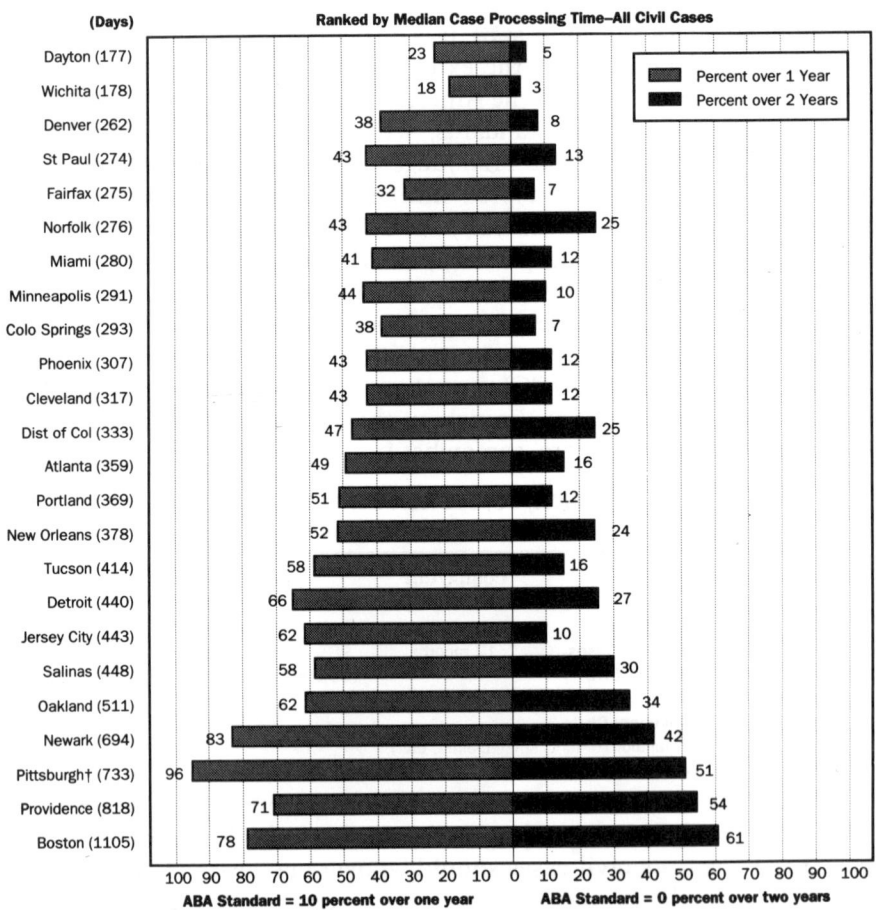

Figure 5
Percent of all Civil Cases over ABA Standards–1987

† Does not include cases disposed by arbitration.

If the ABA and COSCA standards are accepted as reasonable, every court in this study was delayed to some extent, and several had a considerable amount of unnecessary time built into their case processing. Some judges, administrators, and observers might conclude that the standards themselves should be reevaluated if none of the courts studied to this date have met them. It is probably too early to draw such a conclusion; the standards were in effect for only three years before the cases in this study were disposed. Courts will need more time to work toward the goals set out by the ABA and other professional organizations. As it stands now, however, most courts in this study must make considerable improvements in caseflow management to approach the current case processing time standards.

In order to address the problem of unnecessary case processing time, one must first understand the factors that contribute to differences in case processing times within and among courts. This report will examine the impact of case mix, jury trial rates, court size, resources (caseload per judge), and case management procedures on case processing time.

Civil Caseload Mix

In this section, two issues will be addressed. First, the differences in case mix among the courts and the effect of caseload mix on case processing times will be examined. Differences among the courts in the pace of tort and contract case litigation will then be presented.

Figure 6 displays the average civil caseload mix (excluding domestic relations and probate cases) for the 23 courts during 1987.[27] Half (51

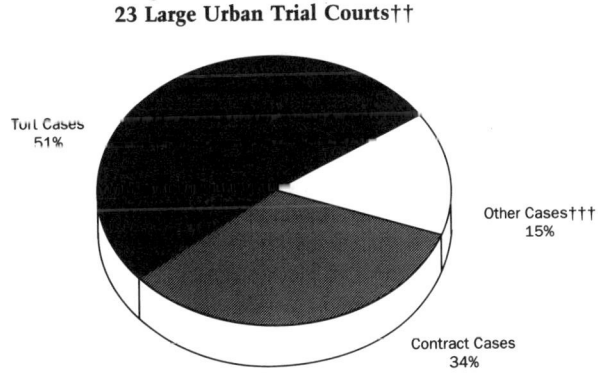

Figure 6
Average Civil Caseload Mix–1987†
23 Large Urban Trial Courts††

Tort Cases 51%

Other Cases††† 15%

Contract Cases 34%

† Average = mean; excludes probate and domestic relations.
†† San Diego includes only trial list cases; Pittsburgh does not include cases disposed by arbitration. Both are excluded.
††† Includes real property, mortgage foreclosures, and eminent domain cases.

percent) of the cases were tort claims; a third (34 percent) were contract or commercial claims; and 15 percent were all other claims, mostly real property issues. Tort (personal injury and property damage) and contract claims dominated the general civil case dockets of these general jurisdiction trial courts.

The averages Figure 6 presents, however, obscure the differences in the types of cases disposed in the 23 courts during 1987. **Figure 7** presents the percentages of tort and contract cases among the caseload for each court. There was significant variation in the percentage of tort cases in the courts' caseloads, ranging from 21 percent in Denver to 87 percent in Jersey City. Note also that the courts in Figure 7 are ranked according to their median processing times for all civil cases. The four courts with the highest percentage of tort cases, Jersey City (87 percent), Newark (82 percent), Oakland (80 percent), and Providence (73 percent), were all among the slowest third of the courts on median time for all civil cases. At first glance, then, it appears that a higher percentage of tort cases were associated with longer case processing times.

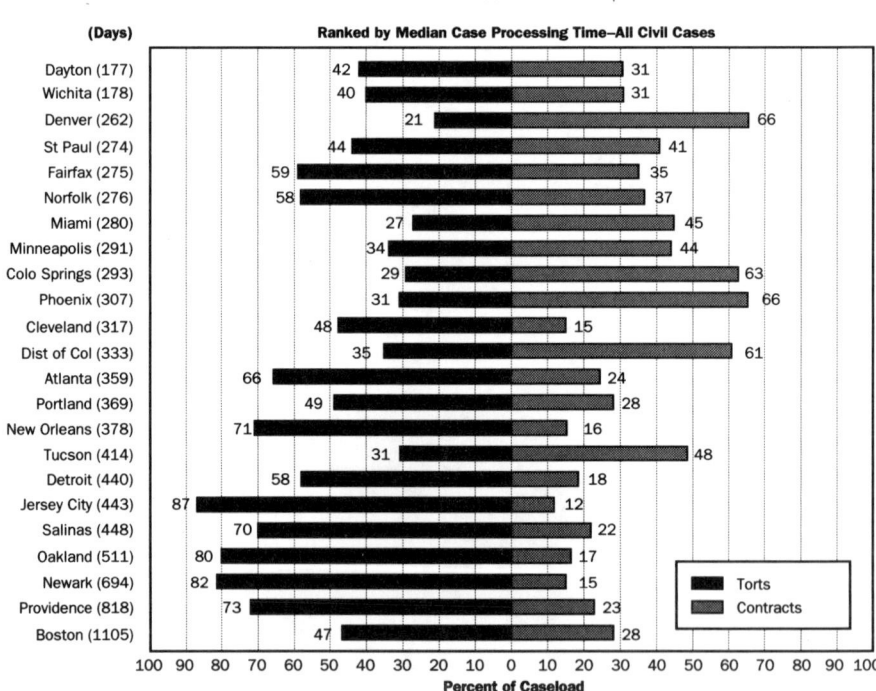

Figure 7
Civil Case Mix–1987†

† Excludes probate and domestic relations. San Diego and Pittsburgh not included; see footnotes in Figure 3. Total for percent torts and percent contracts does not equal 100 percent; the percentage of "other" civil cases is not included.

The percentage of contract cases in the caseload also varied widely. Jersey City had only 12 percent contract cases, while Denver and Phoenix had 66 percent. Denver was among the fastest courts, and Phoenix was among the middle range of courts on median processing time for all civil cases. Three courts with some of the lowest percentages of contract cases (Jersey City, Newark, and Oakland) were among the slowest courts. In general, a higher percentage of contract cases appeared to be associated with a shorter median time for all civil cases.

In order to explore in a more sophisticated manner the relationships between case mix and case processing time, several measures of civil case processing time will be used. In this and subsequent analyses of factors related to civil case processing times, the median and 90th percentile times for *all civil, trial list, tort,* and *contract* cases will be examined. However, only the median time for *jury trial* cases will be examined because some of the jury trial samples are as small as 20 cases. A few unusually long cases could skew the 90th percentile, so the 90th percentile time for jury trial cases is excluded from the analysis. As a result, nine measures of civil case processing time will be used to examine the relationship between explanatory factors (e.g., percent contract and tort cases) and the pace of civil case litigation.

It is important to note that all nine measures of civil case processing time are strongly correlated with each other (see Appendix B). Courts with long case processing times for tort cases, for example, also tended to have long disposition times for contract, trial list, and jury trial cases.

First, the relationship between the percentage of tort cases in the caseload and civil case processing times will be examined. Although one would expect case mix to affect the overall pace of litigation, most studies across several jurisdictions have failed to find such a relationship.[28] In this study, however, the percentage of tort cases in the caseload displays a statistically significant[29] relationship with five of the nine measures of case processing time. Although correlations with the median and 90th percentile for all civil and contract cases are weak to moderate,[30] the percentage of tort cases show a strong relationship with the 90th percentile case processing time for trial list cases.[31] As the percentage of tort cases increased, the 90th percentile time for trial list cases was very likely to be longer. Some types of tort cases, including medical malpractice, products liability, toxic torts, and even some auto torts, are among the most complex of court cases. These types of cases are likely to be among the oldest cases in any court and are probably more likely to go to trial than other case types. Courts with a higher percentage of these tort cases are likely to have longer 90th percentile times, especially among trial list cases.

The correlations are also consistent with the observation made from Figure 7 that the percentage of contract cases in the caseload exhibit a negative correlation with three measures of civil case processing time.[32] In other words, as the percentage of contract cases in the caseload increased, there was some tendency for case processing times to be shorter, especially for the 90th percentile processing time for trial list cases. Contract cases are apparently, overall, somewhat less litigious or complex and, therefore, arrive at a conclusion in a shorter time than tort cases (see Figure 2).

Tort cases generally take longer than contract cases (see Figure 2). However, there are likely to be considerable variations among the courts in the pace of litigation for tort and contract cases. **Figure 8** presents the median, 75th, and 90th percentile processing times for tort cases. The

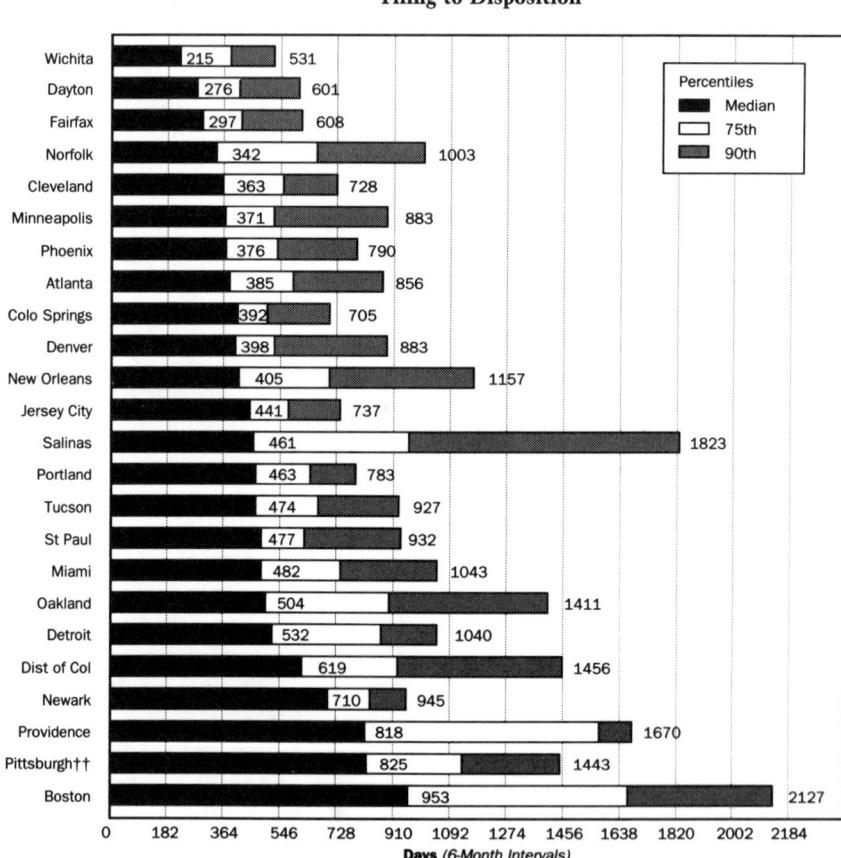

Figure 8
Tort Cases–1987†
Filing to Disposition

† San Diego not included. See footnotes in Figure 3.
†† Does not include cases disposed by arbitration.

fastest court on median tort case time was Wichita at 215 days. The slowest median tort case processing time was in Boston (953 days), which took two years (approximately 4.5 times) longer than in Wichita. The three slowest courts all had median tort disposition times of more than two years, while the five fastest courts had median times of less than one year. In fact, four of the five fastest courts had 90th percentile tort disposition times that were less than the median times of the three slowest courts.

Upon examination of the 90th percentile disposition times, one notices that some courts, including Norfolk, New Orleans, Salinas, Oakland, the District of Columbia, and Boston, exhibited 90th percentile times for tort cases that were considerably longer than for courts that had comparable median times. These courts allowed the last 10 percent of the cases to linger in the system longer than courts with comparable median processing times.[33]

Jersey City and Newark, unlike the courts described above, moved very quickly from the median to their 90th percentile case. In these courts, the problem appeared to be in controlling cases at the early stages of litigation. But once control was established, cases moved relatively quickly.

As suggested earlier, a court's ranking on tort case processing time was usually not very different from its rank on median case processing time for all civil cases. Two noticeable exceptions were St. Paul, which ranked fourth on median time for all civil cases but sixteenth on median tort disposition time, and Miami, which moved from seventh on median time for all civil cases to seventeenth on median time for tort cases (see Figures 3 and 8).

Figure 9 also displays some interesting variations in the median and 90th percentile processing times for contract cases. The median disposition times for contract cases in the two slowest courts, Boston and Providence, were more than three and a half years (1,580 and 1,325 days, respectively). Newark, with the fourth-slowest median in contract cases, had a median time of less than half the time found in Boston and Providence. On the other hand, Wichita, Dayton, Norfolk, and Denver had median times of less than six months in contract cases. Norfolk, Atlanta, Salinas, Oakland, and the District of Columbia displayed unusually long 90th percentile times compared to courts that had similar median times. Jersey City, Newark, and Detroit, however, had short 90th percentile times compared to others that were in their range on median times. Wichita disposed of 90 percent of its cases in less time (430 days) than it took the eight slowest courts to dispose of 50 percent of their cases.

Courts generally required more time to dispose of their tort cases than contract cases (see Figure 2). **Figure 10** compares median tort and contract disposition times in each court. Courts that were fast on median time for

22 / EXAMINING COURT DELAY

all civil cases tended to be fast on both tort and contract processing times. One very interesting pattern emerges from Figure 10. The seven slowest courts on median time for all civil cases were the only courts where the median time for contract cases was longer than for tort cases. Most of these courts had relatively high percentages of tort cases and relatively low percentages of contract cases in their caseloads. The reasons for these patterns are unclear. It is possible that in some of these seven courts, personal injury (tort) cases were given priority over other cases. Because the pattern is concentrated among the slowest courts, further investigation should be performed to determine whether a formal or informal priority system is related to overall delay among these courts (see Figure 7).

Figure 9
Contract Cases–1987†
Filing to Disposition

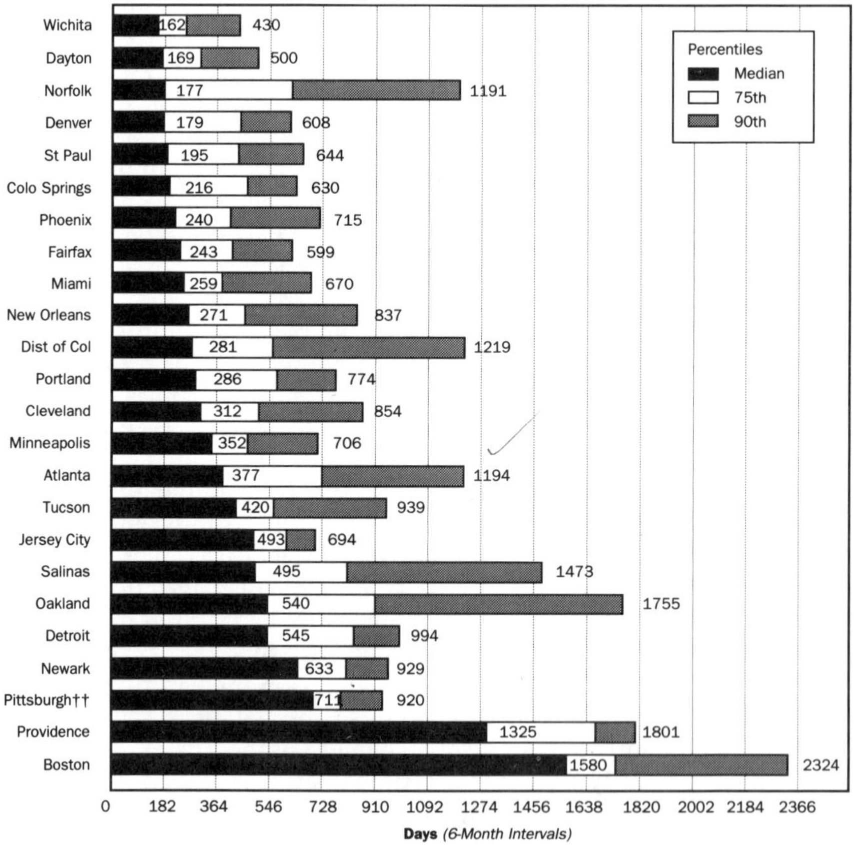

Court	Median	75th	90th
Wichita	162		430
Dayton	169		500
Norfolk	177		1191
Denver	179		608
St Paul	195		644
Colo Springs	216		630
Phoenix	240		715
Fairfax	243		599
Miami	259		670
New Orleans	271		837
Dist of Col	281		1219
Portland	286		774
Cleveland	312		854
Minneapolis	352		706
Atlanta	377		1194
Tucson	420		939
Jersey City	493		694
Salinas	495		1473
Oakland	540		1755
Detroit	545		994
Newark	633		929
Pittsburgh††	711		920
Providence	1325		1801
Boston	1580		2324

Days (6-Month Intervals)

† San Diego not included. See footnotes in Figure 3.
†† Does not include cases disposed by arbitration.

**Figure 10
Tort vs. Contract Cases–1987
Filing to Disposition**

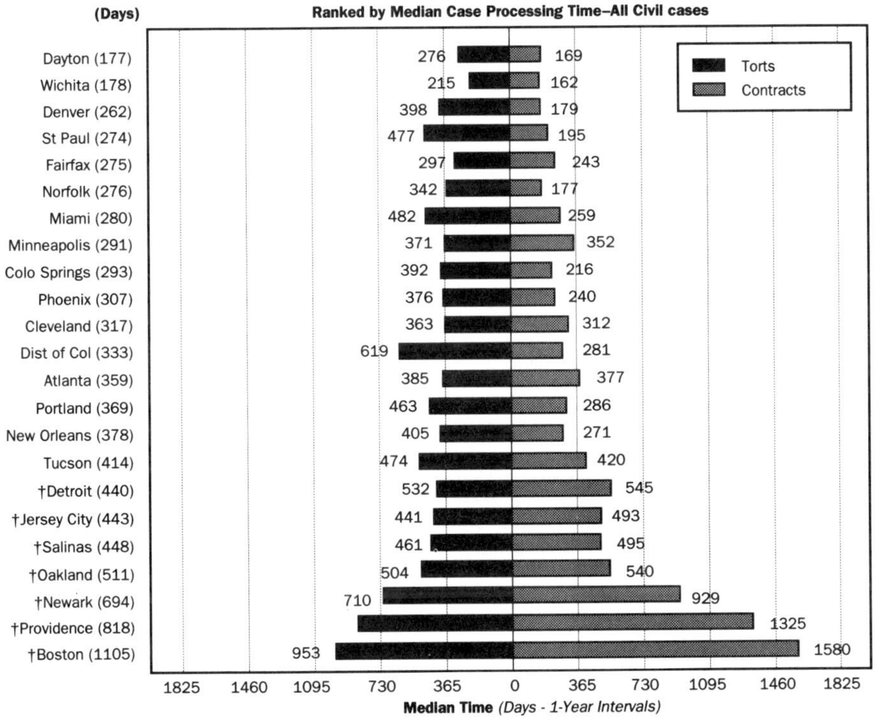

Ranked by Median Case Processing Time–All Civil cases

(Days)	Torts	Contracts
Dayton (177)	276	169
Wichita (178)	215	162
Denver (262)	398	179
St Paul (274)	477	195
Fairfax (275)	297	243
Norfolk (276)	342	177
Miami (280)	482	259
Minneapolis (291)	371	352
Colo Springs (293)	392	216
Phoenix (307)	376	240
Cleveland (317)	363	312
Dist of Col (333)	619	281
Atlanta (359)	385	377
Portland (369)	463	286
New Orleans (378)	405	271
Tucson (414)	474	420
†Detroit (440)	532	545
†Jersey City (443)	441	493
†Salinas (448)	461	495
†Oakland (511)	504	540
†Newark (694)	710	929
†Providence (818)		1325
†Boston (1105)	953	1580

Median Time *(Days - 1-Year Intervals)*

† Contract cases longer than tort cases.

In summary, the percentage of tort cases in the caseload had an impact on the pace of litigation, especially on the 90th percentile time for trial list cases. Courts with more tort cases tended to have longer processing times. A higher percentage of contract cases, moreover, were related to somewhat shorter processing times, especially for 90th percentile for trial list cases.

Jury Trial Rates and Disposition Times

One might expect that the pace of litigation is related to the proportion of cases that are disposed by jury trial. Some courts use jury trials to a much greater extent than others. Jury trials require greater court involvement and resources and, therefore, might inhibit the court's ability to process other cases more expeditiously. **Table 1** displays the percentage of all civil cases disposed by jury trial in each court. The courts are ranked by median disposition time for all civil cases. Again, there is considerable variation among the courts in the percentage of jury trial dispositions, ranging from less than 1 percent in Wichita to 9 percent in Fairfax, Portland, and Newark. The last two courts were among the slower half on overall case processing. On the other hand, 9 percent of the dispositions in Fairfax were jury trials, yet Fairfax was one of the fastest courts in the study.

In **Figure 11**, the median time to verdict in jury trial cases is compared to the median time for all civil cases. Jury trial cases generally exhibited the longest median case processing times across the courts in this study (see Figure 2). It is noteworthy that the fastest median jury trial time (Fairfax) was faster than the median disposition times for all civil cases in nine

Table 1

Jury Trial Rate and All Civil Case Processing Time[a]–1987

	All Civil Median	Percent Jury Trials
Dayton	177	1
Wichita	178	<1
Denver	262	4
St Paul	274	2
Fairfax	275	9
Norfolk	276	4
Miami	280	1
Minneapolis	291	1
Colo Springs	293	2
Phoenix	307	2
Cleveland	317	2
Dist of Col	333	2
Atlanta	359	4
Portland	369	9
New Orleans	378	1
Tucson	414	4
Detroit	440	2
Jersey City	443	4
Salinas	448	2
Oakland	511	1
Newark	694	9
Providence	818	4
Boston	1105	1
Mean	402	3

a San Diego and Pittsburgh excluded; data not comparable.

courts (see Figure 11). Furthermore, the median disposition time for jury trial cases in Fairfax (356 days) was approximately three times faster than in the slowest three courts. Fairfax had the only median time in jury trial cases of less than one year. Twelve courts exhibited a median disposition time in jury trial cases of less than two years. Three courts had median times over two-and-a-half years.

Despite the interesting variations among the courts, however, the percentage of jury trials was not related to any of the nine measures of case processing time (see Appendix B). The percentage of cases disposed by jury trial had no apparent effect on case processing times among the courts in this study.

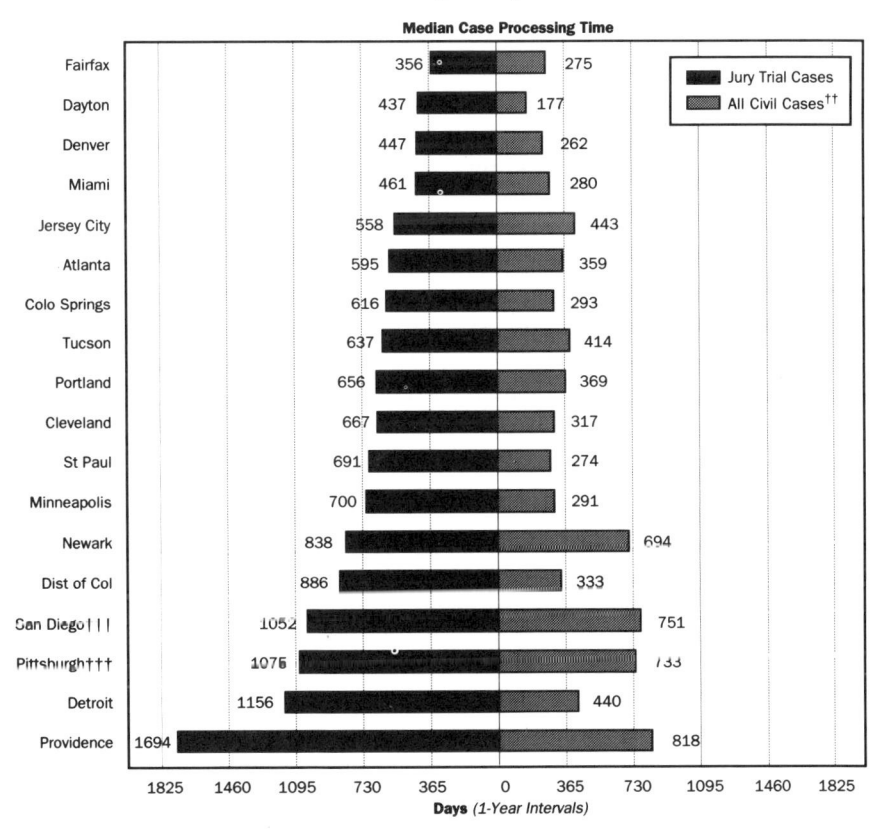

Figure 11
Jury Trials vs. All Civil Cases –1987†
Filing to Disposition

Median Case Processing Time

Court	Jury Trial Cases	All Civil Cases††
Fairfax	356	275
Dayton	437	177
Denver	447	262
Miami	461	280
Jersey City	558	443
Atlanta	595	359
Colo Springs	616	293
Tucson	637	414
Portland	656	369
Cleveland	667	317
St Paul	691	274
Minneapolis	700	291
Newark	838	694
Dist of Col	886	333
San Diego†††	1052	751
Pittsburgh†††	1075	733
Detroit	1156	440
Providence	1694	818

Days (1-Year Intervals)

† Includes only courts from which a minimum of 20 jury trial cases were obtained from the sample.
†† Includes all types of dispositions (e.g., settled, dismissed, and bench and jury trials).
††† San Diego: All civil case data include only cases in which a trial readiness document was filed; Pittsburgh: All civil cases exclude those concluded by arbitration.

Court Size and Court Resources

A long-standing assumption has been that courts in large urban areas, because of the size, diversity, and complexity of court organization and caseload, tend to experience greater delay in case processing than smaller, less complex courts. In this section, the population of the county, the number of civil filings (excluding domestic relations, probate, and small claims), and the number of full-time equivalent judges that handle civil cases are used as indicators of court size and complexity.

Table 2 presents data on population size, number of civil case filings, and the number of civil judges in 1987. First, the population of the counties represented in this study ranges from 275,000 in Norfolk to 2.2 million in San Diego. Detroit, Miami, San Diego, Cleveland, Oakland, Phoenix, and Pittsburgh all have populations over one million. Miami was among the eight fastest courts, but San Diego and Pittsburgh were among the eight slowest courts. Norfolk, Salinas, Colorado Springs, and Wichita had the smallest populations. Wichita and Norfolk were among the six fastest courts; Salinas and Colorado Springs were in the middle group. Correlation analysis suggests that population was not related to any of the nine measures of civil case processing time (see Appendix C).

Examination of the total number of civil case filings (see Table 2) leaves the same impression; there is little or no pattern between total civil filings and all civil case processing time.[34] Again, correlation analysis indicates that there are no substantial correlations between total civil filings and any of the nine measures of civil case processing time (see Appendix C).

Another indicator of court size is the number of civil judges. If only the total number of judges who spend at least part of their time on civil cases is counted, the fact that judges in some courts handle only civil cases and others handle a combination of civil and criminal matters is not taken into account. Through a survey of the court administrators, an estimate of the average amount of time the judges spent on their civil caseload duties (excluding domestic relations, probate, and small claims) was obtained; this is labeled *time on civil cases* in Table 2. The surveys were reviewed and signed by the chief or presiding judge in most courts, so there is reason to believe that the estimates are a reasonable reflection of the average time spent on civil cases. The measure of *FTE (full-time equivalent) civil judges* was derived by multiplying the *total civil judges* by *time on civil cases*. The number of FTE civil judges more accurately reflects the total number of judges that worked on the civil caseload in 1987. A review of Table 2 fails to reveal any discernible link between the number of FTE civil judges and median case processing time for all civil cases. Correlation analysis also indicates that the number of FTE civil judges was not related to any of the nine measures of civil case processing time (see Appendix C).

Table 2

Court Size, Filings per Judge, and Tort Case Processing Time–1987

	All Civil Median	Population[a] 1986	Civil[b] Filings in 1987	Total[c] Civil Judges	Time on[d] Civil Cases	FTE[e] Civil Judges	Filings per FTE Judge
Dayton	177	566	4401	12.00	.60	7.20	611
Wichita	178	391	17122	9.00	.90	8.10	2114
Denver	262	505	26239	11.25	1.00	11.25	2332
St Paul	274	474	6895	20.00	.42	8.40	821
Fairfax	275	710	11269	11.00	.60	6.60	1707
Norfolk	276	275	5488	9.00	.50	4.50	1220
Miami	280	1769	33213	32.00	.50	16.00	2076
Minneapolis	291	988	8095	28.00	.50	14.00	578
Colo Springs	293	380	7154	10.00	.40	4.00	1789
Phoenix	307	1900	45571	26.00	1.00	26.00	1753
Cleveland	317	1445	22562	37.00	.50	18.50	1220
Dist of Col	333	626	*[f]	13.00	.95	12.35	*
Atlanta	359	623	3875	15.00	.40	6.00	646
Portland	369	567	7598	14.00	.40	5.60	1357
New Orleans	378	554	20009	10.50	1.00	10.50	1906
Tucson	414	602	10045	9.10	.95	8.65	1162
Detroit	440	2164	29798	35.20	.80	28.16	1058
Jersey City	443[g]	553	6714	5.50	.98	5.39	1246
Salinas	448	340	2141	7.00	.33	2.31	927
Oakland	511	1209	14537	13.50	1.00	13.50	1077
Newark	694[g]	842	8682	10.00	1.00	10.00	868
Pittsburgh	733[h]	1374	13085	13.50	1.00	13.50	969
San Diego	750[i]	2201	21916	26.00	1.00	26.00	843
Providence	818	582	5751	5.00	1.00	5.00	1150
Boston	1105	661	7661	8.00	1.00	8.00	958
Mean		892	14159	15.62	.75	11.18	1266

a 1986 population in thousands (County and City Data Book, 1988).
b Number of civil cases with a complaint filed, excluding domestic relations and probate cases (data from survey of court administrators).
c "Total civil judges" represents the total number of full-time equivalent judicial staff (including full-time, part-time, or pro-tem judges and/or commissioners/referees) who spent at least part of their time on civil cases in 1987 (data from survey of court administrators).
d "Time on civil cases" is an estimate of the average proportion of judge time spent on civil caseload duties during 1987 (data from survey of court administrators).
e "Full-time equivalent (FTE) civil judges" is calculated by multiplying the number of "total civil judges" with "time on civil cases."
f District of Columbia reported only cases which became "at issue" in 1987.
g The civil case sample does not include cases disposed before an answer was filed.
h Does not include cases disposed by arbitration.
i The San Diego sample included only cases in which a trial readiness document had been filed. See also Appendix A.
* Data unavailable or not comparable.

28 / EXAMINING COURT DELAY

The number of judges or filings, of course, is probably less important than a measure of workload: the number of cases per staff member or judge. In Table 2, *filings per FTE civil judge* provides an indication of the comparative level of judicial resources available among the courts to handle their caseload. Prior studies of the pace of litigation in trial and appellate courts suggested that a larger number of filings per judge was not related to longer case processing times.[35] Table 2 and **Figure 12** tend to support the earlier studies. The eight fastest courts on median case processing time for all civil cases had an average of 1432 civil cases per FTE civil judge while the eight slowest had an average of 1056. Moreover, Wichita had the second-highest number of filings per FTE judge but had the second-fastest median disposition time for all civil cases. In fact, a *larger* number of filings per FTE civil judge was related to *shorter* 90th percentile times in contract and trial list cases.[36] The correlations suggest that as the civil filings per judge increased among these courts, case disposition times tended to be faster.

A partial explanation for larger caseloads per judge being related to faster case processing times may be that the faster/higher caseload courts

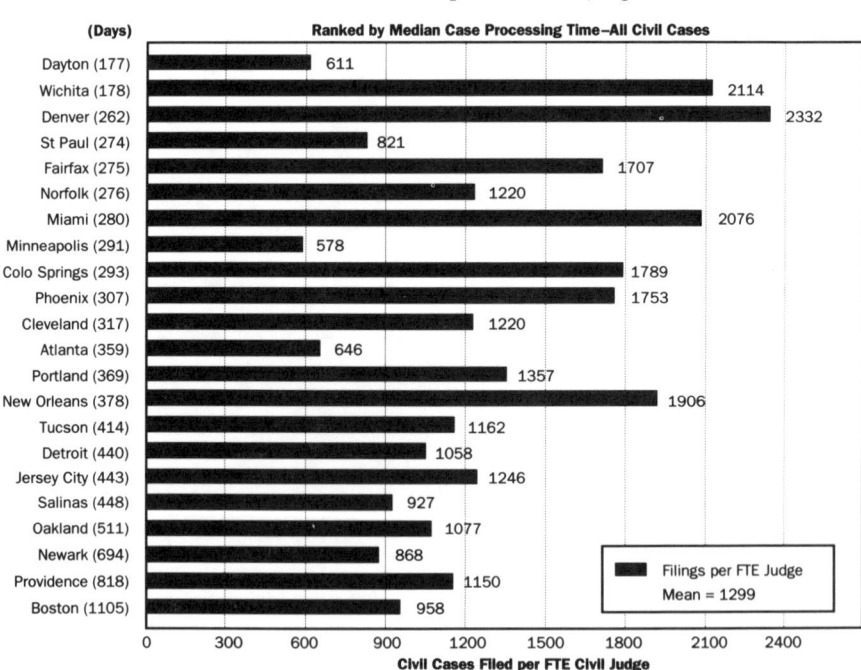

Figure 12
Civil Caseload per FTE Civil Judge–1987†

Ranked by Median Case Processing Time–All Civil Cases

Court (Days)	Filings per FTE Judge
Dayton (177)	611
Wichita (178)	2114
Denver (262)	2332
St Paul (274)	821
Fairfax (275)	1707
Norfolk (276)	1220
Miami (280)	2076
Minneapolis (291)	578
Colo Springs (293)	1789
Phoenix (307)	1753
Cleveland (317)	1220
Atlanta (359)	646
Portland (369)	1357
New Orleans (378)	1906
Tucson (414)	1162
Detroit (440)	1058
Jersey City (443)	1246
Salinas (448)	927
Oakland (511)	1077
Newark (694)	868
Providence (818)	1150
Boston (1105)	958

Mean = 1299

Civil Cases Filed per FTE Civil Judge

† All civil cases excluding probate and domestic relations. Pittsburgh and San Diego are excluded; see footnotes in Figure 3.

had a higher percentage of easier or faster case types. As **Figure 13** indicates, the courts with the largest caseloads per judge tended to have higher percentages of contract cases and lower percentages of tort cases. The percentage of contract and tort cases both displayed correlations with caseload per FTE judge.[37] It has already been noted that the percentage of tort cases in the caseload were related to longer case processing times on five measures, especially the 90th percentile for trial list cases, and the percentage of contract cases in the caseload were related to shorter case processing times on three measures, especially the 90th percentile for trial list cases. Thus, the data provide some basis for understanding why faster courts were generally able to handle more cases per judge; they tended to have a higher percentage of contract cases, which may be easier to process than tort cases. Conversely, slower courts had fewer cases per judge but tended to have a larger percentage of tort cases, which generally required more time than contract cases.

The relationship between caseload per judge and case processing times, then, is very complex. However, there is little evidence here to suggest that larger caseloads per judge were related to longer case processing times. Case

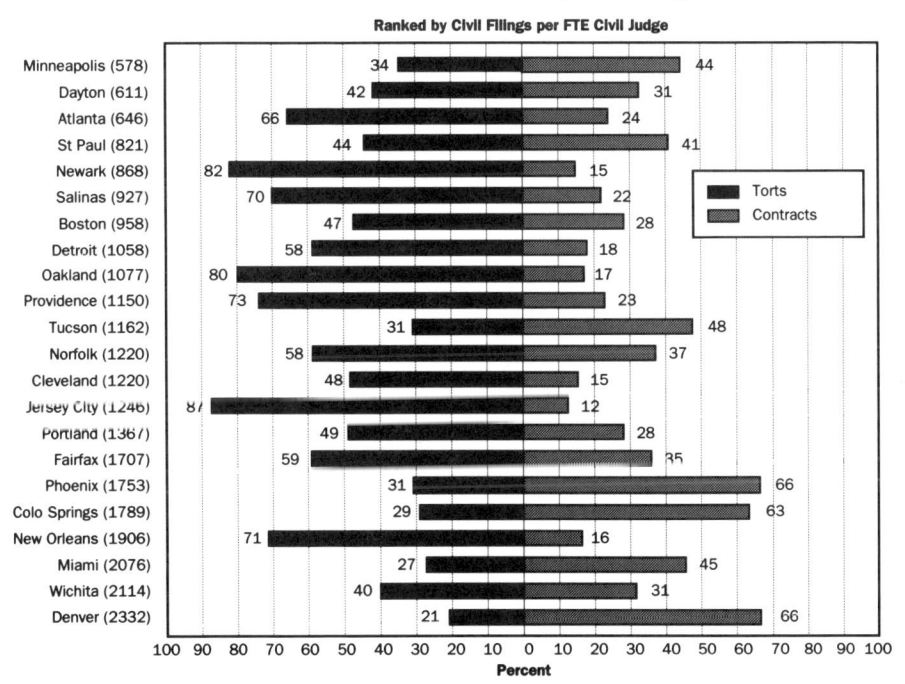

Figure 13
Civil Case Mix and Caseload per FTE Judge–1987†

Ranked by Civil Filings per FTE Civil Judge

City (Filings)	Torts %	Contracts %
Minneapolis (578)	34	44
Dayton (611)	42	31
Atlanta (646)	66	24
St Paul (821)	44	41
Newark (868)	82	15
Salinas (927)	70	22
Boston (958)	47	28
Detroit (1058)	58	18
Oakland (1077)	80	17
Providence (1150)	73	23
Tucson (1162)	31	48
Norfolk (1220)	58	37
Cleveland (1220)	48	15
Jersey City (1246)	87	12
Portland (1367)	49	28
Fairfax (1707)	59	35
Phoenix (1753)	31	66
Colo Springs (1789)	29	63
New Orleans (1906)	71	16
Miami (2076)	27	45
Wichita (2114)	40	31
Denver (2332)	21	66

† Excludes probate and domestic relations. San Diego and Pittsburgh excluded; see footnotes in Figure 3.

mix is one important intervening factor in the relationship. But even the effect of case mix is not clear. Although contract cases generally required less time to process than tort cases, the seven slowest courts (on median time for all civil cases) were the only ones that took longer to dispose of their contract cases than their tort cases (see Figure 10). The slowest courts tended to be slow in processing tort cases but even slower in processing contract cases. Thus, the pattern among the slowest courts suggests that differences in caseflow and resource management are more salient factors than caseload per judge in explaining differences in the pace of litigation among the courts.

The findings reported here support the contention that a higher number of filings per judge is not generally related to longer case processing times.[38] Of course, there will be a point after which a larger caseload cannot be absorbed efficiently so that additional judges will be necessary.[39] The findings simply suggest that many courts have the capacity to handle more cases per judge and to move their cases more quickly.[40] Finally, indicators of court size, including population, number of filings, and number of judges, were not related to civil case processing time.

Caseflow Management Procedures

One reason some courts with larger caseloads per judge may be able to handle their caseloads more quickly than courts with smaller caseloads is that their case management procedures are more effective. Some of the more prominent characteristics of case management that could affect the pace of litigation are examined in this section.

Calendar Type and Judicial Assignments

The calendar system is the method by which cases are assigned to judges. An individual calendar court assigns a case to an individual judge after the complaint is filed, and that judge handles all matters related to the case until its disposition. In a master calendar court, case events are handled by judges who are available at the assigned time; different judges may handle each of the various case events (e.g., scheduling conference, motions, pretrial conference, and trial). Some courts use a combination of individual and master calendars (referred to as hybrid calendars in this report). Evidence from earlier research suggests that all three systems can work quite efficiently.[41] However, the same research indicates that faster civil courts tend to use an individual calendar system, while most of the slower courts tend to use a master calendar. At least in theory, an individual calendar system entails greater accountability than a master calendar. Each judge is responsible for her or his cases from the time of filing through disposition. Furthermore, information for monitoring the pace of a judge's caseload can be relatively easy to maintain. Thus, an individual calendar system could be more conducive to a faster pace of litigation.

Table 3 provides some evidence that individual calendars are faster than master calendars. Eleven of the 13 slowest courts used a master or

Table 3

Calendar, Judicial Assignment, and Tort Case Processing Time–1987

	Torts Median	Calendar[a] Type	Judicial[b] Assignment
Wichita	215	Master	General Civil
Dayton	276	Individual	Civil/Criminal
Fairfax	297	Master	Civil/Criminal
Norfolk	342	Master	Civil/Criminal
Cleveland	363	Individual	Civil/Criminal
Minneapolis	371	Individual	Civil/Criminal
Phoenix	376	Individual	General Civil
Atlanta	385	Individual	Civil/Criminal
Colo Springs	392	Individual	Civil/Criminal
Denver	398	Individual	General Civil
New Orleans	405	Individual	General/Other Civil
Jersey City	441	Hybrid (M)	General Civil
Salinas	461	Master	Civil/Criminal
Portland	463	Master	Civil/Criminal
Tucson	474	Individual	General Civil
St Paul	477	Master	Civil/Criminal
Miami	482	Individual	General/Other Civil
Oakland	504	Master	General Civil
Detroit	532	Hybrid (M)	Civil/Criminal
Dist of Col	619	Hybrid (M)	General Civil
Newark	710	Master	General Civil
San Diego	742[c]	Hybrid (M)	General Civil
Providence	818	Master	General Civil
Pittsburgh	825[d]	Master	General Civil
Boston	953	Master	General Civil

a Hybrid (M) indicates that the court utilizes both an individual and master calendar, but is categorized here by its primary type, master (data from survey of court administrators).
b Indicates the types of cases assigned to judges who handled civil cases: general civil only (all civil cases excluding domestic relations and probate); two or more of civil and domestic relations or probate; and a combination of civil and criminal (data from survey of court administrators).
c Includes trial list cases only.
d Does not include cases disposed by arbitration.

hybrid that was primarily a master calendar, while only 4 of the fastest 12 courts used a master calendar system. Conversely, 8 of the fastest 12 courts, but only 2 of the slowest 13 courts, used individual calendars. Overall, there is a noticeable pattern that favors individual calendars. Correlation analysis indicates that there was a relationship between calendar type and seven of the nine measures of civil case processing time.[42] That is, individual calendars were more likely to produce shorter civil case processing times. However, 3 of the 4 fastest courts used a master calendar. Although an individual calendar might be more likely to produce faster civil case processing times, a master calendar can clearly be made to work efficiently. But overall, the evidence suggests that individual calendars tend to result in faster civil case processing times.

Another important organizational feature of the trial court is the degree of specialization of the judicial assignment system. Some courts assign a combination of civil and criminal cases to all the judges in the court, while others create divisions where judges handle only civil or only criminal cases. One major reason for specialization in most organizations is to improve efficiency. One might expect that where judges are able to specialize, the courts will process cases more quickly. Table 3 shows that the six slowest courts, but only one of the six fastest courts, used specialized judicial assignments (i.e., general civil cases only). However, correlation analysis indicates that the degree of specialization in judicial assignments was not significantly related to any of the measures of civil case processing time (see Appendix C).[43]

In summary, individual calendars were more likely to produce faster civil case processing times, although there were some relatively fast master calendar courts in this study. Whether judges had specialized assignments (i.e., handled only civil cases) or mixed assignments (i.e., both civil and criminal cases) was unrelated to civil case processing times.

Early Control, Trial Backup Systems, and Firm Trial Dates

Merely examining the case assignment systems does not reveal much about the degree to which the court actually exerts control over the flow of cases through the system. Proponents of court control argue that the court should exercise early and continuous control over case processing, scheduling future events at relatively short intervals beginning shortly after the filing of the complaint.[44] In this section, three aspects of court control over the caseflow will be examined: when the court begins to schedule case events, whether the court maintains a backup system to assure the start of trials, and the existence of a firm trial date policy.

Early and continuous control is advocated by almost everyone concerned with caseflow management. In this study, the point when courts routinely established control over the processing of cases was determined through a survey completed by the court administrators. *Point of court control* is the time when judges or administrators usually contacted the parties to set a schedule for case events (e.g., discovery, settlement or pretrial conferences, or submission of joint memoranda on the issues) or acted to dismiss a case on the court's own motion for lack of prosecution. **Table 4** displays *point of court control* over cases in each court. Courts were ranked as establishing control "early" (case events scheduled within 120 days after complaint was filed);[45] in "one year or less" (between 121 days and one year from filing of a complaint);[46] or "at trial readiness" (not until a trial readiness document was filed).

As Table 4 indicates, 3 of the 5 fastest courts used "early" control procedures, while the 5 slowest courts all waited until cases were "trial ready." None of the slowest 11 courts used "early" control procedures. Those that established control in "less than 1 year" were not represented among either the 5 fastest or 5 slowest courts. Correlation coefficients also suggest that there is a moderate to strong relationship between early control and faster disposition times on eight measures of civil case processing time, especially for 90th percentile trial list cases.[47] It should be noted, however, that the Virginia courts (Fairfax and Norfolk) wait for parties to request a trial date before case events are scheduled, and yet they were among the 4 fastest courts on median tort case disposition time. Both courts routinely dismissed cases (after notice to the parties) after two years if no trial date had been requested. Thus, waiting until cases are "trial ready" to establish control over civil cases is not inevitably linked to slow case processing times. But overall, early control by the court over case processing was related to a faster pace of litigation, especially among the oldest trial list cases (90th percentile).

Another aspect of court control over caseflow is reflected in the existence of a system to assure that trials begin on the scheduled dates. If a trial is to be postponed, it should not be due to the inability to find a judge to hear the case. A backup system could be arranged among the full-time judges within the court or by use of part-time judges or those who are brought in from a lower court or other jurisdiction. Table 4 indicates that 6 courts among the slower 13 and 4 courts among the faster 12 had no trial backup system. Correlation analysis suggests that there was a moderate relationship between the existence of a trial backup system and faster civil case processing times at the 90th percentile.[48] Having a trial backup system helps to get older cases to disposition sooner. The way a trial backup system is operated, however, is probably more important than its mere existence. Furthermore, the existence of a trial backup system does not

Table 4

Elements of Caseflow Control and Tort Case Processing Time–1987

	Tort Median	Point[a] of Court Control	Trial[b] Backup System	Percent Jury[c] Trials on First Trial Date	Disposition[d] Time Goals
Wichita	215	Early	Yes	*	More
Dayton	276	Early	Yes	*	More
Fairfax	297	Trial Ready	Yes	74	None
Norfolk	342	Trial Ready	No	*	None
Cleveland	363	Early	Yes	*	Same
Minneapolis	371	< 1 Year	No	*	More
Phoenix	376	< 1 Year	Yes	*	Less
Atlanta	385	Trial Ready	Yes	*	None
Colo Springs	392	< 1 Year	Yes	47	Same
Denver	398	Varies[e]	Yes	29	Less
New Orleans	405	Trial Ready	No	*	None
Jersey City	441	Trial Ready	No	0	More
Salinas	461	Trial Ready	No	*	None
Portland	463	Early	Yes	1	Same
Tucson	474	< 1 Year	Yes	21	Less
St Paul	477	Trial Ready	No	*	Less
Miami	482	Trial Ready	Yes	*	Same
Oakland	504	Trial Ready	Yes	*	None
Detroit	532	< 1 Year	No	*	None
Dist of Col	619	< 1 Year	No	*	More
Newark	710	Trial Ready	No	*	More
San Diego	742[f]	Trial Ready	Yes	16	Same
Providence	818	Trial Ready	Yes	*	Less
Pittsburgh	825[g]	Trial Ready	Yes	*	None
Boston	953	Trial Ready	No	*	None
Mean				27	

a Indicates when the court established control over the progress of a case by setting a schedule for future events. See text for definitions. (Data from survey of court administrators).
b See text for explanation.
c Percent of jury trial cases which went to trial on the first scheduled trial date (for courts where data were available).
d Disposition time goals employed by the court are categorized here in relation to the ABA standards for general civil cases, (i.e. "more"= more strict; "less"= less strict; "same"= approximately the same).
e "Point of Court Control" varies by judge and by case in Denver.
f Includes trial list cases only.
g Does not include cases disposed by arbitration.
* Data unavailable or not comparable.

reveal much about court practices regarding trial scheduling and the granting of continuances, which could impair the effectiveness of a backup system.

A better indicator of a court's commitment to a firm trial date is the percentage of jury trials that started on the first scheduled trial date. A court committed to getting cases to trial when scheduled, and reluctant to grant continuances, would generally start cases on the first scheduled trial date. Furthermore, if a court is tough on continuances and starts cases on the first scheduled date, cases will settle earlier. As a result, these courts will have shorter disposition times overall. Unfortunately, the first scheduled trial date in 20 or more jury trial cases was obtained from only seven courts (see Table 4). Among this small sample of courts, however, it appears that a higher percentage of jury trials that started on the first scheduled trial date was related to shorter median tort case disposition times. The three fastest courts with relevant data started an average of 50 percent of their jury trials on the first scheduled trial date. The three slowest courts with relevant data averaged 13 percent on the first scheduled trial date. Fairfax, which waits until a trial readiness document is filed to begin scheduling case events, had 74 percent of its jury trials begin on the first scheduled trial date. Combined with regular dismissal of cases that are inactive after two years, a firm trial date policy appears to contribute significantly to the relatively fast pace of litigation in Fairfax. In addition, analysis of jury trials in felony cases suggests that the percentage of jury trials that start on the first scheduled trial date were correlated with most measures of felony case processing time.[49] Overall, then, the data from this study suggest that a firm trial date policy is an important factor in reducing court delay.

In summary, early court control over case events showed a moderate association with shorter civil case processing times. Early control could particularly help reduce the processing times in the oldest cases, thus helping courts meet the ABA standards. A firm trial date policy also appeared to be related to faster case processing time. The existence of a trial backup system showed a moderate correlation with only 90th percentile case processing times.

Disposition Time Goals

Adoption of disposition time goals and the collection and dissemination of information to monitor the caseflow management process are also considered fundamental for achieving and maintaining expeditious case processing times.[50] The last column in Table 4 indicates how the state or local disposition time goals, if any, in the various states or localities compared with the ABA time standards (i.e., more strict, same, less strict, none). Nine of the 25 courts were not subject to any state or local disposition time goals for civil cases. According to Table 4, there was no apparent pattern between the existence of disposition time standards and median tort disposition time. Correlation coefficients support this conclusion (see Appendix C). However, the existence of time standards was moderately related to shorter 90th percentile disposition times for each of the civil case categories.[51] Disposition time goals apparently are associated with less delay among the oldest cases on the docket.

Disposition time goals are useful for guiding the efforts of judges and staff in achieving a faster pace of litigation. But progress in meeting the goals must be monitored through the collection and dissemination of relevant caseflow information.[52] Appendix F shows how frequently the courts disseminated various types of caseflow information to their judges during 1987. Most courts reported the number of civil cases pending, filed, and disposed on a monthly basis. Fewer, but approximately half the courts, reported the age of pending and disposed cases on at least a quarterly basis. Eight of the 16 courts with time standards reported on a monthly basis the number of cases that exceeded the time standards. Only five of the courts regularly reported the number of continuances granted. Moreover, there was no pattern evident between the reporting of the various types of information and median tort case processing time. The information must not only be collected and reported, it must also be used by the judges and staff to manage their caseloads.[53] Furthermore, the judges and staff must be committed to achieving the goals, or the goals and information will have little impact.

Overall, the caseflow management factors that were most likely to reduce civil case processing times were early court control of case events and civil case disposition time standards.[54] Individual calendar systems also showed a propensity toward faster case processing times. Naturally, there were exceptions to these general tendencies. Three of the fastest courts on median tort processing time (Wichita, Fairfax, and Norfolk) used a master calendar. Fairfax and Norfolk did not begin to schedule case events until cases were trial ready, and they were not subject to disposition time goals. Exceptions to the general trend, though worth examination, should not obscure the overall associations identified in this study. Early control over case events, firm trial dates, stricter disposition time goals, and an individual calendar were associated with faster civil case disposition times.

Civil Case Backlog Index

Earlier, this report examined one aspect of backlog—the percentage of cases over the ABA disposition time standards. In this section, another measure of backlog is examined. **Table 5** shows the backlog index, which is a ratio of the number of civil cases pending at the beginning of the year divided by the number of civil cases disposed during the year. This index reflects how well the court is keeping up with its pending caseload. If the index is more than 1.0, the court did not dispose of as many cases as it had pending at the start of the year. A lower ratio generally indicates that the court turned over its pending cases once a year. A ratio of .50 suggests that the pending caseload was disposed within approximately six months, or twice during the year. It is noteworthy that Fairfax and Norfolk, two of the faster courts, had two of the highest backlog indexes. Backlogs are clearly growing in these courts, though they had a relatively fast pace of litigation. However, despite the high backlog indexes in Fairfax and Norfolk, the backlog index exhibited a moderate to strong correlation with six measures of case processing time.[55] As we expected, a higher backlog index is

Table 5

Civil Case Backlog Index
and Tort Case Processing Time–1987

	Torts Median	Civil Backlog Index 1987[a]
Wichita	215	.35
Dayton	276	.58
Fairfax	297	1.57
Norfolk	342	1.34
Cleveland	363	.76
Phoenix	376	.74
Atlanta	385	.91
Colo Springs	392	.47
Denver	398	.46
Jersey City	441	.69
Portland	463	.63
Tucson	474	.87
St Paul	477	.37
Miami	482	1.01
Detroit	532	.88
Newark	710	1.14
San Diego	742[b]	.12
Boston	953	1.72
Mean		.81

a Number of pending civil cases as of January 1, 1987 divided by the number disposed in 1987.
b Represents tort cases with a trial readiness document filed.

associated with longer civil case processing times. Thus, the backlog index is a simple tool by which courts can monitor their caseflow.

Summary of Factors Related to the Pace of Civil Case Litigation

The complexity of the relationships related to the pace of civil case litigation is clear. In order to present a more complete picture of the findings thus far, **Figure 14** summarizes these relationships. It is important to note that Figure 14 merely displays graphically the simple two-variable correlations reported above. It does not present the results of a sophisticated multivariate regression analysis.[56]

First, in Figure 14, we see that court size may affect civil case processing times. For instance, although the number of civil case filings did not

Figure 14
Summary: Bivariate Correlations Related to Civil Case Processing Time–1987

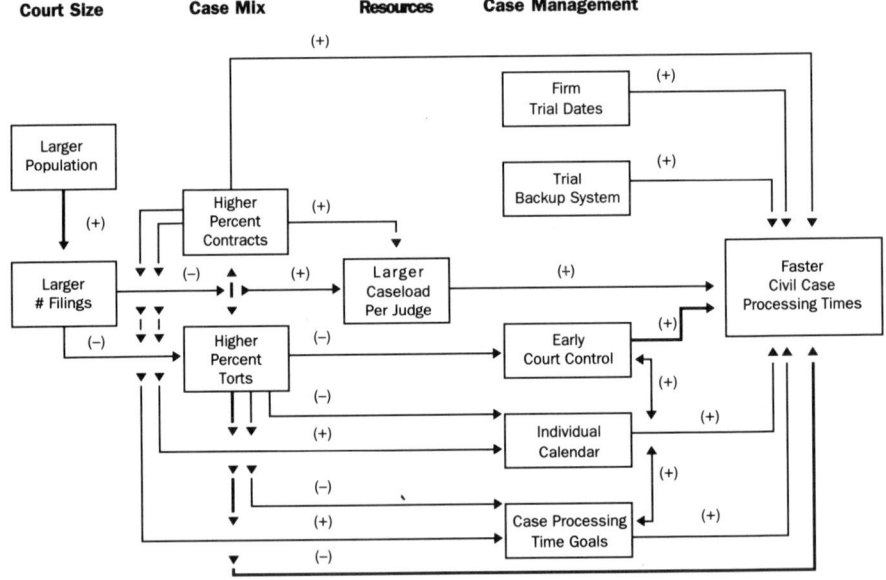

→ (narrow line) r = ± .40 to .59 on at least one measure of civil case processing time; p ≤ .05 (Pearson's r).

→ (bold line) r ≥ ± .60 or higher on at least one measure of civil case processing time; p ≤ .05 (Pearson's r).

(−) When one factor is present, the other factor tends not to be present.

(+) When one factor is present, the other factor tends to be present.

display a direct relationship to case processing times, it was related to case mix (percent torts) and caseload per judge, which were related to case processing time. Its impact is probably indirect rather than direct.

Figure 14 also shows the possible importance of case mix, especially the percentage of torts in the caseload. Not only was a higher percentage of torts directly associated with longer case processing times, it was also related to a lack of early court control, the presence of master calendars, and the lack of case processing time goals. Each of these case management characteristics was, in turn, related to longer case processing time. These findings support the conventional wisdom that case mix is related to differences in civil case processing times.

Contrary to conventional wisdom, courts with a larger caseload per judge were somewhat more likely to have faster case processing times in contract and trial list cases. However, courts with larger caseloads per judge were likely to have a higher percentage of contract cases, which were usually faster, overall, than tort cases.

As indicated in Figure 14, several case management procedures were found to be associated with the pace of civil case litigation. Individual calendar systems were correlated with shorter case processing times on seven of the nine measures examined in this study with some notable exceptions. Early court control was moderately to strongly correlated with shorter case processing times for all case types. Disposition time goals and the existence of a trial backup procedure displayed moderate correlations with 90th percentile processing times. Although the available data were limited to a small number of courts, firm trial dates were associated with faster case processing times. It is noteworthy that courts with more tort cases (usually the slower courts) tended to have master calendars, lack disposition time goals, and lack early control over their cases. Furthermore, individual calendar courts were more likely to establish early control over cases and have disposition time goals. In general, early court control was related to faster median and 90th percentile case processing times; goals and a trial backup system were most likely to shorten the time required to dispose of the oldest (90th percentile) cases in the courts.

Findings from the bivariate correlation analysis presented here are valuable because they present a statistical evaluation of the complex relationships among factors related to the pace of litigation. A form of multivariate analysis, however, provides additional evidence regarding the relative importance of explanatory factors when they are examined simultaneously for their relationship to case processing times.[57]

Figure 15 displays three flow charts that illustrate which factors appeared to be most influential in explaining variations in processing times for all civil, tort, and trial list cases. After other relevant factors were controlled through multivariate analysis, there were two key factors related to the pace of litigation for all civil cases: early court control and shorter case processing time goals.[58] Early court control was an important predictor of shorter case processing times for all three civil case categories. Disposition time goals were related to shorter 90th percentile processing times for all civil cases. The only other factor that retained an important

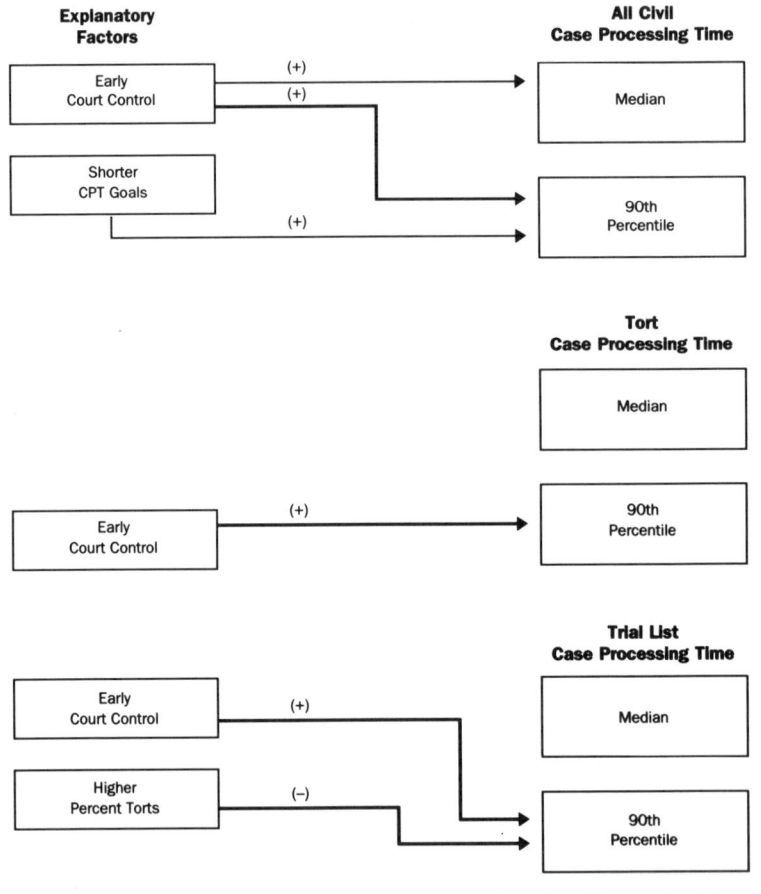

Figure 15
Summary: Multivariate Analysis of Factors Related to Civil Case Processing Time—1987

Explanatory Factors / **All Civil Case Processing Time**

- Early Court Control (+) → Median
- Early Court Control (+) → 90th Percentile
- Shorter CPT Goals (+) → 90th Percentile

Tort Case Processing Time

- Median
- Early Court Control (+) → 90th Percentile

Trial List Case Processing Time

- Early Court Control (+) → Median
- Higher Percent Torts (−) → 90th Percentile

→ (narrow line) The correlation with CPT remained statistically significant after all but one relevant factor were controlled for in a series of three variable-stepwise regression analyses (see Appendices A and N).

→ (bold line) The correlation with CPT remained statistically significant after all other relevant factors were controlled for in a series of three-variable stepwise regression analyses (see Appendices A and N).

(−) The explanatory factor has a negative/detrimental impact on case processing time (i.e., case processing time is longer).

(+) The explanatory factor has a positive/beneficial impact on case processing time (i.e., case processing time is shorter).

role in explaining the pace of civil case litigation was the percentage of tort cases in the caseload. More tort cases were related to longer 90th percentile times, but only for trial list cases.[59]

Factors examined here appear to explain variations in 90th percentile processing times more effectively than they explain median case processing times. Nevertheless, this is an important finding because one of the major goals of delay reduction is to reduce the time it currently takes to dispose of the older cases in the courts.

The key factors identified in this study, early court control and shorter disposition time goals, are largely within the control of the judges and court staff.[60] Courts that are committed to expeditious case processing are likely to take charge of cases earlier and to set disposition time goals that are taken seriously by judges and staff. If such measures are taken and courts are committed to achieving the goals, delay can be reduced.

Perceived Causes of Civil Case Delay

After arriving at some conclusions about the most important factors related to civil case processing time, it is interesting to examine what leaders (judges and court administrators) in these courts regard as the major causes of delay in their courts. One would expect that, at least in some of the areas of concern, there would be notable differences between the faster and slower courts. In order to examine the causes of delay as perceived by key court leaders, a list of potential problems was given to the court administrators who were asked to rate them from "not a problem" (1) through "a very serious problem" (4). The surveys, including the ratings of the problems related to court delay, were reviewed and signed by the presiding judge in most courts.[61]

Table 6 displays the average ratings from the six fastest and six slowest courts on median tort case processing time. The potential problems are grouped into five general categories: procedural problems, commitment to delay reduction, resources, communication and accountability, and caseload. The table shows that there was little or no difference between the fastest and slowest courts on most of the potential problems. There were, however, significant differences on ratings of problems related to court delay in the area of court resources.[62] The slowest courts ranked "insufficient number of judges" (3.7) and "insufficient number of courtrooms" (3.8) as "very serious problem(s)," whereas the fastest courts ranked these between "not a problem" and "minor problem" (1.8 and 1.5, respectively). These differences are predictable. Lack of sufficient resources, especially too few judges, has commonly been cited as the primary cause of court delay.[63] Empirical data on the issue of insufficient courtrooms are not presented here. Too few courtrooms, for example, could affect the ability to set early and firm trial dates. This is a legitimate area of concern, one that may contribute to the differences between fast and slow courts. However, there was little difference in the average number of filings per judge between the six fastest courts (1,242) and the six slowest courts (1,198). Yet leaders from the slower courts believed that an insufficient number of judges was a very serious problem. Conversely, leaders from the faster courts viewed the number of judges as only a minor problem. One of the benefits of this research is that it could help the judges and administrators

Table 6

Rating Problems Affecting Civil Case Delay[a]–1987

	Six Fastest Courts (Average)[b]	Six Slowest Courts (Average)[b]
1. Procedural Problems		
Too many continuances	1.8	1.8
Lack effective "firm trial date"	1.5	2.0
Inefficient calendar/assignment system	1.8	1.5
Court leaders unable to change case management procedures	1.7	1.4
2. Commitment to Delay Reduction		
Lack CPT goals/standards	2.0	1.5
Lack of knowledge about case management procedures	1.7	1.7
Judges lack concern about delay	1.3	1.7
Lawyers lack concern about delay	2.3	3.0
Resistance among lawyers to court control	2.2	1.8
3. Resources		
Insufficient number of judges	1.8[c]	3.7[c]
Insufficient number of court rooms	1.5[c]	3.8[c]
Insufficient staff for caseflow management	1.5	2.7
4. Communication and Accountability		
Lack of caseflow information reports	2.0	1.8
Inadequate communication within court about delay	1.7	2.0
Lack of accountability within court for caseflow	1.8	2.0
5. Caseload		
Large case backlog	1.8[c]	3.8[c]
Increase in number of civil case filings	2.2	2.2

a 1 = no problem; 2 = minor problem; 3 = moderately serious problem; 4 = very serious problem.
b Based on median tort case processing time; San Diego and Pittsburgh excluded due to noncomparable data.
c The difference between the fastest and slowest courts is statistically significant at the .05 level (Fisher's Exact Test).

in the slower courts identify more clearly the factors that contribute to delay in their courts.

A second issue in Table 6, which manifested a significant difference between fast and slow courts, was backlog. The slowest courts rated "large case backlog" as a "very serious problem" (3.8), while the fastest courts rated backlog as only a "minor problem" (1.8). This finding is not surprising. The data discussed earlier show a relationship between the backlog index and case processing times. Slower courts also had a higher percentage of cases over the ABA time standards (see Figure 5). But one must be cautious about how the relationship between backlog and case processing time is interpreted. Any delay reduction effort must address the problem posed by a large number of older pending cases before, or at least simultaneously with, the implementation of a delay reduction program.[64]

One of the most interesting findings is that faster courts, which tended to carry larger caseloads per judge than the slower courts, viewed "insufficient number of judges" as only a minor problem, whereas slower courts viewed it as a "very serious problem." Data presented earlier on caseload per judge should assist the slower courts in reassessing their court delay problem and organizational needs. However, these ratings were from one or two people in each court and do not represent an objective indicator of the actual problems in the courts. Nor do they necessarily represent a consensus among judges or administrators regarding factors that affect court delay. The ratings do provide us some indication of what key court leaders consider to be the problems faced by their courts and, therefore, should be considered in evaluating the causes of delay in their courts.

Trends in the Pace of Civil Case Litigation: 1976–1987

One of the advantages of tracking case processing times in the same courts as Church et al. (1978a), Neubauer et al. (1981), and Mahoney et al. (1985, 1988) is that changes in the pace of litigation over time can be tracked. The data in this study were collected in a manner that was as consistent as possible with the methodology employed by these four studies. However, changes in recordkeeping procedures in some courts over the years, changes in the staff who carried out the sampling, and changes in coders could have affected to some extent the outcomes of the research at each time period. Despite these caveats, the data provide a reasonable basis for assessing general trends in the pace of litigation.

Table 7 displays median tort case processing times for 1976, 1983, 1985, and 1987. Only 5 of the 16 courts with 1976 data reduced their median tort case processing time from 1976 to 1987. Nine of the courts increased their tort case processing time by 18 percent or more; four increased by 41 percent or more during this time. Of those that reduced their case processing time between 1976 and 1987, Minneapolis made the most substantial reduction (310 days, 44 percent), followed by Detroit (256 days, 32 percent). Wichita, among the fastest courts in 1976 on tort case processing time, also reduced substantially its median tort case processing time (75 days, 26 percent). Each of these courts implemented delay reduction programs during the past several years. On the other hand, Portland (up 153 days, 49 percent) displayed the largest percentage increase from 1976 to 1987. New Orleans, Pittsburgh, and Miami also experienced increases in median tort disposition time of more than 40 percent since

Table 7

Tort Case Processing Time Trends
Filing to Disposition, 1976–1987

	Median Tort Case Processing Time				Percent Change in Median Tort Case Processing Time		
	1976[a]	1983[a]	1985[a]	1987	1976-87	1983-87	1985-87
Wichita	290[b]	492	411	215	−26	−56	−48
Dayton	*	345	279	276	*	−20	−1
Cleveland	384	318	343	363	−5	14	6
Phoenix	308	317	292	376	22	19	29
Atlanta	402[c]	*	*	385	−4	*	*
Minneapolis[d]	710	818	603	400	−44	−51	−34
New Orleans	288	401	403	405	41	1	0
Jersey City	584[b]	425	394	441	−24	4	12
Portland	310	393	389	463	49	18	19
Miami	331	408	325	482	46	18	48
Oakland	421	528	637	504	20	−5	−21
St Paul[d]	440[e]	*	*	520	18	*	*
Detroit	788	721	648	532	−32	−26	−18
Newark	654	544	624	710	9	31	14
San Diego[f]	574	816	697	742	29	−9	6
Providence	*	516	697	818	*	59	17
Pittsburgh[g]	583	657	651	825	42	26	27
Boston	811	701	782	953	18	36	22

a   Data obtained from Mahoney et al. 1988.
b   Represents median tort case processing time for 1979, obtained as part of study by Mahoney et al. 1988.
c   Data obtained from Church et al. 1978.
d   Data for all years is for all civil cases with a trial list document filed only.
e   Time from service, not case filing.
f   Tort times for all years are for trial list cases only.
g   1983-1987 data exclude cases disposed by arbitration.
*   Data unavailable or not comparable.

1976. Despite these increases, however, Portland, New Orleans, and Miami all remain in the faster half of the courts in this study.

In the four years from 1983 to 1987, six courts reduced their median tort case processing times. Leading the list was Wichita, which reduced its median time by a remarkable 277 days (56 percent), from 492 to 215 days (see Table 7). Even more impressive, Wichita reduced its tort processing time by 196 days between 1985 and 1987. It should be noted that Wichita's progress was not steady. Rather, it showed a substantial increase in processing time from 1976 to 1983 (290 to 492 days) before it began to bring its median case processing time down. Wichita's reduction in case processing time between 1983 and 1987 is even more impressive given its 32 percent increase in filings per FTE civil judge between 1983 and 1987 (see **Table 8**). It should be noted that Wichita initiated a delay reduction effort in 1980.[65] Wichita, therefore, provides a very good example of how a court can reduce its case processing time, despite a significant increase in its filings per judge, if a commitment to delay reduction exists among court leaders.[66]

Dayton is interesting because it was already among the fastest courts (345 days) in 1983. Yet Dayton steadily improved in the past few years by reducing its median tort processing time by 69 days (20 percent) between 1983 and 1987 (see Table 7). Dayton has manifested its commitment to

Table 8

Trends in Civil Case Filings per FTE Civil Judge, 1976–1987

	Tort Median	Civil Filings per FTE Civil Judge				Percent Change Filings per FTE Civil Judge		
	1987	1976[a]	1983[b]	1985[c]	1987[d]	1976-87	1983-87	1985-87
Wichita	215	*	1446[c]	1598	1902[e]	*	32	19
Phoenix	376	1104	1186	1473	175	359	48	19
Jersey City	441	*	747	1005	1221	*	63	21
Miami	482	1073	801	1070	1038	-3	30	-3
Detroit	532	943	*	743	1058	12	*	42
Newark	710	785	*	784	868	11	*	11
San Diego	742[f]	1312	*	*	843	-36	*	*
Boston	953	1317	708	879	958	-27	35	9

a 1976 civil filings divided by 1976 civil judges (Church et al. 1978).
b Mahoney et al. 1985.
c Mahoney et al. 1988 (unpublished data).
d Judges were counted in a manner as comparable to Mahoney et al. (1985 and 1988) as possible.
e Used "total civil judges." Does not account for the 5 percent of judge time spent on other civil or criminal matters. (see Table 2).
f Represents tort cases with a trial readiness document filed.
* Data unavailable or not comparable.

expeditious case processing by adopting case processing time goals for its own judges that are more strict than goals for other courts in Ohio.[67] Naturally, it is encouraging that courts with relatively fast disposition times (e.g., Wichita and Dayton) can become even faster. Both courts have leaders and staff who are committed to reducing court delay. It should be noted that Dayton had the second fewest civil filings (611) per full-time equivalent civil judge in 1987 (see Figure 12) and therefore had more judicial capacity to improve its case processing times. Wichita, however, had a comparatively large caseload per judge. Thus, caseload per judge did not determine the ability of these courts to reduce delay.

Two courts that were among the slowest in 1976 also showed improvement through 1987. Detroit, which had the second-longest median tort disposition time in 1976, made steady progress in reducing tort case processing time through 1987. It made most of its progress from 1985 to 1987, when it reduced its time from 648 to 532 days (18 percent) even though its number of civil cases per judge increased by 42 percent (see Table 8). Detroit showed a commitment to delay reduction by implementing a new case management system in 1986. A substantial degree of credit for the reduction in case processing time can be traced to the new case management program.[68] Because many cases disposed in 1987 were filed before 1986, the full impact of the new case management program was probably not evident in the 1987 data. Even greater progress toward delay reduction should be observed shortly. Oakland saw a steady rise in its median tort processing time from 1976 to 1985 but experienced considerable improvement between 1985 and 1987, reducing its median time from 637 to 504 days (21 percent). Detroit and Oakland, however, had relatively long median tort disposition times in 1985 and could reduce their disposition times more easily. Despite the significant improvements made by Detroit and Oakland, both courts continue to rank among the slower half of the courts in this study on civil case disposition times (see Figures 3 and 8).

Most courts, however, experienced an increase in median tort case processing time since 1983. Providence, which was already one of the slower courts, increased its time by 302 days (up 59 percent) between 1983 and 1987. Boston, Pittsburgh, and Newark were also among the slower courts in 1983, and all experienced considerable increases in median tort disposition time between 1983 and 1987 (see Table 7). Boston's tort disposition time improved from 1976 to 1983, but it has risen substantially since then. Pittsburgh experienced an increase in tort disposition time from 1976 to 1983, saw little change from 1983 to 1985, then increased its time substantially between 1985 and 1987.[69] Newark improved its median tort disposition time from 654 to 544 days between 1976 and 1983, but jumped to 710 days in 1987. Part of the increase in case processing time in Newark between 1983 and 1987 might be attributed to an 11 percent increase in the number of cases filed per FTE civil judge from 784 in 1985 to 868 in 1987 (see Table 8). However, five of the fastest seven courts had more than 1,000 civil cases filed per FTE civil judge in 1987 (see Figure 12). Thus, Newark probably had the judicial capacity to handle its cases more expeditiously.

Phoenix, Miami, and Jersey City are interesting because they were among the fastest half of the 15 courts on median tort case processing time in 1985, but experienced a substantial increase in disposition time between 1985 and 1987 (see Table 7). Miami, for instance, had a median tort disposition time of 325 days in 1985, but dramatically increased its disposition time to 482 days in 1987 (a 48 percent increase). The rise in case processing time coincided with a 30 percent increase in filings per full-time civil judge from 801 in 1983 to 1,038 in 1987. Phoenix also experienced a significant rise in median tort case processing time (292 to 376 days) between 1985 and 1987. This 29 percent rise in case processing time coincided with a 48 percent increase in the number of civil cases filed per full-time civil judge (from 1,186 in 1983 to 1,753 in 1987). In a similar manner, Jersey City's 12 percent rise in median tort disposition time from 394 days in 1985 to 441 days in 1987 paralleled a 63 percent rise in the number of filings per full-time civil judge (from 747 in 1983 to 1,221 in 1987) (see Table 8).

Phoenix, Miami, and Jersey City shared the following characteristics: a relatively expeditious median tort case processing time in 1983 and a rapid increase in filings per judge in a four-year period. Each court had at least 747 filings per civil judge in 1983. Moreover, each exceeded 1,000 filings per civil judge in 1987 (see Figure 12 and Table 8). The number of filings per FTE civil judge alone was not related to longer case processing times in 1987 (see Figure 15). But the data suggest that a substantial increase in filings per judge in a short period in a relatively expeditious court was related to an increase in civil case processing time where courts had relatively high caseloads (i.e., 800 to 1,000 cases) per judge and relatively expeditious case processing times in previous years. In other words, even among courts that operate at a relatively high degree of efficiency, there appears to be a caseload saturation point or threshold. The caseflow management system, already operating at relatively high capacity and efficiency compared to other courts, are unable to absorb a rapid increase in filings per judge. Additional judges may be required to maintain or improve case processing times in these courts.

Wichita, however, provides evidence that fails to support the saturation point explanation derived from the trends in Phoenix, Jersey City, and Miami. Wichita had the largest caseload (1,446 cases) per judge in 1983, almost twice as large as Jersey City's caseload (747 cases) per judge (see Table 8). Wichita had a median tort case disposition time in 1983 that was in the middle range of the 15 courts with comparable data (see Table 7).

From 1983 to 1987, Wichita's caseload per judge increased by 32 percent (more than Miami's increase but less than those of Phoenix and Jersey City) (see Table 8). Despite the 32 percent increase in caseload per judge and the largest initial (in 1983) caseload per judge of any of the 15 courts, Wichita reduced its tort case processing time by 48 percent between 1985 and 1987. Wichita's success is attributable in large part to the civil case management system adopted in the early 1980s.[70] It also suggests that when courts are committed to delay reduction, expeditious case processing can be achieved and maintained even in the face of substantial increases in caseload per judge.

In general, though, the data are somewhat discouraging. Considerable emphasis has been placed on delay reduction in the past decade, yet most of these courts slipped further from achieving of the ABA disposition time standards. The long-term (1976 to 1987) trend in the pace of civil litigation is toward longer disposition times regardless of whether the courts were fast or slow a decade ago. The short-term (1983 to 1987) pattern is similar, though the courts that were the slowest in 1983 generally experienced the greatest increases in civil case processing time.

A silver lining of sorts can be found, however, in the performance of some of the courts in this study. Detroit and Oakland, for instance, were among the slower courts in 1983 but have shown considerable improvement. Dayton and Wichita, two courts that were already relatively fast in previous years, also have shown considerable improvement; they are now nearly in compliance with the ABA disposition time standard that all cases be disposed within two years after filing (see Figure 5). Compliance with the ABA standard, therefore, appears achievable. Wichita's achievement is especially remarkable given its large caseload in 1987. While time will tell whether Wichita can maintain expeditious case processing times with such a large caseload, it is encouraging that cases can be moved quite expeditiously despite relatively large caseloads. Moreover, it is encouraging to know that when courts commit themselves to comprehensive delay reduction initiatives, as Dayton, Detroit, Minneapolis, and Wichita have done in the past decade, delay can be reduced substantially.

Summary: The Pace of Civil Case Litigation, 1987

The first and possibly most important finding regarding the pace of civil case litigation in this study is that several courts are close to achieving the ABA disposition time goal of disposing all civil cases within two years after they are filed. The data, therefore, lead one to conclude that the two-year time standard (all cases disposed within two years) is achievable. None of the 25 courts in this study, however, were in compliance with the ABA disposition time standard that courts dispose of 90 percent of their cases within one year of filing. In fact, none were even very close (within 5 percent of meeting the standard; see Figure 5). Overall, considerable improvement in caseflow management must occur in most of these courts before they will achieve complete compliance with the ABA standards.

One key factor was identified as the best predictor of faster case processing times: early court control over the caseflow. Early control was related to shorter median case processing times for all civil cases and shorter 90th percentile times for all civil, tort, and trial list cases. Case processing time goals were related to shorter 90th percentile times for all civil cases. A higher percentage of tort cases in the caseload was related to longer 90th percentile times for trial list cases only.

In general, these findings should be encouraging. The key factors related to faster case processing (early court control and disposition time goals) are within the capacity of the courts to change. These factors could be key elements in a delay reduction program.

It is noteworthy that the number of filings per judge was not related to civil case processing times when the effects of other factors were controlled through multivariate analysis. When asked about court resources, however, court administrators and judges in slower courts generally rated a lack of resources (especially judges and courtrooms) as being a very serious problem, whereas administrators and judges from faster courts viewed "insufficient judges" as a minor problem. The findings from this study should help slower courts assess more accurately the source of their court delay problems and organizational needs.

Backlog index (number of pending cases at the start of the year divided by the number of disposed cases for the year) displayed a moderate-to-strong correlation with all nine measures of case processing time. Court managers and judges could use this index as a simple means for monitoring the case processing performance of their courts.

Finally, trends in the pace of litigation were examined in 18 courts. Ten courts experienced an increase in their median tort case processing times since 1976, while only five courts reduced their times. Ten of 16 courts experienced an increase in disposition times between 1983 and 1987. Thus, despite the emphasis on delay reduction during the past decade, the trend is toward longer case processing times in these urban trial courts. Some good news can be found, however, in the few courts that managed to reduce their case processing times despite increases in caseloads. Four of the courts that showed substantial improvement, including Wichita, Dayton, Detroit, and Minneapolis, had instituted delay reduction programs during the past decade. If courts are committed to the improving their case management procedures, court delay can be reduced.

Notes

20. There are only 25 courts in the study of civil case litigation because civil case data from the Bronx Supreme Court could not be obtained in time to be included in this report. Bronx is included in the study of felony case processing time.

21. In all figures involving case processing times, the shaded bars indicate the number of days required to dispose of the median, 75th, and 90th percentile cases. The first number displayed on the bar for a particular court is the median time. The number at the right end of the bar is the 90th percentile time. The reader can approximate the 75th percentile time from the chart.

22. In Salinas, this reflects recent efforts to close out the oldest cases.

23. Providence does not take action to move cases to the trial-setting stage, and cases are not dismissed routinely for failure to prosecute.

24. It is not clear whether the COSCA/CCJ Standards require 100 percent of a court's cases to be disposed within the stated time periods or whether the average case should meet these standards.

25. This overestimates the percentage of cases Pittsburgh typically has over two years old. First, the sample does not include cases that went to mandatory arbitration and did not seek review in the general jurisdiction court. Thus, the sample does not include what might have been many of the simpler and faster cases. Second, a new administrative judge in Pittsburgh purged many of the oldest cases during 1987.

26. San Diego data are excluded because they include only cases in which a trial readiness document was filed; Pittsburgh is excluded because their data do not include cases disposed by arbitration.

27. See footnote 26.

28. See, e.g., Grossman et al. (1981) p. 103; Mahoney et al. (1988) p. 49.

29. The .05 level is used to determine statistical significance. This means that the relationship (i.e., the correlation coefficient) is likely to have occurred by chance in only 5 samples out of 100. (See also Blalock (1979) pp. 415-25.) Hereafter, only those relationships that are statistically significant at the .05 level or better are reported in the text.

30. For instance, percentage torts is related to the median case processing times for all civil ($r = .42$), contract ($r = .35$); 90th percentile for all civil ($r = .37$) and contract ($r = .39$). All these correlations are statistically significant ($p \leq .05$). See Appendix B.

31. $r = .71$; $p = .002$. See Appendix B.

32. Median all civil ($r = -.37$) and contract cases ($r = -.36$); and 90th percentile for trial list cases ($r = -.55$); $p < .05$. See Appendix B.

33. Some factors about these courts should be considered in trying to understand their disposition times. Norfolk is the site of the largest naval base in the United States, and many of the old cases, according to court administrators, involve naval personnel who are out of the country. The same explanation could apply to San Diego, which also is host to a large naval base. Boston purged many old cases during 1987 in preparation for meeting the demands of the new statewide delay reduction act which became effective in July 1988. But Boston has displayed very slow disposition times since 1976. The slow median time in Boston, therefore, is not totally attributable to the purge of old cases that occurred in 1987, though the increase in case processing time since 1985 could be attributable to the purge of old cases in 1987 (see pp. 43-48). Like Boston, Salinas purged a large number of old cases (over five years old) during 1987, so its median and especially 90th percentile times are longer than

in a more typical year. Oakland, site of World War II military shipbuilding yards, has a large proportion of old cases because there have been approximately 2,000 pending asbestos (toxic tort) cases, which involve large numbers of plaintiffs and defendants. The comparatively long 90th percentile disposition times in the District of Columbia and New Orleans may be due to the lack of systematic procedures for checking (and possibly dismissing) old cases.

34. Counting and comparing cases across courts is one of the most difficult tasks in research on the pace of litigation. For instance, courts vary in the types of cases that are within their jurisdiction and when they begin to count cases (at filing of a complaint or when assigned to a trial judge). In order to maintain comparability of data, some courts were excluded from the Tables and Figures if their data were not comparable to other courts. Some courts are included in the Tables and Figures with footnotes that identify the factor that affects comparability (see, e.g., Pittsburgh in the Tables and Figures).

35. See, e.g., Flanders (1977); Church et al. (1978a); Friesen et al. (1978); Neubauer et al. (1981); Martin and Prescott (1981); Weller et al. (1982); Mahoney et al. (1985, 1988).

36. Contract cases 90th percentile ($r = -.38$); trial list 90th percentile ($r = -.43$). All are statistically significant ($p \leq .05$). See Appendix C.

37. Percent contract cases ($r = .44$; $p = .02$); percent tort cases ($r = -.38$; $p < .04$). See Appendix C.

38. See also Flanders (1977); Church et al. (1978a); Friesen et al. (1978); Neubauer et al. (1981); Martin and Prescott (1981); Weller et al. (1982); Mahoney et al. (1988).

39. See the section, "Trends in the Pace of Civil Case Litigation," p. 43. Trend data support a saturation point argument that fast courts, if they experience an increased caseload per judge, will need additional judges to process cases expeditiously.

40. It is possible that courts with a smaller caseload per judge do not have as many administrative and/or support staff per judge as courts with a larger caseload. This is an important measure of resources that was *not* examined in this study.

41. See Church et al. (1978a) pp. 36-38; Mahoney et al. (1985) p. 15; (1988) p. 73.

42. All civil cases: median ($r = -.42$), 90th percentile ($r = -.43$); tort cases: median and 90th percentile ($r = -.38$); contract cases: median ($r = -.38$); 90th percentile ($r = -.43$); jury trials median ($r = -.48$). All were statistically significant ($p < .04$). See Appendix C.

43. San Diego and Pittsburgh were excluded from this correlation analysis due to non-comparable data. See footnote 26.

44. See, e.g., Solomon (1973); Friesen et al. (1978); Friesen (1984); Solomon and Somerlot (1987); Mahoney et al. (1988).

45. Including courts that, by rule, had a status or scheduling conference of some kind within 120 days after the filing of the complaint, regardless of whether all answers had been filed by that time.

46. Including those courts that had the authority to dismiss a case on their own motion if a trial date had not been requested within one year after the complaint was filed.

47. 90th percentile: trial list ($r = .75$), $p = .000$ (see also Appendix C).

48. All civil ($r = -.40$) and tort cases ($r = -.40$); $p = .03$. See Appendix C.

49. See Appendix I and pp. 80-83.

50. See Solomon (1973) p. 36; Mahoney et al. (1988) p. 199; Mahoney and Sipes (1985) pp. 11-13.

51. All civil ($r = -.50$); torts ($r = -.41$); contracts ($r = -.50$); trial list cases ($r = -.53$). All were statistically significant ($p < .03$). See Appendix C.

52. See Murray (1984) p. 19; Mahoney and Sipes (1985) pp. 12-13.

53. See Mahoney et al. (1988) p. 200.

54. Firm trial dates were also related to shorter disposition times. But because relevant data were obtained from only seven courts, this finding should not be overemphasized at this time.

55. (r) ranged from .51 to .69; (p) ranged from .001 to .02. See Appendix C.

56. A sample of 26 courts is too small to allow for multivariate regression analysis involving simultaneously all relevant explanatory variables. If a substantially larger number of courts were included, more sophisticated analysis could reveal which of the many variables, if any, retain significant relationships with other factors when the influence of the other independent variables are controlled simultaneously.

57. For a description of the series of three variable "stepwise" regression analyses used in this study, see Appendix A. For a description of the results of the multivariate analyses depicted in Figure 15, see Appendix N. A more common multivariate technique that could have been used in this study is partial correlation analysis (see, e.g., Blalock (1979), Chapter 19). However, Blalock notes that partial correlation and regression techniques usually rank variables in the same order of importance.

58. "Firm trial dates" (i.e., the percentage of jury trial cases that started trial on the first scheduled trial date) were not included in the multivariate analysis because there were too few courts (7) that had relevant data. "Firm trial dates" were very important in the analysis of felony case processing times.

59. See Appendix N.

60. See, e.g., Mahoney et al. (1989), which discusses successful civil case delay reduction in Dayton and Phoenix.

61. There were a few administrators who returned the survey without having the presiding judge sign it. The views of court administrators and judges sometimes conflict regarding the nature and extent of certain kinds of problems in the court. It cannot be known from our survey whether the ratings reflect a consensus score (arrived at after discussion between the administrator and judge) or if the administrator (or judge) simply deferred to the other's judgment.

62. Statistical significance determined by means of the chi square statistic.

63. See, e.g., Zeisel et al. (1959).

64. See Solomon and Somerlot (1987) pp. 48-51; Mahoney et al. (1988) p. 204.

65. See Schwartz (1984) p. 22.

66. See Mahoney et al. (1988). Chapter 8 explains the nature of Wichita's delay reduction program.

67. Dayton civil disposition time goals: mortgage foreclosure and administrative appeals (120 days); workers' compensation and appropriation (180 days); personal injury (270 days); medical malpractice (360 days); injunctions and all other civil cases (150 days). See Mahoney et al. (1988). Chapter 6 discusses the civil and criminal case management program in Dayton.

68. See Mahoney et al. (1988). Chapter 7 includes a description of the new civil case management program in Wayne County Circuit Court.

69. Pittsburgh also purged many of its oldest cases in 1987 at the direction of a new administrative judge. Disposition times are thus somewhat longer than might have been projected from previous years. It also should be reiterated that Pittsburgh's sample does not include cases disposed by arbitration. Because arbitration cases are usually shorter, the numbers reported here probably overstate the median case processing times in Pittsburgh.

70. See Mahoney et al. (1988). Wichita's civil case management and delay reduction program is described in Chapter 7. Wichita has a unified district court so that the court has jurisdiction over all civil cases, regardless of the dollar amount at issue. For purposes of case processing time analysis, only major civil cases were counted (those in which there was more than $5,000 in damages at issue). For purposes of filings per judge, however, all civil cases were counted, including limited action cases (those $5,000 or less), because the judges were required to handle both limited action and major civil cases. Probate and domestic relations cases were excluded. Judges who handled only domestic relations, probate, or small claims cases were excluded from the "filings per judge" ratio.

The Pace of Felony Case Litigation, 1987

Felony Case Processing Times in 26 Urban Trial Courts

This section presents an overview of felony case processing times. Two primary measures of case processing time are used to capture the complex nature of criminal litigation. First, total disposition time includes time from arrest to disposition. In most jurisdictions, total disposition time measures the time it takes the local criminal justice system to conclude its cases. It reflects the coordination and cooperation among the various agencies, including the police, prosecutor's office, lower court, and general jurisdiction court. The second measure is from the filing of an indictment or information in the general jurisdiction court[71] to disposition, or upper court disposition time. Although interagency cooperation remains important, during this time period the upper court can independently exercise considerable influence over the pace of criminal litigation.

Figure 16 displays the overall median disposition times from across the 26 courts for various case categories. It is not surprising that the most serious cases (murder, rape, and robbery) required the longest time (148 days) from arrest to disposition. Drug sale and drug possession cases took about the same amount of time from arrest to disposition (118 and 120 days, respectively). The median time from arrest to disposition for other felonies (104 days) was approximately two weeks shorter than for drug cases. In general, the typical felony case (see *all felonies* in Figure 16) required 119 days from arrest to disposition. The patterns are similar when only upper court time (indictment or information to disposition) is considered. Most serious cases were longest (113 days), followed by drug sale cases (89 days). Drug possession cases, however, generally took the same amount of time in the upper court as all other felonies (74 days). Drug possession cases, on the other hand, displayed the longest overall time from arrest to indictment or information (46 days); all other case types were notably shorter for this phase of case processing. This anomaly might be explained by the need for lab tests on the suspected substance in drug possession cases, though lab tests would also be necessary in drug sale cases.

As was true of civil case processing times, the overall median case processing times for large urban trial courts obscure variations among the courts. Focusing on the individual courts, **Figure 17** presents the 50th, 75th, and 90th percentile disposition times for total disposition times for all felony cases for all courts in the study.[72] Dayton (56 days) and Salinas (62 days) had the fastest median times from arrest to disposition. Newark, at 308 days, had a median total disposition time that was more than five times longer than Dayton's. The average median total disposition time was 126 days.

At the 90th percentile time, Salinas (162 days) was the fastest, while Providence (859 days) was the slowest. St. Paul is notable because it had the fourth fastest median time from arrest to disposition (77 days), but dropped to 18th place with its 90th percentile time (434 days). Conversely,

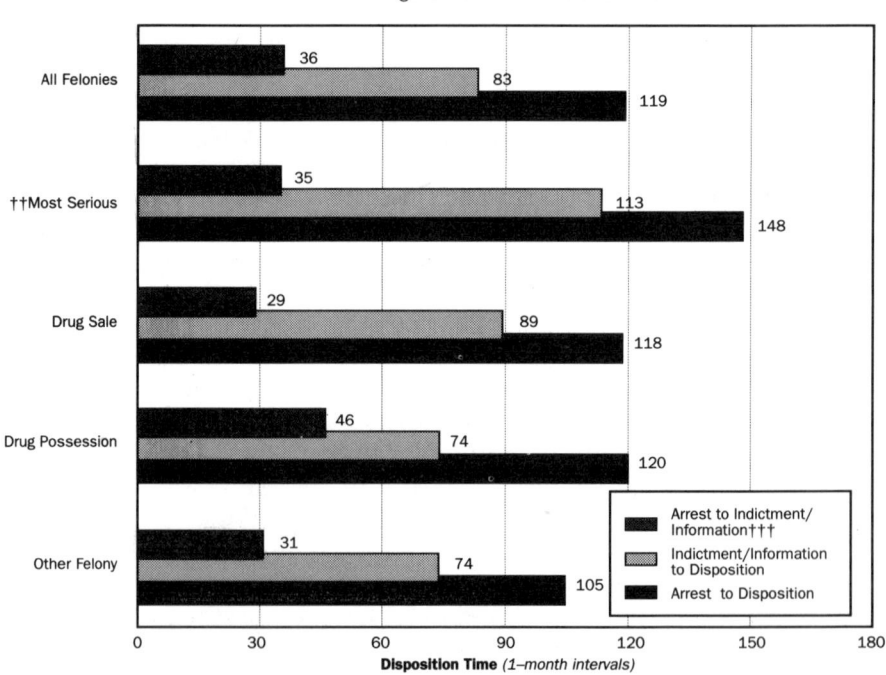

Figure 16
Median Felony Case Processing Times†
for Large Urban Trial Courts–1987

Case Type	Arrest to Indictment/Information†††	Indictment/Information to Disposition	Arrest to Disposition
All Felonies	36	83	119
††Most Serious	35	113	148
Drug Sale	29	89	118
Drug Possession	46	74	120
Other Felony	31	74	105

Disposition Time (1–month intervals)

† Medians from among the median CPT's for 18-26 courts depending upon case type and whether total or upper court time.
†† Murder, rape, and robbery.
††† Arrest to disposition minus indictment/information to disposition.

Pittsburgh moved from 19th place on median total disposition time (153 days) to 7th place with its 90th percentile time (283 days). The average 90th percentile total disposition time among these courts was 370 days.

Figure 18 displays upper court disposition times (indictment or information to disposition). Salinas had the fastest median upper court time (22 days), followed by Fairfax (29 days). At the other end, Boston (233 days) was by far the slowest to dispose of 50 percent of its cases after they reached the upper court. Jersey City was the second slowest at 150 days. The average median time from indictment/information to disposition among the 26 courts was 86 days.

Figure 18 also reveals the disparities among the courts at the 90th percentile upper court disposition time. Newark (894 days), Providence

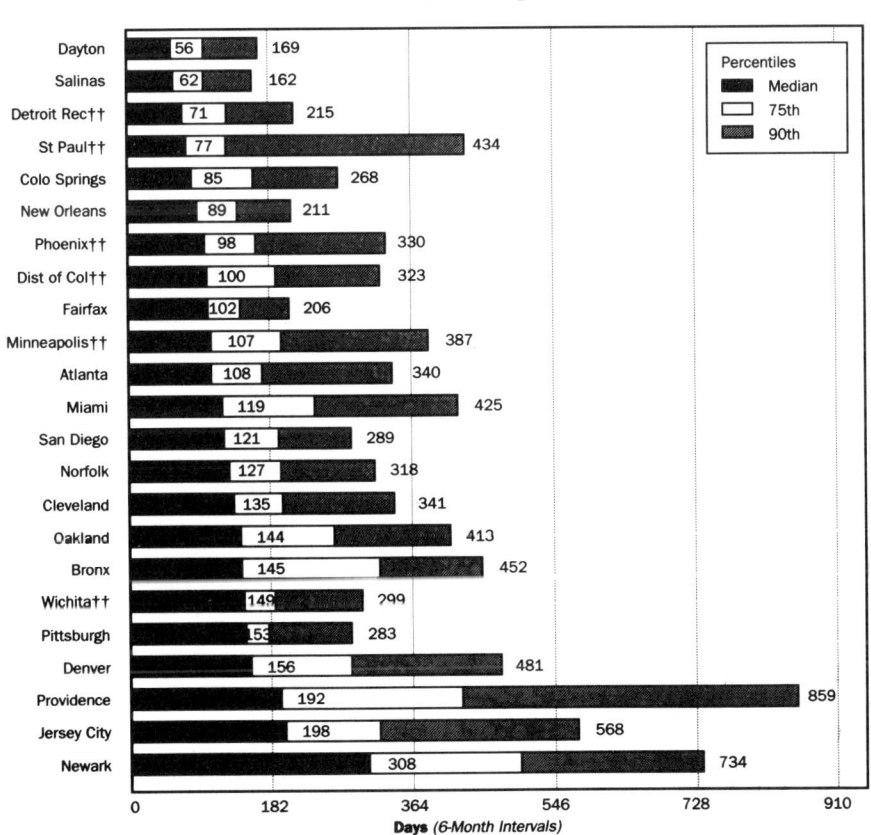

Figure 17
Felony Case Processing Time–1987†
Arrest to Disposition

Court	Median	90th
Dayton	56	169
Salinas	62	162
Detroit Rec††	71	215
St Paul††	77	434
Colo Springs	85	268
New Orleans	89	211
Phoenix††	98	330
Dist of Col††	100	323
Fairfax	102	206
Minneapolis††	107	387
Atlanta	108	340
Miami	119	425
San Diego	121	289
Norfolk	127	318
Cleveland	135	341
Oakland	144	413
Bronx	145	452
Wichita††	149	299
Pittsburgh	153	283
Denver	156	481
Providence	192	859
Jersey City	198	568
Newark	308	734

Days (6-Month Intervals)

† Original arrest and complaint dates not available or obtained from Boston, Portland, and Tucson.
†† Used date complaint filed as starting point; original arrest dates not or infrequently available.

(811), Jersey City (605 days), and Miami (624 days) had very slow 90th percentile times. These courts are especially notable because they required a considerably longer proportion of time to move from their median to their 90th percentile cases than to dispose of the first 50 percent of their cases. Wichita, on the other hand, was the fourth slowest court at the median upper court disposition time (133 days), but moved up to the 9th fastest at the 90th percentile time (231 days). Fairfax (65 days) and Salinas (69 days) had the fastest 90th percentile upper court disposition times. In fact,

Figure 18
Felony Case Processing Time–1987
Indictment/Information to Disposition

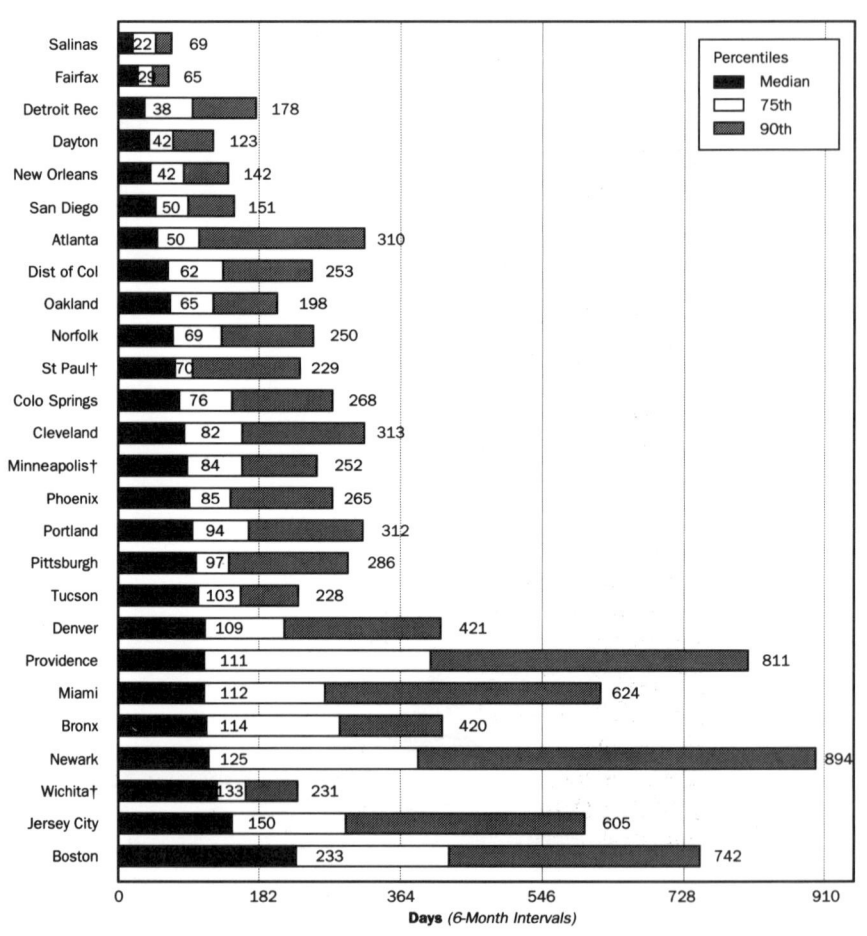

Court	Median	75th	90th
Salinas	22		69
Fairfax	29		65
Detroit Rec	38		178
Dayton	42		123
New Orleans	42		142
San Diego	50		151
Atlanta	50		310
Dist of Col	62		253
Oakland	65		198
Norfolk	69		250
St Paul†	70		229
Colo Springs	76		268
Cleveland	82		313
Minneapolis†	84		252
Phoenix	85		265
Portland	94		312
Pittsburgh	97		286
Tucson	103		228
Denver	109		421
Providence	111		811
Miami	112		624
Bronx	114		420
Newark	125		894
Wichita†	133		231
Jersey City	150		605
Boston	233		742

Days (6-Month Intervals)

† Used time from first appearance in upper court to disposition; date indictment/information filed was unavailable.

Fairfax and Salinas had 90th percentile upper court disposition times that were shorter than or equal to the median disposition times in 18 of the courts. The average 90th percentile upper court disposition time among the 26 courts was 333 days.

The variation in disposition times within and among the courts is interesting and informative. These statistics alone, however, do not tell the extent to which there is unnecessary delay in the courts. The ABA standards provide guidance on this issue.

The ABA Criminal Case Disposition Time Standards

The COSCA/CCJ and ABA disposition time standards for felony cases are listed below. Most states have speedy trial rules for criminal cases to assure that the constitutional rights of defendants are met. But COSCA/CCJ and ABA standards are useful because they provide the courts with some generally acceptable standards for defining delay. The ABA standards are more specific[73] and are used here as the guide for defining unnecessary case processing time.

COSCA/CCJ and ABA Felony Cases
Disposition Time Standards

	COSCA/CCJ	ABA
Felonies (arrest to disposition)	180 days	90 % in 120 days 98 % in 180 days 100 % in 1 year

Figure 19 indicates the percentage of cases in each court that exceeded the ABA standards at 180 days (98 percent of all cases should be completed) and one year (100 percent of all cases should be completed). At the 180-day goal, only two courts (Dayton and Salinas) were even close to having 98 percent of their cases disposed. The courts ranged from having 8 percent of their cases over 180 days old at disposition (Dayton and Salinas) to 81 percent over 180 days old (Newark). No court met the ABA standard of having only 2 percent of felony cases beyond 180 days old. At the one-year mark, several courts were close to having 100 percent of their cases disposed, in compliance with the ABA standards. Dayton, with only 1 percent of its cases older than one year, virtually met the standard. Likewise, Salinas, Detroit, New Orleans, and Fairfax (all at 2 percent over one year), and San Diego and Wichita (both at 5 percent over one year) were all close to meeting the ABA standards. At least three courts, however, had more than 20 percent of their cases over one year old at disposition; nine

courts had more than 10 percent of their cases exceeding the one-year time standard.

Wichita is notable because it is among the slower half of the courts on median processing times (see Figures 17 and 18). Yet it exceeded the ABA one-year standard by only 5 percent. By this measure, Wichita is among the top half of the courts, displaying minimal delay. In general, though, slower courts tended to have a higher percentage of cases over the ABA time standards.

More courts were close to meeting the ABA's criminal disposition time standards than were close to meeting the civil case time standards. Fourteen courts, for instance, exceeded the ABA's one-year felony disposi-

Figure 19
Percent of All Felony Cases Over ABA Standards–1987†

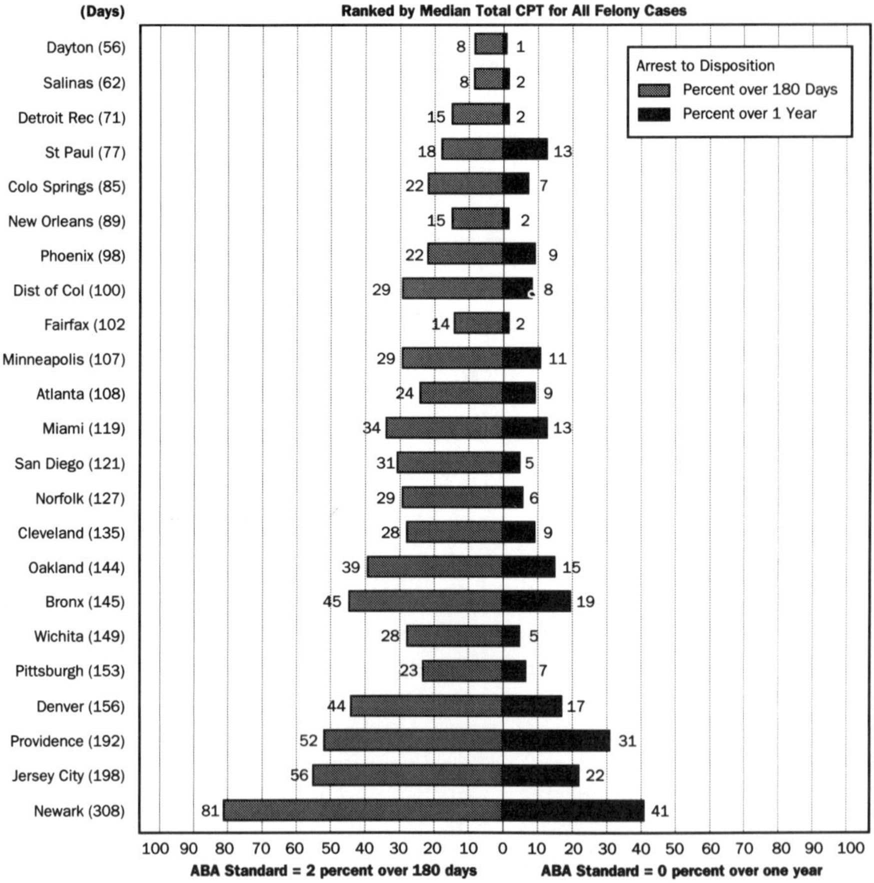

Ranked by Median Total CPT for All Felony Cases

Arrest to Disposition
- Percent over 180 Days
- Percent over 1 Year

Court (Days)	% over 180 Days	% over 1 Year
Dayton (56)	8	1
Salinas (62)	8	2
Detroit Rec (71)	15	2
St Paul (77)	18	13
Colo Springs (85)	22	7
New Orleans (89)	15	2
Phoenix (98)	22	9
Dist of Col (100)	29	8
Fairfax (102)	14	2
Minneapolis (107)	29	11
Atlanta (108)	24	9
Miami (119)	34	13
San Diego (121)	31	5
Norfolk (127)	29	6
Cleveland (135)	28	9
Oakland (144)	39	15
Bronx (145)	45	19
Wichita (149)	28	5
Pittsburgh (153)	23	7
Denver (156)	44	17
Providence (192)	52	31
Jersey City (198)	56	22
Newark (308)	81	41

ABA Standard = 2 percent over 180 days   ABA Standard = 0 percent over one year

† Boston, Portland, and Tucson are not included; arrest dates were unavailabe.

tion time standard by ten percent or less.[74] But 21 courts exceeded the 180-day felony standard by more than 10 percent. Overall, no court in the study complied with the ABA disposition time standard of only 2 percent of felony cases over 180 days old at disposition.

Felony Caseload Mix

In order to address the problems involved in reducing disposition times in these and other courts, it is necessary to understand the impact of case mix, caseload, and resource and case management factors on case processing times among the courts. In this section, the impact of case mix on the pace of litigation will be examined. Some courts, due to jurisdictional and demographic differences, have a higher percentage of more serious cases than other courts. Because the most serious cases are likely to take longer, courts with a higher percentage of serious cases are expected to produce longer case processing times overall.

Figure 20 illustrates the overall median felony caseload mix for the 26 urban trial courts in this study. Fourteen percent of all cases were in the *most serious* category (murder, rape, robbery). Drug-related cases constituted 26 percent of the average caseload (16 percent drug sale cases and 10 percent drug possession cases). Sixty percent of the cases were *other felony*, mostly larceny and burglary. Case types were defined by the most serious charge in the indictment or information. Thus, the percentage of drug-related cases reported here underestimates the total number of cases in

Figure 20
Average Felony Caseload Mix–1987†
23 Large Urban Trial Courts

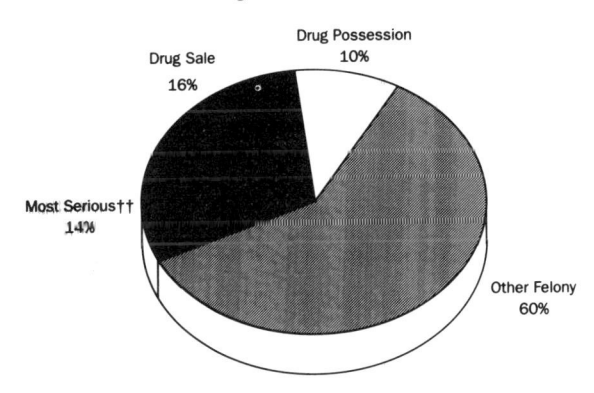

- Drug Possession 10%
- Drug Sale 16%
- Most Serious†† 14%
- Other Felony 60%

† Based on the most serious charge in the indictment or information. District of Columbia excluded from all case types (see footnote f in Table 9). Norfolk and Pittsburgh excluded from all drug cases (see footnote g in Table 9).
†† Includes murder, rape, robbery.

which drug charges were involved. For example, cases were not categorized as *drug possession* cases if they included more serious charges (e.g., rape, robbery, assault). Furthermore, conversations with judges and administrators in many of the courts in this study suggest that the percentage of drug cases in their caseloads were even higher in their courts in 1988 than during 1987.

Concentrating on the typical caseload mix obscures the substantial variations among the individual courts. **Figure 21**, therefore, illustrates the percentages of drug and most serious cases in the caseload for each court in the study. The percentage of most serious cases ranged from 31 percent in Boston to 6 percent in Atlanta and New Orleans.[75] Boston had the longest median upper court processing time; New Orleans was among the

Figure 21
Felony Caseload Mix–1987
Ranked by Median Upper Court Case Processing Time

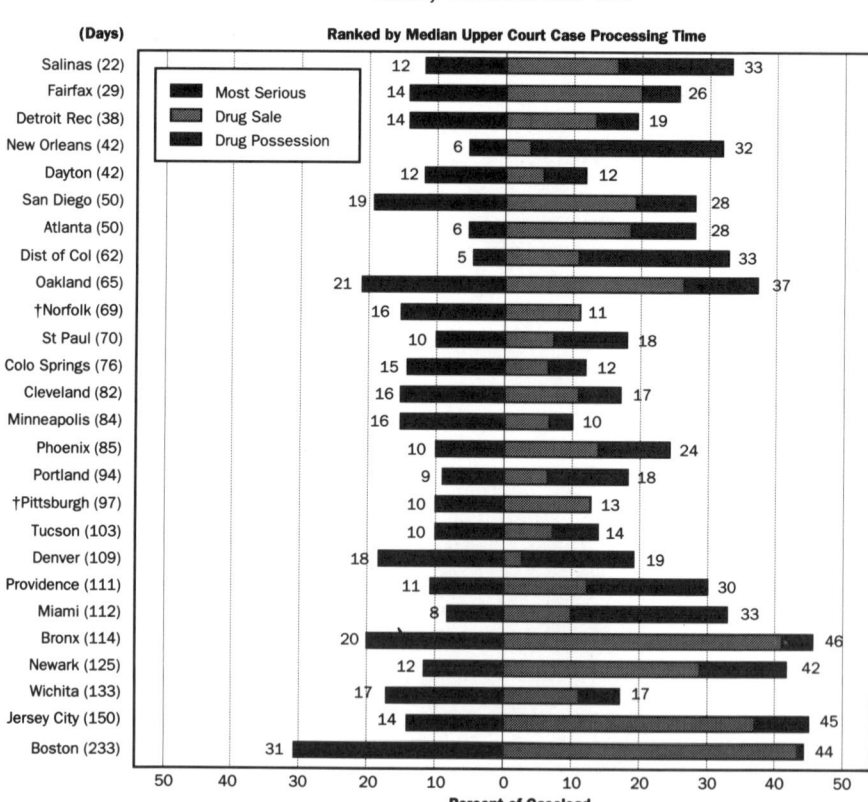

Court (Days)	Most Serious	Drug Sale	Drug Possession (combined %)
Salinas (22)	12		33
Fairfax (29)	14		26
Detroit Rec (38)	14		19
New Orleans (42)	6		32
Dayton (42)	12		12
San Diego (50)	19		28
Atlanta (50)	6		28
Dist of Col (62)	5		33
Oakland (65)	21		37
†Norfolk (69)	16		11
St Paul (70)	10		18
Colo Springs (76)	15		12
Cleveland (82)	16		17
Minneapolis (84)	16		10
Phoenix (85)	10		24
Portland (94)	9		18
†Pittsburgh (97)	10		13
Tucson (103)	10		14
Denver (109)	18		19
Providence (111)	11		30
Miami (112)	8		33
Bronx (114)	20		46
Newark (125)	12		42
Wichita (133)	17		17
Jersey City (150)	14		45
Boston (233)	31		44

Percent of Caseload

† Norfolk and Pittsburgh; drug possession included under "drug sale."

faster courts. But the pattern among most of the other courts between the percentage of most serious cases and median upper court time is not clear.

Figure 21 also shows that the percentage of drug sale cases ranged from 43 percent in Boston to 2 percent in Denver. Four of the five courts with the largest percentage of drug sale cases (Bronx, Boston, Jersey City, and Newark) were among the five slowest courts on median upper court disposition time. Denver, however, was also among the slowest third of the courts but had the lowest percentage (2 percent) of drug sale cases. Fairfax had a moderately high percentage of drug sale cases (20 percent), but was among the fastest courts on upper court processing time. Nonetheless, the relationship between percentage of drug sale cases and median upper court time appears to be substantial: slower courts tended to have more drug sale cases.

It is possible that case mix and other factors could have different impacts on different types of felony cases. In order to check for such variations, several measures of felony case processing time will be used in this section. These measures include the median for total (arrest to disposition) and upper court (indictment/information to disposition) case processing times for

(1) all felony cases;
(2) most serious (murder, rape, robbery) cases;
(3) drug sale cases;
(4) drug possession cases;
(5) all other felony cases; and
(6) jury trial cases.

These measures will provide a basis for determining the impact of various factors on the typical (median) cases. In addition to these 12 measures, the 90th percentile total and upper court case processing times for all felony cases will be examined to determine the impact of various factors on the disposition times for the oldest cases in each court. In all, then, 14 measures of felony case processing time will be used.

Regarding the impact of case mix, correlation analysis confirms earlier observations about the importance of drug cases. The percentage of drug sale cases displayed a correlation with 12 of the 14 measures of case processing time (see Appendix H). Thus, as the percentage of drug sale cases in a caseload increased, the disposition times for all felony case types were likely to be longer.

As noted earlier, most serious cases generally took longer than other case types (see Figure 16). Correlation analysis shows that the percentage of most serious cases in a caseload were moderately correlated with median upper court time in four case categories.[76] But it was not related to total or 90th percentile case processing times.

The percentage of drug possession cases, however, had very little impact on case processing times; it failed to show a significant correlation with any measure of felony case processing time. Even the combination of drug possession and drug sale cases (percentage of all drug cases) failed to produce a substantially stronger[77] correlation with any felony case processing times than was established by the percentage of drug sale cases alone (see Appendix H).

It is worth exploring whether the combination of drug sale and most serious cases exerted a correlation that was significantly greater than the relationship established by the percentage of drug sale cases alone. Combining the percentages of drug sale cases and most serious cases did not significantly increase any correlations beyond those established by the percentage of drug sale cases alone (see Appendix H).

There was a substantial correlation between the percentage of drug sale cases and the percentage of most serious cases in the caseload.[78] As the apparent magnitude of the drug problem increased, so did the proportion of violent crime cases in a jurisdiction. Also noteworthy is the negative correlation between the percentage of most serious and the percentage of drug possession cases in the caseload.[79] As the percentage of most serious cases increased, the percentage of drug possession cases tended to decrease. This phenomenon probably occurs because as the percentage of serious violent crime cases increases, prosecutors may file most "possession only" cases as misdemeanors in order to spend more time on the more serious (violent) offenses.

This is the first time research on the pace of litigation has included an examination of the impact of drug-related cases on case processing time. The finding of a relationship between the percentage of drug sale cases in the caseload and court delay calls for more sophisticated study of the issue because of its potential policy implications. A first step toward a better understanding of the complex relationship between the percentage of drug sale cases in the caseload and court delay is to examine the variations among the courts in case processing times for the various case types.

Examination of case processing times for drug sale cases is relevant because of the apparent relationship between the percentage of drug sale cases in the caseload and court delay. Drug sale cases are potentially complex. Drug dealers frequently can afford private counsel, and their cases may be more likely to involve motions to suppress evidence based on questions surrounding the search of the defendant's person, car, or home. Lab tests also can slow the processing of drug cases. Furthermore, longer and mandatory sentences for drug dealing increase the likelihood that defendants will seek a jury trial. Among the 26 courts, only the most serious cases took longer than drug sale cases in the upper court (see Figure 16).

There was considerable variation among the courts in their comparative times on drug sale and most serious cases. **Table 9** displays the median total and upper court processing times in each court for the various case types. Fairfax, San Diego, Newark, and Jersey City are interesting because their total processing times were longer for drug sale than for most serious cases, but their median upper court processing times for drug sale cases were shorter than for most serious cases. In other words, the preindictment processing time was longer for drug sale cases than for most serious cases in these courts. The greatest difference was in Newark, where the typical time from arrest to indictment (total time minus upper court time) was approximately 213 days for drug sale cases but 87 days for most serious cases.

Figure 22 compares the median upper court times for drug sale and most serious cases. It shows that in 8 of the 26 courts, the median drug sale cases required more time than the median most serious cases (see also Table 9). The differences between most serious and drug sale cases in these 8 courts were not very great. Moreover, the 8 courts that processed drug sale cases more slowly than their most serious cases tend to be found in the middle range of courts on median upper court time for all felony cases. Therefore, taking more time in the upper court to process drug sale cases than most serious cases was not associated with longer case processing times overall among the courts.

A more interesting pattern exists in the comparative processing times for drug sale and less serious (other felony) cases. Most courts processed less serious cases more quickly than drug sale cases. But **Figure 23** shows that seven courts processed their drug sale cases faster than their less serious cases. The most striking differences were in the Bronx (a 51-day difference) and Newark (a 49-day difference). Six of these seven courts (Boston, Bronx, Jersey City, Miami, Newark, and Providence) were among the seven slowest courts on median upper court time for all felony cases (see Figure 18). In Newark, moreover, other (less serious) felonies took longer from arrest to disposition (352 days) than either drug sale (304 days) or most serious (251 days) cases (see Table 9). This anomaly did not occur in any other court. Courts and/or the prosecutors in these seven jurisdictions may have given priority to processing drug sale cases at the expense of less serious cases. Without more in-depth case study data on the policies and practices of the prosecutors in these and other jurisdictions, the foregoing interpretation must remain tentative. The data, however, suggest that courts and prosecutors should proceed with caution if they intend to expedite drug sale cases at the expense of less serious cases. Such a policy could result in greater court delay overall.

64 / Examining Court Delay

Table 9

Median Felony Case Processing Times by Case Types–1987

	Upper Court: Indictment to Disposition[a]					Total: Arrest to Disposition[b]				
	All Cases	Most Serious	Drug Sale	Drug Possess.	Other Felony	All Cases	Most Serious	Drug Sale	Drug Possess.	Other Felony
Salinas	22	52	25	4	9	62	96	58	70	52
Fairfax	29	43	30	30	23	102	114	128	*	90
Detroit Rec[c]	38	85	32	14	35	71	114	59	64	65
New Orleans	42	117	*	45	36	89	159	*	90	81
Dayton	42	45	54	47	40	56	59	62	142	52
San Diego[d]	50	66	58	36	42	121	115	181	96	101
Atlanta	50	90	59	37	47	108	147	123	120	87
Dist of Col[e,f]	62	95	119	76	49	100	152	134	101	86
Oakland[d]	65	109	68	70	57	144	172	164	191	107
Norfolk	69	87	174[g]	*	58	127	146	230[g]	*	114
St Paul[e,h]	70	66	76	74	70	77	68	91	75	77
Colo Springs	76	133	118	56	66	85	142	106	68	74
Cleveland	82	104	78	84	74	135	149	114	147	133
Minneapolis[e,h]	84	98	105	87	79	107	104	126	109	105
Phoenix[c]	85	113	122	70	73	98	110	110	97	96
Portland[i]	94	85	92	112	90	*	*	*	*	*
Pittsburgh	97	134	91[g]	*	93	153	169	160[g]	*	147
Tucson[i]	103	146	132	106	96	*	*	*	*	*
Denver	109	148	*	95	103	156	188	*	144	147
Providence	111	217	100	74	117	192	291	202	183	183
Miami	112	148	89	91	116	119	176	97	106	113
Bronx[d]	114	238	67	98	118	145	277	87	132	184
Newark	125	164	91	113	140	308	251	304	262	352
Wichita[e,h]	133	149	153	155	126	149	160	165	168	139
Jersey City	150	155	143	120	156	198	186	216	158	197
Boston[i]	233	274	225	*	236	*	*	*	*	*
Mean	86	121	93	74	83	126	154	133	126	121

a Date indictment or information filed in the court (dispositions included dismissals, guilty pleas, diversions, deferred adjudications, and verdicts after trial).
b Used date of original arrest.
c Arrest dates generally unavailable; used date lower court complaint filed as start date for total CPT.
d Total and upper court case processing time measures include some felony cases in which the defendant pled guilty in the lower court.
e Arrest dates generally unavailable; used date complaint filed in clerk's office as start date for total CPT (no lower court in these jurisdictions).
f Case types determined by the most serious charge at *conviction*, not in indictment/information; CPT's for most serious, drug sale, drug possession, and less serious were not used to calculate the means.
g Could not distinguish drug sale cases from drug possession cases; included all drug-related cases under drug sale cases in this table.
h Date indictment or information filed unavailable; used date of first appearance by defendant in upper court as start date for upper court CPT.
i Arrest date and date complaint filed unavailable.
* Data unavailable or not comparable.

Evidence presented here suggests that some of the longer case processing times among the courts were attributable to higher percentages of most serious and drug sale cases in their caseloads. A higher percentage of drug sale cases in the caseload were related to longer case processing times, not only for categories of cases that included drug sale cases (e.g., "all" and "jury trials") but also for nondrug cases as well. However, the courts with the largest drug sale caseloads in 1987 (Boston, Bronx, Jersey City, and Newark) were among the slowest courts in earlier studies of felony case processing times (see Table 19; see also Mahoney et al. (1988)). Moreover, Table 21 in this study indicates that the size of the drug-related caseload increased most dramatically between 1983 and 1987 in the courts that were among the slowest on median upper court time in 1983 (see also Goerdt et al. (1989)). The most convincing interpretation of all the available data suggests that a higher percentage of drug cases in the caseload is not the

Figure 22
Drug Sale vs. Most Serious Cases–1987*
Indictment/Information to Disposition

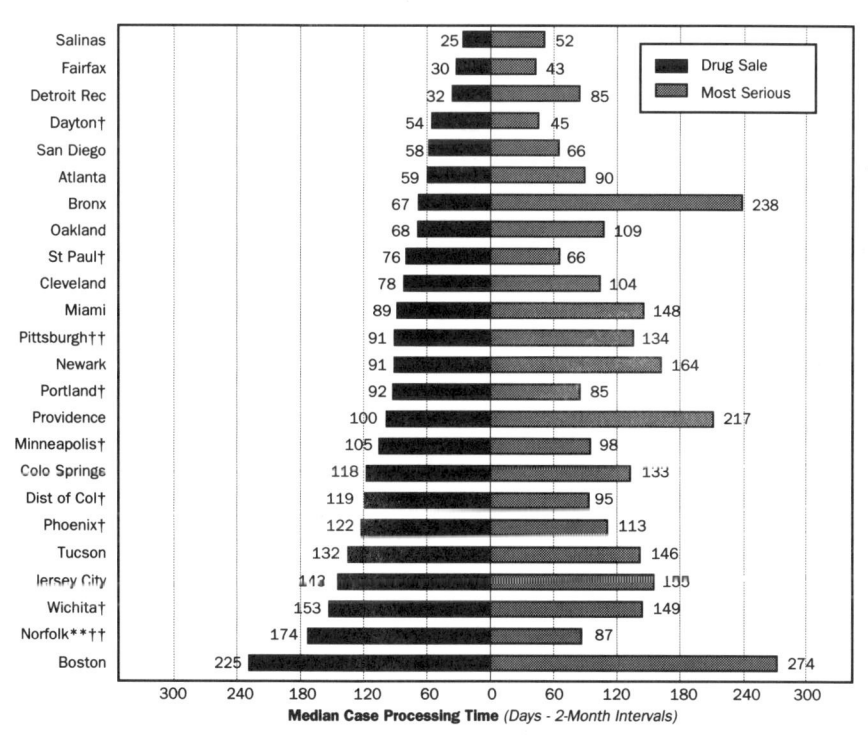

Court	Drug Sale	Most Serious
Salinas	25	52
Fairfax	30	43
Detroit Rec	32	85
Dayton†	54	45
San Diego	58	66
Atlanta	59	90
Bronx	67	238
Oakland	68	109
St Paul†	76	66
Cleveland	78	104
Miami	89	148
Pittsburgh††	91	134
Newark	91	164
Portland†	92	85
Providence	100	217
Minneapolis†	105	98
Colo Springs	118	133
Dist of Col†	119	95
Phoenix†	122	113
Tucson	132	146
Jersey City	143	155
Wichita†	153	149
Norfolk**††	174	87
Boston	225	274

Median Case Processing Time (Days - 2-Month Intervals)

* New Orleans and Denver excluded; too few drug sale cases.
** All drug cases combined were slower than most serious.
† Drug sale slower than most serious.
†† Includes drug sale and possession cases.

66 / EXAMINING COURT DELAY

**Figure 23
Drug Sale vs. Less Serious Cases–1987*
Indictment/Information to Disposition**

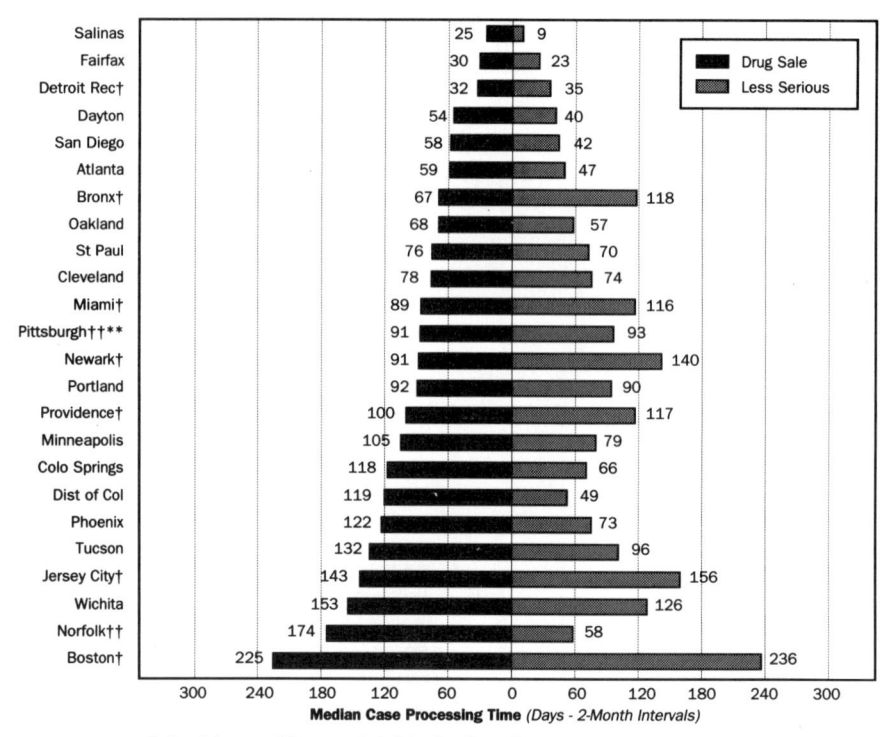

City	Drug Sale	Less Serious
Salinas	25	9
Fairfax	30	23
Detroit Rec†	32	35
Dayton	54	40
San Diego	58	42
Atlanta	59	47
Bronx†	67	118
Oakland	68	57
St Paul	76	70
Cleveland	78	74
Miami†	89	116
Pittsburgh††**	91	93
Newark†	91	140
Portland	92	90
Providence†	100	117
Minneapolis	105	79
Colo Springs	118	66
Dist of Col	119	49
Phoenix	122	73
Tucson	132	96
Jersey City†	143	156
Wichita	153	126
Norfolk††	174	58
Boston†	225	236

Median Case Processing Time *(Days - 2-Month Intervals)*

* New Orleans and Denver excluded; too few drug sale cases.
** All drug cases combined were faster than less serious.
† Drug sale faster than less serious.
†† Includes drug sale and possession cases.

cause of longer felony case processing times. Rather, the courts that were already slow were the ones that experienced the greatest increase in drug-related cases in recent years — creating the appearance that drug-related (especially drug sale) cases were a cause of court delay.

Jury Trial Rates and Disposition Times

The mix of cases, as the preceding discussion indicates, can affect the overall case processing times in a court. It is also anticipated that the court's (and prosecutor's) inclination to take cases to trial will influence the overall pace of felony litigation in a court. A jury trial is the ultimate recourse for a defendant who stands accused of a crime. Delay in processing jury trial cases, where the availability and memory of witnesses are paramount, has significant implications for the quality of justice. **Figure 24** displays the median upper court disposition times for jury trial and all felony cases. Median upper court disposition time in jury trial cases ranged from 33 days in Fairfax to 395 days in Bronx. Fairfax's upper court disposition time in jury trial cases was shorter than the upper court disposition times for all cases (including guilty pleas and dismissals) in 24 of the courts (see Figures 18 and 24).

Jury trial cases, overall, require a longer time to disposition than other case types. One would expect, then, that a higher jury trial rate would lead to longer case processing times overall. **Table 10** suggests that there was no relationship between the percentage of jury trials and the median upper court time for all felony cases. However, the percentage of jury trials displayed a weak-to-moderate negative association with the median and

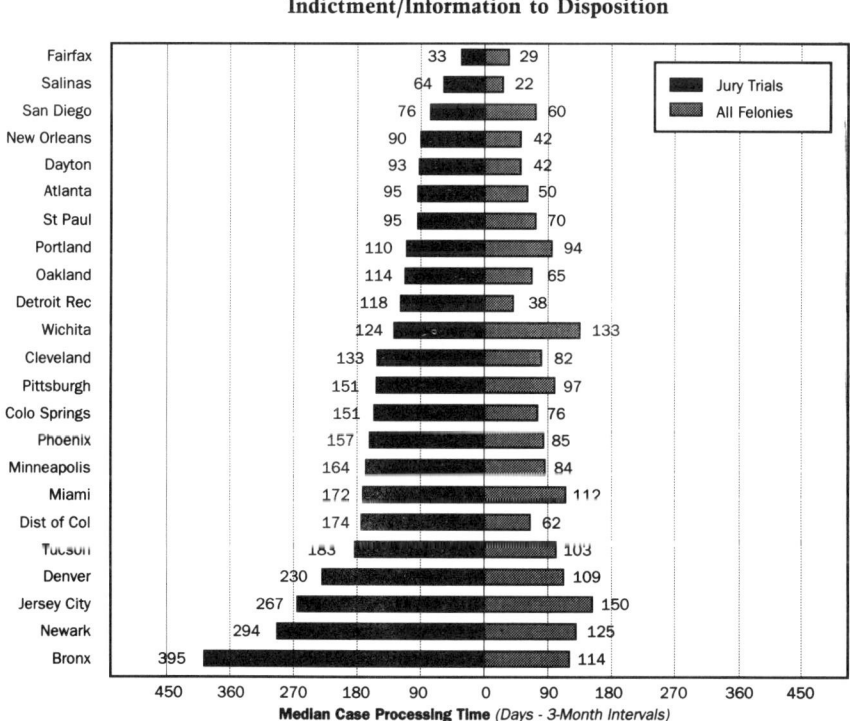

Figure 24
Jury Trial Cases vs. All Felony Cases –1987†
Indictment/Information to Disposition

Court	Jury Trials	All Felonies
Fairfax	33	29
Salinas	64	22
San Diego	76	60
New Orleans	90	42
Dayton	93	42
Atlanta	95	50
St Paul	95	70
Portland	110	94
Oakland	114	65
Detroit Rec	118	38
Wichita	124	133
Cleveland	133	82
Pittsburgh	151	97
Colo Springs	151	76
Phoenix	157	85
Minneapolis	164	84
Miami	172	112
Dist of Col	174	62
Tucson	183	103
Denver	230	109
Jersey City	267	150
Newark	294	125
Bronx	395	114

Median Case Processing Time *(Days - 3-Month Intervals)*

† Boston, Norfolk, and Providence are not included; less than 20 jury trial cases in the samples.

90th percentile for upper court processing time in all felony cases.[80] Courts with higher jury trial rates produced, overall, comparatively shorter upper court disposition times. A larger percentage of jury trials increased the likelihood that cases would be concluded sooner. But, overall, the jury trial rate had very little association with felony case processing times. Most courts had such a small percentage of cases that were disposed by jury trial that the impact of the court's jury trial rate on overall case processing times was minimal.

Table 10

Jury Trial Rate and Felony Case Processing Time–1987

	All Felonies Upper Court	All Felonies Total	Percent Jury[a] Trials
Salinas	22	62	7
Fairfax	29	102	15
Detroit Rec	38	71	8
New Orleans	42	89	8
Dayton	42	56	3
San Diego	50	121	9
Atlanta	50	108	3
Dist of Col	62	100	12
Oakland	65	144	8
Norfolk	69	127	2
St Paul	70	77	2
Colo Springs	76	85	5
Cleveland	82	135	7
Minneapolis	84	107	6
Phoenix	85	98	2
Portland	94	*	6
Pittsburgh	97	153	6
Tucson	103	*	6
Denver	109	156	6
Providence	111	192	3
Miami	112	119	2
Bronx	114	145	7[b]
Newark	125	308	5
Wichita	133	149	10[c]
Jersey City	150	198	5
Boston	233	*	3
Mean			6

a   Cases disposed by jury verdict.
b   Could not distinguish jury trials from non-jury trials.
c   If a trial started, the case was coded as one disposed by trial.
*   Data unavailable or not comparable.

Bench Warrant Rates

Felony case disposition times cannot be discussed without addressing the role that bench warrants play in the pace of felony litigation. Because disposed felony cases are examined here, the samples include cases in which defendants failed to appear for a scheduled court appearance and were not brought back into custody for some period of time. These cases are included in the analysis, as they were in Church et al. (1978a) and Mahoney et al. (1985, 1988). Moreover, **Table 11** shows the percentage of cases in which at least one bench warrant was issued because a defendant failed to appear for court proceedings after the initial arrest. There was considerable variation among the courts in the problem they experienced with defendants failing to appear. The percentage of cases with bench warrants ranged from 6 percent in Fairfax to 36 percent in Providence. Three of the slowest eight courts had bench warrants issued in at least 25 percent of their cases. The eight slowest courts had bench warrants in an average of approximately 22 percent of their cases; the eight fastest courts had bench warrants in an average of approximately 15 percent of their cases. The data suggest that the percentage of cases with a bench warrant issued had an impact on overall case processing times.

Correlation analysis shows that the percentage of cases with bench warrants exhibited a moderate association with seven measures of case processing time and was strongly related to median upper court time for most serious cases and 90th percentile times for all felonies.[81] It also was strongly related to the percentage of all felony cases over 180 days old and over one year old at disposition.[82] But it is even more interesting that the percentage of cases with a bench warrant issued showed an equally strong association with the percentage of nonbench warrant cases over 180 days old and one year old at disposition.[83] This suggests that courts with a high percentage of bench warrant cases also tended to have the most difficulty in processing nonbench warrant cases expeditiously. In other words, courts with problems in caseflow management were also likely to have problems screening and monitoring defendants on bail/ROR.

Including bench warrant cases in the analysis, moreover, has only a minimal impact on the percentage of cases that exceed the ABA disposition time standards. Table 11 shows that if cases in which bench warrants were filed are excluded from the analysis, most courts were closer to achieving the ABA disposition time standard of disposing all felony cases within one year. But the improvements are not very great for most courts. The average change in percentage of cases over one year old at disposition was only 2.9 percent among the 19 courts with bench warrant data. Exclusion of bench warrant cases did not help any court to meet the ABA's one-year disposition time standard (to have none of their cases over one year old at disposition).

Among courts that had more than 10 percent of their cases over one year old at disposition, exclusion of bench warrant cases brought only four

Table 11

Percent Bench Warrants,
Cases Over ABA Standards, and Felony Case Processing Time–1987

	All Felonies		Percent[a] Bench Warrants	Percent Over 180 Days[b]		Percent Over One Year[b]	
	Total	Upper Court		All Cases	Non-BW[c] Cases	All Cases	Non-BW[c] Cases
Dayton	56	42	19	8	6	1	1
Salinas	62	22	16	8	9	2	2
Detroit Rec	71	38	13	15	12	2	1
St Paul	77	70	15	18	9	13	6
Colo Springs	85	76	20	22	16	7	3
New Orleans	89	42	18	15	13	2	2
Phoenix	98	85	13	22	18	9	6
Dist of Col	100	62	*	9	*	8	*
Fairfax	102	29	6	14	12	2	2
Minneapolis	107	84	21	29	24	11	9
Atlanta	108	50	18	24	15	9	4
Tucson[d]	*	103	26	*	*	*	*
Miami	119	112	30	34	29	13	9
San Diego	121	50	21	31	23	5	3
Portland[d]	*	94	20	*	*	*	*
Norfolk	127	69	*	29	*	6	*
Cleveland	135	82	25	28	23	9	6
Oakland	144	65	15	39	32	15	12
Bronx	145	114	23	45	41	19	17
Wichita	149	133	15	28	23	5	3
Pittsburgh	153	97	12	23	20	7	4
Denver	156	109	18	44	36	17	8
Providence	192	111	36	52	43	31	25
Jersey City	198	150	*	56	*	22	*
Newark	308	125	*	81	*	41	*
Boston[d]	*	233	30	*	*	*	*
Mean			20	30		11	
				26[e]	21[e]	9[e]	6[e]

a Percentage of cases in which at least one bench warrant was issued between arrest and disposition (guilty plea, dismissal, verdict, etc.).
b Original arrest to disposition.
c Cases in which no bench warrants were issued against the defendant.
d Original arrest dates unavailable; courts ranked here in general position based on upper court CPT.
e Means only for courts (20) with data on arrest dates and bench warrants.
* Data unavailable or not comparable.

courts (St. Paul, Minneapolis, Miami, and Denver) within 10 percentage points or less of meeting the ABA one-year standard. It is interesting that three of the six fastest courts showed no change in the percentage of cases over one year old when bench warrant cases were excluded. Thus, the presence of bench warrant cases in the samples of disposed cases had only a marginal impact on how close the courts were to meeting the ABA case processing time standards.

In general, evidence suggests, at least indirectly, that effective case-flow management and effective management of released defendants among these courts were generally related. Jurisdictions with better-managed courts—those with faster case processing times—tended to screen and monitor their released defendants better as well. Jurisdictions with slower courts tended to do a poorer job of managing their released defendants. This suggests that an overall organizational evaluation of management practices in jurisdictions with slow courts may be warranted.

Overall, the percentage of bench warrant cases in the caseload was associated with felony case processing time. However, excluding bench warrant cases from the analysis did not improve substantially any court's performance in relation to the ABA disposition time standard that all felony cases be disposed within one year or that 98 percent be disposed within 180 days.

Court Size: Population and Number of Filings and Judges

Naturally, knowledge about the types of cases and the percentage of bench warrant cases in the caseload is not sufficient to explain differences among the courts in overall case processing time. Many other factors influence a court's pace of litigation, including the size of the caseload and the number of judges. Conventional wisdom suggests that the greater the size and complexity of the court, the greater the likelihood that delay will occur in case processing. In order to examine this issue, relationships among population, number of felony filings, number of felony judges, and felony case processing times will be examined.

Table 12 indicates the population of the counties over which the courts in this study have jurisdiction. There does not appear to be any substantial relationship between population size and upper court processing time. San Diego, for example, had the largest population but was among the fastest third of the courts. Wichita, however, had the fourth smallest population but the fourth slowest median upper court processing time. In fact, correlation analysis suggests that there were no substantial relationships between population and any of the 14 measures of case processing time (see Appendix I).

72 / EXAMINING COURT DELAY

The number of felony cases filed in 1987 also indicates the size and complexity of the court system. It should be noted that cases are difficult

Table 12

Court Size, Filings per Judge, and Felony Case Processing Time–1987

	Upper Court Median	Population[a] 1986	Felony[b] Filings 1987	Total[c] Felony Judges	Time on[d] Felony Cases	FTE[e] Felony Judges	Filings per FTE Felony Judge
Salinas	22	340	1342	7.00	.50	3.50	383
Fairfax	29	710	2832	11.00	.40	4.40	644
Detroit Rec	38	1086	16312	34.00	1.00	34.00	480
New Orleans	42	554	6243[f]	15.00	.70	10.50	595
Dayton	42	566	2220	10.00	.40	4.00	555
San Diego	50	2201	9258	19.00	1.00	19.00	487
Atlanta	50	623	8378	14.00	.55	7.70	1088
Dist of Col	62	626	11130	17.00	.97	16.49	675
Oakland	65	1209	5070	16.00	.44	7.04	720
Norfolk	69	275	4530	9.00	.50	4.50	1007
St Paul	70	474	2475	20.00	.25	5.00	495
Colo Springs	76	380	3401[f]	10.00	.40	4.00	850
Cleveland	82	1445	9472	33.00	.50	16.50	574
Minneapolis	84	988	3620	39.00	.20	7.8	464
Phoenix	85	1900	12410[f]	14.25	.95	13.54	917
Portland	94	567	6338	14.00	.50	7.00	905
Pittsburgh	97	1374	5904	17.50	.40	7.00	843
Tucson	103	602	3222[f]	8.00	.95	7.60	424
Denver	109	505	2910[f]	6.75	1.00	6.75	431
Providence	111	582	3020[f]	6.00	.90	5.40	559
Miami	112	1769	23884	24.00	1.00	24.00	995
Bronx	114	1194	8799[f]	37.00	1.00	37.00	238
Newark	125	842	7217	19.50	.95	18.52	390
Wichita	133	391	1694	7.00	.80	5.60	302
Jersey City	150	553	2385	7.80	.85	6.63	360
Boston	233	661	1646[f]	8.00	1.00	8.00	206
Mean		862	6373	16.30	.70	11.21	599

a 1986 population in thousands (County and City Data Book, 1988).
b Number of felonies with an indictment/information filed; generally includes all charges arising from one incident against one defendant (data from survey of court administrators).
c "Total felony judges" represents the total number of full-time equivalent judicial staff (including full-time, part-time, or pro-tem judges and/or commissioners/referees) who spent at least part of their time on felony cases in 1987 (data from survey of court administrators).
d "Time on felony cases" is an estimate of the average proportion of judge time spent on felony caseload duties during 1987 (data from survey of court administrators).
e "Full-time equivalent (FTE) felony judges" is calculated by multiplying the number of "total felony judges" by "time spent on felony cases."
f Indicates courts which count multiple incidents in one indictment or information; all others count single criminal incidents in one indictment or information.

to count in a manner that is comparable across all courts. Most courts counted their cases in a comparable manner, but comparisons should be made with some caution.[84]

Table 12 shows that there is little, if any, relationship between the number of filings and case processing time. Miami had the largest caseload with over 23,000 felonies filed in 1987, and it ranked among the lower half of the courts on case processing time. Detroit, however, had the second largest number of filings but was among the fastest courts. Again, there were no substantial correlations between the number of filings and felony case processing time (see Appendix I).

A third indicator of court size is the number of full-time equivalent (FTE) felony judges.[85] Table 12 shows that the fastest ten courts had an average of 11 FTE felony judges; the slowest ten had an average of 12.6 FTE felony judges. Thus, there is little relationship between the number of FTE judges and median upper court processing time. However, the total number of FTE felony judges exhibited a moderate relationship with median total disposition and upper court time for jury trial cases.[86] Larger courts, by this measure, had some tendency to produce longer median disposition times in jury trial cases. But the number of FTE judges was not related to any of the other 12 measures of criminal case processing time.

Court size, therefore, had very little direct association with felony case processing time. Population and number of felony filings were unrelated to the pace of felony litigation. But a larger number of FTE felony judges were associated with longer median times in jury trial cases.

Court Resources: Felony Caseload per Judge

Caseload per judge, rather than mere size of the court, is more likely to influence case processing times. Measurement of caseload per judge, however, is more difficult than one might expect. Caseload entails some measure of active cases per judge at a given time. As noted earlier, there are difficulties in counting cases.[87] In addition, courts differ in whether they count fugitive cases in their active pending caseload.[88] Thus, for purposes of this study, the number of cases filed during 1987 is used as the primary measure of caseload. The proportion of time judges spend on felony cases also varies considerably among the courts. In some courts, there are separate criminal divisions where judges spend all their time handling felony case matters. In other courts, judges handle a variety of case types, both civil and criminal, and may spend only part of their time on felony matters. Comparisons regarding felony caseload per judge are difficult to make under these circumstances. An extensive study of how the judges in the courts spend their time would be the best way to measure time spent on felony matters. In this study, each court administrator was asked to estimate the overall average amount of time their judges spent on felony case matters during 1987 (*time on felony cases*). The presiding judge in each court was asked to review the responses in the survey and to sign it to express his or her belief that the responses were accurate. In the absence of a better measure of overall judge time spent on felony matters, the estimates made by court administrators and approved by the presiding judges provide an acceptable starting point for making the felony caseload per-judge figures more comparable.

Multiplying the estimate of *time on felony cases* by the number of judges who handled felony cases (*total felony judges*) provided the number of FTE felony judges (see Table 12). **Figure 25** illustrates the substantial variation among the courts on the number of felony cases filed per FTE felony judge. Boston (206) and the Bronx (238) had the fewest, while Atlanta

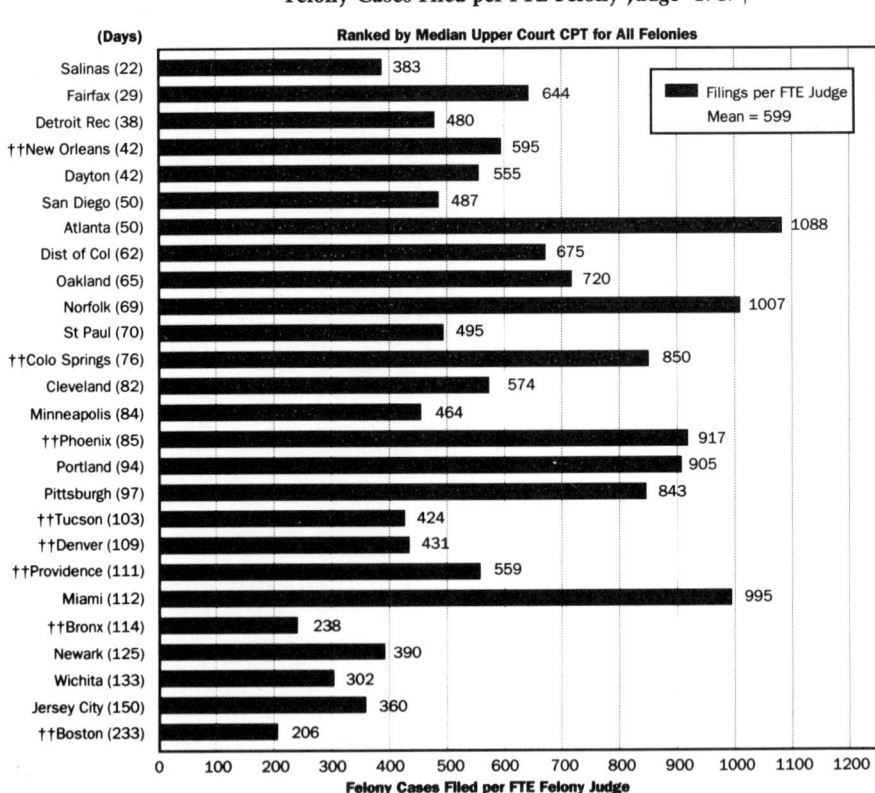

Figure 25
Felony Cases Filed per FTE Felony Judge – 1987†

Ranked by Median Upper Court CPT for All Felonies

Filings per FTE Judge
Mean = 599

Court (Days)	Filings per FTE Judge
Salinas (22)	383
Fairfax (29)	644
Detroit Rec (38)	480
††New Orleans (42)	595
Dayton (42)	555
San Diego (50)	487
Atlanta (50)	1088
Dist of Col (62)	675
Oakland (65)	720
Norfolk (69)	1007
St Paul (70)	495
††Colo Springs (76)	850
Cleveland (82)	574
Minneapolis (84)	464
††Phoenix (85)	917
Portland (94)	905
Pittsburgh (97)	843
††Tucson (103)	424
††Denver (109)	431
††Providence (111)	559
Miami (112)	995
††Bronx (114)	238
Newark (125)	390
Wichita (133)	302
Jersey City (150)	360
††Boston (233)	206

Felony Cases Filed per FTE Felony Judge

† Most courts count all charges against one defendant arising from one criminal incident as a "case."
†† May count all charges against one defendant arising from multiple criminal incidents as a "case."

(1,088) and Norfolk (1,007) reported the most filings per FTE felony judge. Boston and the Bronx were among the five slowest courts on upper court processing time, yet they had the lowest number of filings per FTE felony judge. The ten fastest courts averaged 663 filings per FTE felony judge, while the ten slowest courts averaged 475 filings per FTE felony judge (a difference of 40 percent). If there was a relationship, it appears to be negative: a larger number of filings per FTE judge, therefore, was related to *faster* case processing times. In fact, Appendix I shows a larger number of filings per FTE judge was weakly related to faster case processing times for all felonies, most serious, less serious, and jury trial cases. The finding that larger caseloads per judge were generally not related to longer case processing times supports what others have found in earlier studies in state and federal trial and appellate courts.[89]

This study supports the argument that there is little or no relationship between caseload per judge and felony case processing time among these courts. Of course, another interpretation of the data could suggest that most of the courts have too many cases per judge and that, after a certain point, the relationship between caseload and court delay tends to become obscured. Furthermore, measures of nonjudicial and physical facility resources were not included in the analysis. The current data do not support the hypothesis that caseload per judge is related to court delay. However, more and better measures of court and other justice agencies' resources should be considered in future research.[90]

Charging and Caseflow Management Procedures

Charging, Calendar, and Judicial Assignment Systems

Procedures for bringing felony charges and, once the charges are filed, assigning the cases to judges within the court have been the focus of considerable attention in courts that have sought to reduce felony case delay. Many states, for example, have reduced the role of the grand jury in bringing felony charges in order to expedite the caseflow process. Courts have also tried to use judges and staff more efficiently by trying different types of calendaring systems: individual, master, or combinations of both. Research suggests that there is a tendency for courts that use an information-based system to be somewhat faster than those that use the grand jury.[91] However, empirical evidence fails to support an argument in favor of any particular type of calendaring system for felony cases.[92]

Table 13 shows that there was no relationship among these courts between the charging procedure and total case processing times in felony cases. Five of the fastest ten courts and five of the slowest ten courts used information-based charging systems. Correlation analysis shows that information-based systems were associated with faster case processing times, but only in drug possession cases.[93] Thus, the charging procedure had little or no impact on the pace of felony case litigation.

Table 14 indicates the type of calendar system used by each court. Eight of the slowest 13 courts, but only 7 of the fastest 13 courts, had

Table 13

Charging Procedure and Felony Case Processing Time–1987

	Arrest to Disposition Median	Charging[a] Procedure
Dayton	56	Indictment[b]
Salinas	62	Information
Detroit Rec	71	Information
St Paul	77	Information
Colo Springs	85	Information
New Orleans	89	Combination
Phoenix	98	Combination
Dist of Col	100	Indictment
Fairfax	102	Indictment
Minneapolis	107	Information
Atlanta	108	Indictment
Tucson[c]	*	Indictment
Miami	119	Information
San Diego	121	Information
Portland[c]	*	Indictment
Norfolk	127	Indictment
Cleveland	135	Indictment
Oakland	144	Information
Bronx	145	Indictment
Wichita	149	Information
Pittsburgh	153	Information
Denver	156	Information
Providence	192	Information
Jersey City	198	Indictment
Newark	308	Indictment
Boston[c]	*	Indictment

a If a court used information 80 percent of the time or more, it was coded as an information based system (same for indictments). Less than 80 percent was coded as a "combination" of indictment and information (data from survey of court administrators).
b Dayton used "information" in 20 percent of its cases.
c Original arrest dates unavailable; courts are ranked here in general position based on upper court CPT.
* Data unavailable or not comparable.

individual calendars (including Detroit's hybrid, but primarily individual, calendar). Neither calendar type affected median upper court processing times for all felony cases. However, the type of calendar system does display a moderate association with median total and upper court disposition times in jury trial cases: master calendars tended to be faster.[94]

Another aspect of the calendar or case assignment system that might affect case processing time is the division of labor between civil and

Table 14

Calendar Type, Judicial Assignment, and Felony Case Processing Time–1987

	Upper Court Median	Calendar[a] Type	Judicial[b] Assignment
Salinas	22	Master	Felony/Civil
Fairfax	29	Master	Felony/Civil
Detroit Rec	38	Hybrid (I)	Felony Only
New Orleans	42	Individual	Felony/Misdemeanor
Dayton	42	Individual	Felony/Civil
San Diego	50	Master	Felony Only
Atlanta	50	Individual	Felony/Civil
Dist of Col	62	Individual	Felony Only
Oakland	65	Master	Felony Only
Norfolk	69	Master	Felony/Civil
St Paul	70	Master	Felony/Civil
Colo Springs	76	Individual	Felony/Civil
Cleveland	82	Individual	Felony/Civil
Minneapolis	84	Master	Felony/Civil
Phoenix	85	Individual	Felony Only
Portland	94	Master	Felony/Civil
Pittsburgh	97	Individual	Felony/Misdemeanor
Tucson	103	Individual	Felony Only
Denver	109	Individual	Felony Only
Providence	111	Master	Felony Only
Miami	112	Individual	Felony Only
Bronx	114	Individual	Felony Only
Newark	125	Hybrid (I)	Felony Only
Wichita	133	Master	Felony Only
Jersey City	150	Individual	Felony/Misdemeanor
Boston	233	Master	Felony Only

a   Hybrid (I) indicates that the court utilized both an individual and master calendar, but is categorized here by its primary type, individual (data from survey of court administrators).

b   Indicates the types of cases handled by judges in the court; felony only, felony and misdemeanor, and a combination of civil and criminal. If felony case duties required 90 percent or more of judges' time, courts were classified as "felony only." See Table 12 (data from survey of court administrators).

criminal caseload duties among judges. One might expect, for instance, that courts that have separate civil and criminal divisions, where felony judges hear only felony cases, would have faster case processing times than courts where judges handle both civil and criminal cases. Specialization, for both judges and administrators, should lead to greater efficiency in caseflow management. Table 14, however, shows that seven of the ten slowest courts, but only four of the ten fastest courts, had specialized criminal divisions where felony judges handled only felony cases. None of the slowest ten courts, but five of the fastest ten courts, had judges that concurrently handled civil and felony case matters.

In order to explore the correlation between specialized judicial assignments and felony case processing time, the courts were ranked according to the degree of specialization (felony and civil, felony and misdemeanor, felony only). The type of judicial assignment displayed a correlation with 11 measures of case processing time.[95] In other words, those courts where judges handled only felony cases were more likely to produce longer case processing times. An explanation of this finding may involve the court's size. The number of FTE felony judges displayed a moderate association with the type of judicial assignment.[96] As the number of judges increased, courts were more likely to have judges who handled only felony cases. Court size, therefore, appeared to be indirectly related to case processing time.

In conclusion, calendar type and charging procedure were at best only weakly to moderately related to felony case processing times among these 26 courts. But those courts where judges had mixed case assignments (civil and criminal) tended to process their felony cases more quickly in the upper court than courts where judges handled only felony cases. The relationship between the type of judicial assignment and case processing time is generally moderate to strong. It could be explained in part by the influence of court size. The relationship between specialized assignments and the pace of litigation bears further examination.[97]

Disposition Time Goals and Caseflow Information

Many factors make an organization perform effectively. Some of the more important features of the court environment, like leadership and staff commitment to expeditious case processing, were beyond the scope of this study. However, every effective organization has goals and priorities. Courts, of course, aspire to achieve many important goals, including equality and fairness, access to justice, independence and accountability, and public trust and confidence. Although achievement of expeditious case processing does not guarantee the accomplishment of these other lofty goals, case processing may be related to their achievement. Having explicit case processing time goals arguably can contribute to achieving not only greater efficiency but also a higher quality of justice.

Almost all criminal courts are subject to a state requirement that cases be disposed within a specified time to satisfy constitutional requirements for a speedy trial. The existence of time standards alone does not determine the pace of felony litigation. Court leadership and commitment to accomplishing stated goals are probably more salient factors.[98] But one would expect, in an effective and efficient court, an information system that allows court leaders and staff to monitor the court's success in achieving time standards. Information concerning four issues seem pertinent to effective caseflow management: the number of cases in the system (pending and filed), the number of cases leaving the system (disposed), the age of the cases in the system and at disposition, and the frequency of postponements of scheduled trials and other court appearances. Court administrators and judges should find data on these issues useful in managing their caseloads and identifying areas of possible concern. Appendix L displays the frequencies with which each court disseminates information to its judges on these four topics. Twenty-one courts disseminated information on the numbers of cases pending and 17 courts on the number of cases filed on a weekly or monthly basis. There does not appear to be any distinction between fast and slow courts (based on median upper court processing time) on the frequency with which this information was disseminated. Only 10 of the 26 courts regularly (weekly or monthly) disseminated some kind of information related to the age of their caseloads. But again, there seems to be little difference between fast and slow courts on either the existence or frequency of distribution of such information. Finally, only seven courts monitored the number of continuances granted to postpone trials or other scheduled court appearances. Slower courts were slightly more likely to report the number of continuances: 5 of the slowest 13 courts reported continuances granted, while only 3 of the fastest 13 courts did so. Slower courts probably began monitoring the number of continuances granted because continuances were perceived as an area of concern, while they were not perceived as a problem among the faster courts.[99]

The mere existence of case processing time goals and the dissemination of certain types of information within the court obviously do not automatically lead to a quicker pace of litigation. There must be a commitment to the goals on the part of the court's leaders and staff and information must be used by leaders and staff to manage their caseloads, anticipate problems, and allocate resources. There must also be an effective caseflow management system through which judges and administrators can work to achieve speedy resolution of felony cases.

Early Resolution of Pretrial Motions and Firm Trial Dates

Recent research suggests that there are several characteristics shared by courts that display expeditious processing in felony cases.[100] **Table 15** presents three factors that indicate the degree of control the courts exercise over felony case processing. First, the estimated average time the courts required to resolve pretrial motions in most cases after the upper court

Table 15

Elements of Caseflow Control and Felony Case Processing Time–1987

	Upper Court Median	Pretrial[a] Motions Decided	Trial[b] Backup System	Median[c] First Trial Date to Trial Start Date	Percent Jury[d] Trials on First Trial Date
Salinas	22	3-6 Weeks	No	3	41
Fairfax	29	<3 Weeks	Yes	0	69
Detroit Rec	38	3-6 Weeks	Yes	0	66
New Orleans	42	<3 Weeks	No	12	42
Dayton	42	3-6 Weeks	Yes	0	58
San Diego	50	3-6 Weeks	Yes	12	3
Atlanta	50	<3 Weeks	Yes	*	*
Dist of Col	62	>6 Weeks	Yes	*	*
Oakland	65	3-6 Weeks	Yes	*	*
Norfolk	69	3-6 Weeks	No	*	*
St Paul	70	>6 Weeks	Yes	*	*
Colo Springs	76	>6 Weeks	Yes	54	12
Cleveland	82	3-6 Weeks	Yes	14	24
Minneapolis	84	<3 Weeks	Yes	*	*
Phoenix	85	>6 Weeks	Yes	93	0
Portland	94	3-6 Weeks	Yes	16	14
Pittsburgh	97	3-6 Weeks	Yes	41	31
Tucson	103	3-6 Weeks	Yes	31	23
Denver	109	3-6 Weeks	Yes	85	10
Providence	111	>6 Weeks	Yes	*	*
Miami	112	3-6 Weeks	Yes	*	*
Bronx	114	>6 Weeks	Yes	*	*
Newark	125	>6 Weeks	Yes	*	*
Wichita	133	3-6 Weeks	Yes	42	19
Jersey City	150	>6 Weeks	No	*	*
Boston	233	>6 Weeks	No	*	*
Mean				29	29

a   Time from arraignment on indictment/information to when pretrial motions are usually decided (data from survey of court administrators).
b   Indicates whether the court enforces a plea cut-off date policy (data from survey of court administrators).
c   Median time from first scheduled trial date to actual trial start date.
d   Percent of jury trial cases which went to trial on the first scheduled trial date.
*   Data unavailable or not comparable.

arraignment was obtained from a survey of the court administrators. Deciding pretrial motions quickly, one would expect, should lead to earlier guilty pleas and trial dates. As Table 15 indicates, there is a relationship between the length of time it takes to resolve pretrial motions and upper court processing time. Six of the slowest 13 courts, but only 3 of the fastest 13 courts, required more than six weeks after the upper court arraignment to resolve pretrial motions. Three of the fastest 13 courts, but only 1 of the slowest half of the courts, resolved pretrial motions in less than three weeks after the arraignment. Early resolution of pretrial motions shows a moderate correlation with faster case processing times on 9 of the 14 measures.[101]

Naturally, getting pretrial motions resolved quickly requires considerable cooperation among the prosecutor, defense attorney, and the court. Slower courts could focus on ways to improve communication and cooperation and, therefore, the time it takes to make and decide pretrial motions in order to reduce overall processing time.

A firm trial date policy is another hallmark of a well-managed and coordinated criminal court system. Trial dates should allow a reasonable amount of time for both sides to prepare their cases. The court should then expect the trial to begin on the assigned date except when very good reasons are presented to justify a postponement. When postponements are granted for good cause, the case should typically be rescheduled for trial without delay. In order for the court to assure that postponements are not due to its inability to provide a judge on the scheduled trial date, excessive overscheduling must be avoided. Moreover, some kind of backup system, whereby other judges within the court, part-time or pro tem judges, or judges from another (e.g., lower) court are available to hear overscheduled trials, could be useful in reducing trial continuances. Table 15 shows that all but five courts had some kind of backup system to assure that trials are heard when scheduled. In general, there appeared to be no substantial correlation between the existence of a trial backup system and court processing time (see Appendix I).

A better indicator of a firm trial date policy is the extent to which trials begin on or near the first scheduled trial date. Where a high percentage of trial cases begin on or near the first scheduled trial date, the court is likely to have established an expectation among the defense and prosecuting attorneys that trials will commence when scheduled (i.e., the court probably has a relatively strict continuance policy). It also indicates that the court is generally effective in the scheduling of its cases, judges, and courtrooms. Table 15 shows the percentage of jury trial cases that began on the first scheduled trial date and the median time from the first scheduled trial date to the actual start of the trial. Although the first scheduled trial date was not available from almost half of the courts, the data suggest that there was a strong relationship between the median time from the first scheduled trial date (FSTD) to the actual start of trial and overall felony case processing time.[102] The shorter the median time from FSTD to the actual trial start date, the shorter the case processing times for all types of cases (except drug possession cases). As one might expect, courts with a shorter median FSTD to trial start also had a smaller percentage of cases exceeding the ABA disposition time standards at 180 days and one year,[103] and they had a lower backlog index.[104]

Even more interesting is that median FSTD to trial start is associated with the jury trial rate. As the percentage of jury trial dispositions increased, the median FSTD to trial start was shorter.[105] If a court was more likely to use jury trials, it was more likely to have a firm trial date policy, and a firm trial date was associated with shorter overall disposition times. Although the jury trial rate had only a weak direct association with the overall pace of litigation, it might have been indirectly related to faster case processing. Furthermore, courts that decided pretrial motions earlier were more likely to start jury trials on or near the first scheduled trial date.[106]

Table 15 also displays the percentage of jury trials in each court that started on the first scheduled trial date, another indicator of a firm trial date policy. As the percentage of cases that started trial on the FSTD decreased, the overall case processing time in the court increased. Correlation analysis shows that the percentage of jury trials that started on the FSTD displays a moderate-to-strong negative relationship with ten measures of felony case processing time.[107] Thus, a firm trial date policy was related to shorter case processing times for all types of cases, not just cases disposed by jury trial. If a court had a firm trial date policy, it was more likely to obtain earlier guilty pleas (by far the most common type of disposition). It is not surprising, then, that a larger percentage of jury trials starting on the FSTD were associated with a lower percentage of cases over the ABA time standards.[108]

Differences among the courts on the percentage of jury trials starting on the FSTD can be partially explained by the percentage of bench warrant cases. Not surprisingly, as the percentage of bench warrant cases increased, there was a tendency for firm trial dates to decrease.[109]

In summary, the type of charging system, the existence of speedy trial rules, and the dissemination of various types of caseload and caseflow information to judges did not distinguish fast from slow courts in this study. Master calendar courts tended to be faster but only in jury trial cases. On the other hand, there were several caseflow management procedures and characteristics that tended to be associated with the faster courts in this study. First, as expected, early resolution of pretrial motions was clearly related to faster disposition times. Second, there was a strong relationship between a firm trial date policy (i.e., the ability to get jury trial cases to trial on or near the first scheduled trial date) and faster processing times for all cases. In general, these findings suggest that particular caseflow management procedures (e.g., calendar or charging procedures) may not be as important for achieving faster case processing as firm trial dates and early resolution of pretrial motions.

Backlog Index

Finally, the backlog index measures the rate at which a court turns over its pending caseload. **Table 16** presents a backlog index, which is the number of pending felony cases at the start of the year divided by the

Table 16

Backlog Index[a] and Felony Case Processing Time–1987

	Upper Court Median	Total Median	Felony[b] Backlog Index 1987
Salinas	22	62	.03
Fairfax	29	102	.19
Detroit Rec	38	71	.17
New Orleans	42	89	.10
Dayton	42	56	.17
San Diego	50	121	.09
Atlanta	50	108	.18
Dist of Col	62	100	.22
Oakland	65	144	.09
Norfolk	69	127	.47
St Paul	70	77	.25
Colo Springs	76	85	.74
Cleveland	82	135	.22
Minneapolis	84	107	.28
Phoenix	85	98	.48
Portland	94	*	.45
Tucson	103	*	.71
Providence	111	192	.64
Bronx	114	145	.33
Newark	125	308	.65
Wichita	133	149	.31
Jersey City	150	198	.39
Boston	233	*	.88
Mean			.35

a Denver, Miami, and Pittsburgh are not included; data unavailable or not comparable.
b Number of pending cases as of January 1, 1987, divided by the number of dispositions in 1987.
* Data unavailable or not comparable.

number of felony dispositions during the year. Backlog index measures the extent to which the court is keeping up with its pending caseload. A backlog ratio of more than 1.00 indicates that the court increased its number of pending cases during the year by disposing of fewer cases than were pending at the start of the year. It suggests that the court required more than one year to turn over its pending caseload. On the other hand, a ratio of .50 indicates that the court disposed of twice as many cases as it had pending at the start of the year—i.e., the court turned over its pending caseload twice during the year. In earlier research on the pace of litigation, a higher backlog index was found to be related to longer felony case processing time.[110]

The data in Table 16 also show a relationship between the backlog index and felony case processing time. The average backlog index among the ten fastest courts was .17, while the average among the ten slowest courts was almost three times as high at .51. It is not surprising, then, that the backlog index shows a moderate to strong relationship with 13 of the 14 measures of case processing time (see Appendix I). The backlog index itself was explained to some extent by two factors: it was higher where the percentage of bench warrant cases were higher[111] and where the jury trial rate was lower.[112] As the percentage of jury trials increased, there was some tendency for the backlog index to be lower. Contrary to conventional wisdom, then, a higher jury trial rate had some tendency to be related to a faster turnover of pending cases.

Overall, a higher backlog index was strongly correlated with longer felony case processing times. Judges and court administrators should find it to be a useful barometer of their courts' case processing performance.

Jail Crowding

Jail crowding is one of the most serious concerns of administrators in the criminal justice system.[113] Citizens and officials worry that jail crowding leads to the pretrial release of defendants who would not be released if there was sufficient jail capacity. Pressure on the jail system can be intense. The impact of jail crowding on case processing, however, is unclear. Courts in jurisdictions with jails operating significantly over capacity may attempt to expedite cases in order to help alleviate crowding in local jails. Conversely, courts that are slow are more likely to contribute to the jail-crowding problem by their failure to move cases quickly enough. Courts could respond to the jail-crowding problem by releasing more defendants on bail or their own recognizance than they might have released if the jails were not so crowded. It is difficult, therefore, to predict the relationship between jail crowding and case processing times.

Table 17 shows the average weekly jail capacity of the local jails during 1987, the intended capacity of the jails, and a ratio of the average weekly jail population divided by the intended jail capacity. Identifying the intended capacity of a jail is sometimes difficult. The perception of what

Table 17

Jail Crowding and Information Received About Jail Population

	Upper Court Median	Average Weekly Jail Population[b]	Intended Jail Capacity[b]	Average Population/ Intended Capacity[c]	# in Jail Awaiting Trial	Time Def. in Jail Before Trial	Total Population/ Intended Capacity
Salinas	22	922	483	1.91	*	*	*
Fairfax	29	641	587	1.09	Month	Month	Month
Detroit Rec	38	1700	1680	1.01	Month	Week	Month
New Orleans	42	*	*	*	*	*	*
Dayton	42	394	361	1.09	Week	*	*
San Diego	50	3763	1470	2.56	Year	Year	Week
Atlanta	50	1300	1200	1.08	Week	Week	Week
Dist of Col	62	1657	1694	.98	*	*	*
Oakland	65	2780	1250	2.22	*	*	*
Norfolk	69	778	347	2.24	*	*	*
St Paul	70	153	209	.73	†	†	†
Colo Springs	76	380	240	1.58	*	*	*
Cleveland	82	950	870	1.09	Week	Week	Month
Minneapolis	84	400	394	1.02	Week	Week	Week
Phoenix	85	3318	2634	1.26	*	*	*
Portland	94	1042	1042	1.00	*	*	*
Pittsburgh	97	975	975	1.00	Month	Month	Month
Tucson	103	800	700	1.14	Month	Month	*
Denver	109	1000	650	1.54	*	*	*
Providence	111	*	*	*	*	*	*
Miami	112	1797	1338	1.34	Week	*	Week
Bronx	114	17000	17000	1.00	Week	†	*
Newark	125	*	1136	*	Week	Week	Week
Wichita	133	180	195	.92	*	*	*
Jersey City	150	800	462	1.73	Month	Week	*
Boston	233	425	386	1.10	Month	Week	Week
Mean				1.33			

a   Indicates how often various types of information relating to jail population are disseminated to judges.
b   Data from survey of court administrators.
c   Average weekly jail population divided by intended jail capacity.
*   No information disseminated on a regular basis.
†   St. Paul data unavailable.

was intended also may have changed over time. Given this caveat, the data obtained from the court administrators provide a reasonable basis for examining the jail crowding problem.[114] The ratio of average weekly jail population divided by the intended jail capacity indicates that the jails in 21 of the 26 jurisdictions operated at full capacity or more during 1987 (including the District of Columbia at 98 percent of capacity). Seven of these jurisdictions had jails that operated at more than 150 percent of intended capacity; three operated at more than 200 percent of their intended capacity. Four jurisdictions with the most serious jail-crowding problem (Salinas, San Diego, Oakland, and Norfolk) were all among the ten fastest courts on median upper court processing time (see Figure 18), though San Diego, Norfolk, and Oakland dropped to the slower half on total disposition time (see Figure 17). But correlation analysis shows that greater jail crowding was moderately associated with only longer median total times in drug sale cases.[115]

Table 17 also examines potentially useful information that judges might receive regarding the jail population. For the 10 courts (with relevant data) in which the judges received no information, or received it only yearly, on the number of defendants in jail awaiting trial, the average weekly jail population was 162 percent of the intended capacity. In the 12 courts that received such information weekly or monthly, the average jail population was 114 percent of intended capacity. In fact, there is a moderate negative correlation between the receipt of information on the number of defendants in jail awaiting trial and jail crowding.[116] That is, courts that received such information were somewhat more likely to have a less serious jail-crowding problem in their jurisdictions.

Jail crowding among these courts was a problem in 1987; most had jails that were filled well beyond their intended capacity. The data suggest, however, that jail crowding was related to longer processing times only in drug sale cases. Courts where judges regularly received information on the number of defendants in jail awaiting trial, however, were somewhat more likely to have less of a jail-crowding problem. Further study on both of these findings could be helpful to judges, prosecutors, and sheriffs.

Summary of Factors Related to the Pace of Felony Case Litigation

The preceding sections illustrate the complex relationships among factors associated with the pace of felony case litigation. **Figure 26** displays these relationships. The flow chart shows the results of bivariate correlations only. It is not derived from more sophisticated (i.e., multivariate) statistical analysis. Moreover, the lines denote only correlations, not causal relationships.

First, population and number of filings were not related to case processing time. But having more FTE judges was related to longer processing times in jury trial cases and to specialized (felony only) judicial assignments, which were related to longer case processing times. Court size therefore, could, be related to felony case processing time.

Higher percentages of most serious and drug sale cases were directly related to longer processing times. A higher percentage of drug sale cases were also related to later resolution of pretrial motions;[117] early resolution of pretrial motions was related to faster processing times. Thus, the impact of case mix could be both direct and indirect.

Caseload per judge was not directly or indirectly related to felony case processing time, at least as indicated by the bivariate correlations.

Figure 26
Summary: Bivariate Correlations Related to Felony Case Processing Time–1987

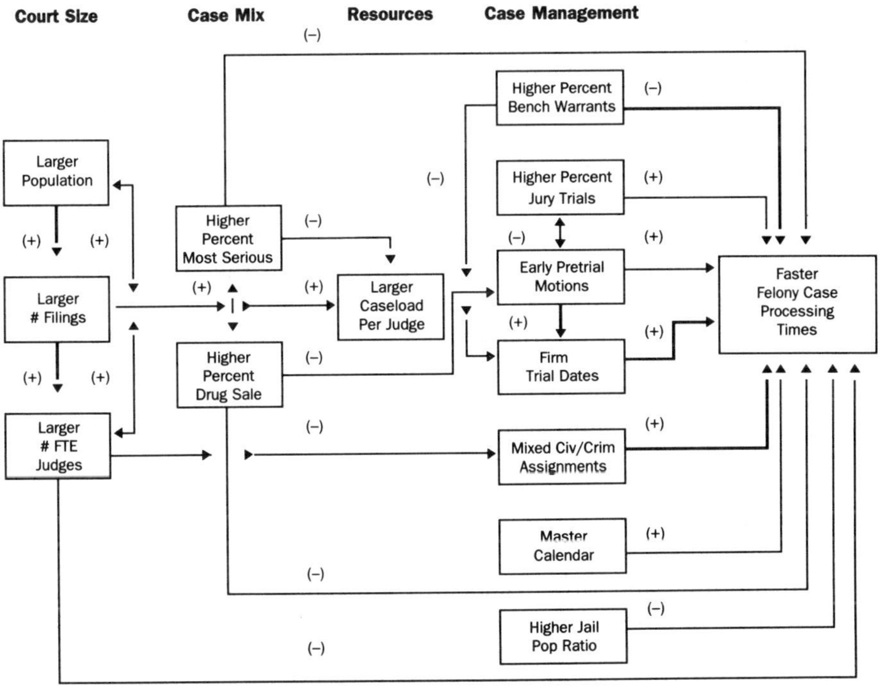

→ (narrow line) r = ± .40 to .59 on at least one measure of felony case processing time; p ≤ .05 (Pearson's r).

→ (bold line) r ≥ ± .60 on at least one measure of felony case processing time; p ≤ .05 (Pearson's r).

(−) When one factor is present, the other factor tends not to be present.

(+) When one factor is present, the other factor tends to be present.

Six case management characteristics displayed a relationship with the pace of felony case litigation: master calendars were related to faster jury trial case processing times; more bench warrants[118] and specialized (felony only) judicial assignments were related to longer processing times for all case types; early resolution of pretrial motions and firm trial dates were associated with shorter processing times for all case types; and a higher rate of jury trials was related to faster upper court disposition times. Specialized judicial assignments can be explained in part by court size (a higher number of FTE judges were related to specialized assignments). Firm trial dates are explained by the early resolution of pretrial motions, but there were fewer firm trial dates where there was a higher bench warrant rate.

Explaining the pace of felony case litigation is a complex matter. In order to identify the factors that were most clearly related to felony case processing times, a multivariate statistical analysis is necessary. After using a form of regression analysis, a simpler model emerges that includes only those factors that retained a statistically significant correlation after controlling for the influence of other factors (see Figure 27).[119] As **Figure 27** indicates, the most important factor related to felony case processing time was firm trial dates.[120] Firm trial dates were most clearly related to shorter case processing times at the 90th percentile for all felonies (total and upper court) and median upper court time in drug sale cases. They also were related to median upper court time for all felony cases. Firm trial dates, set at a reasonably early date, are likely to lead to earlier guilty pleas or dismissals because the parties realize that the court does not generally grant postponements. And because jury trial cases tend to be among the oldest cases, a firm trial date policy will shorten the time required to dispose of the older cases (i.e., the 90th percentile).

The finding that a firm trial date policy is a key factor related to shorter case processing times should be good news to judges and administrators. Although firm trial dates may be difficult to achieve, they are within the control of judges and court staff through cooperation with relevant criminal justice agencies.

Data also indicate some of the factors that could facilitate or inhibit the achievement of firm trial dates. Figure 26 shows that early resolution of pretrial motions was strongly associated with firm trial dates. Early pretrial motions and firm trial dates are indicators of active judicial involvement in caseflow management. Courts that established control early in their cases also tended to have firm trial dates. On the other hand, courts with a higher percentage of bench warrant cases were less likely to have firm trial dates.

While firm trial dates were related to faster case processing times, a larger percentage of bench warrant cases were related to longer processing **times** at the 90th percentile (the oldest cases) for each of the felony categories in Figure 27. This finding is understandable: if a bench warrant is issued, a case could be several years old before the defendant is rearrested. More bench warrant cases will lead to more old cases. However, as noted

Figure 27
Summary: Multivariate Analysis of Factors Related to Felony Case Processing Times–1987

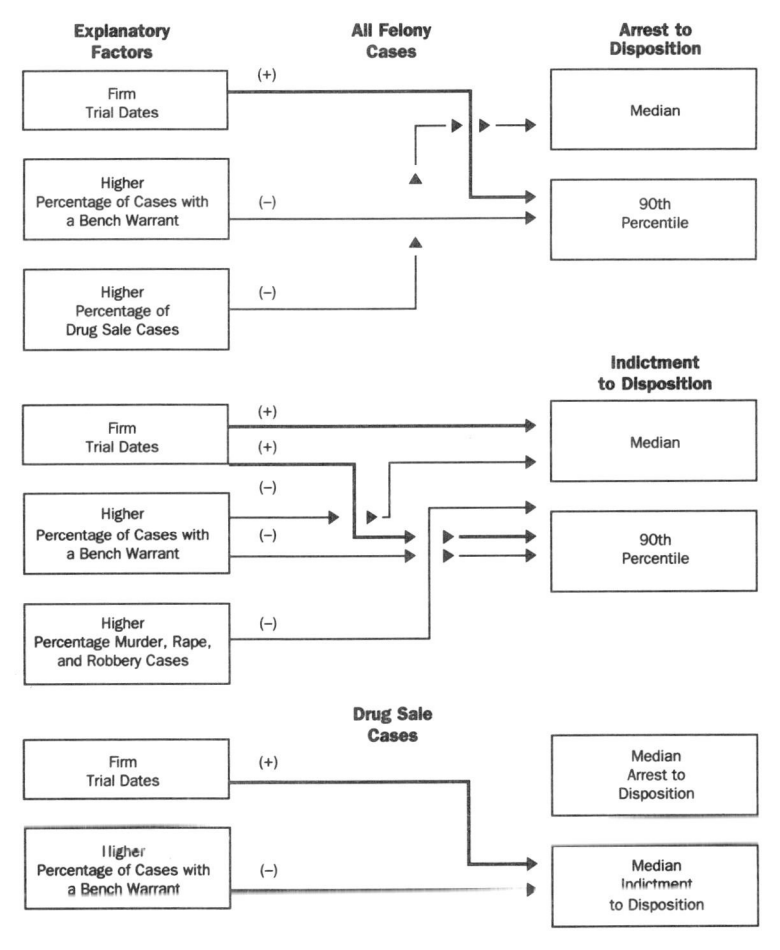

All Felony Cases

- Firm Trial Dates (+) → Arrest to Disposition: Median
- Higher Percentage of Cases with a Bench Warrant (−) → 90th Percentile
- Higher Percentage of Drug Sale Cases (−)

Indictment to Disposition

- Firm Trial Dates (+) → Median
- Firm Trial Dates (+) (−) → 90th Percentile
- Higher Percentage of Cases with a Bench Warrant (−)
- Higher Percentage Murder, Rape, and Robbery Cases (−)

Drug Sale Cases

- Firm Trial Dates (+) → Median Arrest to Disposition
- Higher Percentage of Cases with a Bench Warrant (−) → Median Indictment to Disposition

→ (narrow line) The correlation with CPT remained statistically significant after all but one relevant factor were controlled for in a series of three factor stepwise regression analyses (see Appendices A and O).

▶ (bold line) The correlation with CPT remained statistically significant after all other relevant factors were controlled for in a series of three factor stepwise regression analyses (see Appendices A and O).

(−) The explanatory factor has a negative/detrimental impact on case processing time (i.e., case processing time is longer).

(+) The explanatory factor has a positive/beneficial impact on case processing time (i.e., case processing time is shorter).

earlier, jurisdictions with a higher percentage of bench warrant cases also tended to have a higher percentage of nonbench warrant cases over the ABA disposition time standards. Thus, courts that displayed more delay also experienced more problems screening and monitoring defendants released before trial. To some extent, then, the "bench warrant factor" is an indirect indicator of the effectiveness of management policies within the jurisdictions.

Besides firm trial dates and the bench warrant rate, case mix retained a prominent role after the multivariate analysis was performed. Figure 27 indicates that a higher percentage of most serious cases in the caseload were most clearly related to longer median case processing times in the upper court for all felonies. Moreover, the percentage of drug sale cases in the caseload displayed a significant relationship with median total case processing times for all felony cases after the influence of other factors was controlled. As explained earlier, the relationship between a high percentage of drug sale cases and longer case processing times probably exists because the slowest courts in 1987 tended to be the slowest in 1983; and the slowest courts experienced the largest increase in drug-related cases between 1983 and 1987 (see Table 21). Knowledge of the trends in these courts, therefore, suggests that relationship between the drug caseload and court delay in these courts is primarily coincidental rather than causal.

In summary, the findings suggest that courts can reduce their pace of felony case litigation by focusing on a firm trial date policy. In general, this factor indicates early and active judicial control over the caseflow and a commitment to having events take place when scheduled. The data also suggest that, all other factors being equal, a higher percentage of most serious cases and bench warrant cases will be associated with longer overall case processing times.

Perceived Causes of Felony Case Delay

Until now, the analysis has focused on the structural, procedural, and caseload factors related to the pace of felony litigation. It is also worth considering the opinions of court administrators and presiding judges regarding the causes of delay in their courts. Are there some problems faced by all courts, both fast and slow? Are there some problems that are perceived to be more serious in slower as compared to faster courts? By means of a survey, each court administrator rated the degree to which various factors in the justice system were problems that affected delay. The presiding judge was asked to sign the survey to acknowledge agreement with the responses on the survey. These ratings are only opinions, but they are the opinions of those who are intimately aware of the problems faced by their respective courts.

In order to determine what problems distinguished fast and slow courts, **Table 18** presents the average ratings from the six fastest and six slowest courts. Each factor was rated from 1 (not a problem) through 4 (very serious problem).

Table 18 shows that there were no statistically significant differences between the ratings of problems regarding felony case processing in the fast

Table 18

Rating Problems Affecting Felony Case Delay[a]–1987

		Six Fastest Courts (avg)[b]	Six Slowest Courts (avg)[b]
1.	**Interagency Coordination**		
	Obtaining lab test results	2.2	2.8
	Obtaining documents from lower court	1.2	1.5
2.	**Procedural Problems**		
	Policy regarding exchange of evidence	2.0	1.5
	Inefficient calendar/assignment system	1.2	1.5
	Prosecutor's charging/plea policy	2.3	2.3
	Lack effective "firm trial date"	1.0	2.3
	Too many continuances	1.7	2.4
	Court leaders unable to change case management procedures	1.0	1.8
3.	**Commitment to Delay Reduction**		
	Judges lack concern about delay	1.2	1.8
	Defense attorneys lack concern about delay	1.5	2.3
	Prosecutors lack concern about delay	1.7	2.5
	Lack of knowledge about case management procedures	1.2	2.0
	Lack CPT goals/standards	1.5	1.0
4.	**Resources**		
	Insufficient number of courtrooms	2.2	2.2
	Insufficient number of judges	2.8	2.6
	Jail crowding	2.8	3.8
5.	**Communication and Accountability**		
	Inadequate communication within court about delay	1.2	1.8
	Inadequate communication with agencies about delay	1.3	1.7
	Lack of accountability within court for caseflow	1.2	1.8
6.	**Caseload**		
	Large case backlog	2.2	3.0
	Increase in drug-related cases	3.3	3.8
	Increase in felony cases	2.8	3.5

a   1 = no problem; 2 = minor problem; 3 = moderately serious problem; 4 = very serious problem.
b   Based on median upper court case processing time.

and slow courts.[121] It is also noteworthy that there were very few problems that were rated even moderately serious (3.0), on the average, by either the fast or slow courts. *Increase in drug-related cases* received the most serious ratings: 3.3 by the fast courts and 3.8 by the slow courts. This is consistent with reports over the past two years that drug-related cases have been on the rise. Slower courts rated this problem only slightly more serious than faster courts. The slower courts, as noted earlier, tended, in fact, to have more drug sale cases than the faster courts. Also consistent with data regarding jail populations presented above, *jail crowding* was also rated as a very serious problem (3.8) by the slower courts and moderately serious by the faster courts (2.8). Slow courts rated *increase in felony cases* as moderately to very serious (3.5), while faster courts rated it as somewhat less serious (2.8). And slower courts ranked *large case backlog* as a moderately serious problem (3.0), but the faster courts ranked it as a minor problem (2.2). Again, as noted above, slower courts tended to have a more serious backlog problem as measured by the backlog index and by the percentage of cases over the ABA disposition time standards.

There was virtually no difference between the fastest and slowest courts in their ratings of *insufficient number of judges* as a problem (2.8 and 2.6, respectively). There were substantial differences in the seriousness ratings fast and slow courts gave to *insufficient number of judges* and *insufficient number of courtrooms* for civil case processing (see Table 6). The lack of any difference in ratings by the fastest and slowest felony courts on the issue of court resources may be because, in most jurisdictions, criminal cases tend to get priority in the distribution of judge and staff time. Thus, even though their courts were relatively slow, judges and administrators may believe they generally received sufficient resources relative to other divisions (e.g., civil, traffic, domestic relations).

In summary, only jail crowding and an increase in felony, especially drug-related, cases were rated as moderate or very serious problems by the faster and slower courts. There were no statistically significant differences between fast and slow courts on any of the ratings.

Trends in the Pace of Felony Case Litigation: 1976–1987

Due in part to the relatively recent increase in empirical research, much attention has been given to the problem of court delay in the past 20 years. One might expect, therefore, that some progress has been made in reducing overall case processing times since 1976. **Table 19** displays the median upper court processing times from 1976, 1983, 1985, and 1987. From 1976 to 1987, 9 of the 17 courts experienced an increase in the median time it took for felony cases in the upper court. All of the increases were greater than 10 percent, though the increase of seven days in Oakland is small. Other increases from 1976 to 1987 were substantial. Six courts experienced an increase of 25 percent or more. Among those with the highest percentage increases in case processing time, Portland was up 84 percent (51 to 94 days), Wichita was up 75 percent (76 days to 133 days), and Pittsburgh was up 67 percent (58 to 97 days).

On the bright side, eight courts reduced their upper court case processing time by 10 percent or more. Three of the slowest courts in 1987 were among the most improved courts since 1976. Jersey City was down 60 percent (376 to 150 days); Providence was also down 60 percent (277 to 111 days); and Bronx was down 65 percent (328 to 114 days).[122] Jersey City and the Bronx have implemented changes to speed felony case processing in the lower court, where judges are allowed to take guilty pleas to felony charges. Some of the faster courts also showed improvement. Dayton, which had

Table 19

Felony Case Processing Time Trends, Indictment/Information to Disposition, 1976–1987, Ranked by 1987 Median Case Processing Time

	Upper Court Indictment to Disposition				Percent Change in Upper Court CPT		
	1976[a]	1983[a]	1985[a]	1987	1976-87	1983-87	1985-87
Detroit Rec	40[b]	43	31	38	−5	−12	23
New Orleans	50	49	48	42	−16	−14	−13
Dayton	69[b]	64	47	42	−39	−34	−11
San Diego	45	*	*	50	11	*	*
Oakland	58	*	*	65	12	*	*
Cleveland	71	88	90	82	15	−7	−9
Minneapolis	60	84	88	84	40	0	−5
Phoenix	98	44	58	85	−13	93	47
Portland	51[c]	52[c]	56	94	84	81	68
Pittsburgh	58	90	120	97	67	8	−19
Providence	277[b]	*	*	111	−60	*	*
Miami	81	92	108	112	38	22	4
Bronx	328	*	*	114	−65	*	*
Newark	99	146	124	125	26	−14	1
Wichita	76[d]	108	115	133	75	23	16
Jersey City	376[d]	121	115	150	−60	24	30
Boston	281	307	332	233	−17	−24	−30

a   Data obtained from Mahoney et al. 1988.
b   Data obtained from Neubauer (1981) (Detroit and Providence data are from cases disposed in 1976; Dayton data are from cases disposed in 1978).
c   Upper court case processing time here reflects the median time from arraignment to disposition (Mahoney et al. 1988).
d   Represents median upper court case processing time for 1979, obtained as part of study by Mahoney et al. 1988.
*   Data unavailable or not comparable.

relatively fast disposition times in 1979, was down 39 percent (69 to 42 days). New Orleans, one of the faster courts in 1976, was also down 16 percent (50 to 42 days); and Phoenix was down 13 percent since 1976. Phoenix had shown great improvement between 1976 and 1983 (98 to 44 days) but showed increasingly longer times from 1983 to 1987.

As shown in Table 19 six courts reduced their upper court times from 1985 to 1987. Boston was down 30 percent; Pittsburgh was down 19 percent; and New Orleans was down 13 percent during these two years. Six courts, however, increased their case processing times by more than 10 percent in just two years. Portland (up 68 percent) increased its upper court processing time most strikingly, followed by Phoenix (up 47 percent) and Jersey City (up 30 percent).

The evidence in Table 19 suggests that significant strides can be made in reducing felony case processing times not just in courts that have been seriously delayed (e.g., Bronx, Boston, and Jersey City) but in courts that have performed relatively well in past years (e.g., Dayton and New Orleans). The data also suggest it is difficult to make generalizations about overall trends among these courts. Few courts displayed either a steady increase or decrease in case processing time during the past decade. But overall, there were more courts that increased their upper court case processing times since the 1970s than there were that decreased their times.

Simply tracking case processing times over a period of years, however, is not sufficient. It is also important to know what happened during the past decade, especially in those courts that experienced significant changes in case processing time. Case studies would be useful to identify changes in procedures, leadership, and organization.[123] Although case studies were not performed in this study, changes over time in the number of filings per judge can be examined in some courts. Comparing case filings and the number of felony judges across the years covered in this study is very difficult. However, it is worth examining the available comparable data (see **Table 20**) to see what occurred in some of the courts that experienced significant changes in case processing time in the past few years.

First, Table 19 indicates that Portland was one of the fastest courts on upper court processing time in 1985 (56 days) but was up to 94 days in 1987, an increase of 68 percent. During this time, their felony filings per judge increased from 627 to 905, up 44 percent (see Table 20). It should also be noted that Portland had the fifth largest caseload per full-time equivalent felony judge (905) among the courts, a caseload that far exceeded the average (599) among the 26 courts studied here.[124]

Phoenix was among the faster courts in 1983. However, it experienced a considerable increase in upper court case processing time from 44 to 85 days (a 93 percent increase) between 1983 and 1987. From 1983 to 1987, their filings per felony judge increased from 590 to 917 cases, up 55 percent.[125] Note in Table 12 that Phoenix had the fourth largest number of 1987 case filings per FTE felony judge (917) of the 26 courts in this study. The increase in case processing times in Portland and Phoenix should be considered in light of the following factors: the courts' relatively fast processing times in 1983, their relatively large caseloads, and the dramatic increases in filings per judge. In combination, these factors could explain, at least in part, the increase in case processing times experienced in Portland and Phoenix. These courts may have reached a caseload/case processing saturation point.

Between 1976 and 1987, Bronx experienced the largest percentage rise in filings per judge of any court in the study: from 121 to 238 filings per judge, a 97 percent increase. Their filings per judge were up 75 percent from 1983 to 1987 alone.[126] Unlike Phoenix and Portland, however, Bronx decreased its upper court case processing time by 65 percent during this

Table 20

Trends in Filings per FTE Felony Judge, 1976–1987

	Upper Court Median	Filings per FTE Felony Judge			Percent Change Filings/Judge	
	1987	1976[a]	1985[b]	1987	1976-87	1985-87
Detroit Rec	38	*	351	480	*	37
New Orleans[c]	42	275	274	416	51	52
San Diego	50	437	619	487	11	-21
Oakland[c]	65	265	373	317	20	-15
Minneapolis	84	384	376	453	17	20
Phoenix	85	522	725	917	76	26
Portland	94	*	627	905	*	44
Pittsburgh	97	471	*	843	79	*
Providence[c]	111	*	533	503	*	-6
Miami	112	*	804	995	*	24
Bronx	114	121	186	238	97	28
Newark	125	443	367	370	-16	1
Wichita[c]	133	*	241	242	*	0
Jersey City	150	*	318	360	*	13
Boston	233	218	151	206	-6	36

a 1976 felony filings divided by 1976 criminal judges (Church et al. 1978a).
b Data obtained from Mahoney et al. (1988).
c Used "total felony judges" rather than "FTE felony judges" (see Table 12) in order to compare 1987 data to earlier years. "Filings per total felony judges" does not account for the percentage of time judges spent on nonfelony matters, and underestimates the caseload compared to "filings per FTE felony judge." Consequently, data from these courts are comparable *within* the courts over time, but not comparable to the other courts.
* Data unavailable or not comparable.

period, largely due to a delay reduction effort that allows lower court judges to accept guilty pleas in felony cases upon waiver of an indictment. In 1976, however, Bronx had the lowest number of felony filings per judge (121) and relatively slow case processing times. Even with the large increase to 238 filings per judge, Bronx still had among the lowest number of filings per judge in 1987. Thus, Bronx probably had the judicial capacity to absorb the additional cases and still reduce its felony case processing time.

Detroit Recorder's, among the fastest courts in each of the previous years, experienced an increase in felony filings per judge from 362 in 1983 to 480 in 1987 (an increase of 33 percent).[127] During this time, they decreased their median upper court processing time by five days. New Orleans, also one of the fastest courts, reduced its upper court processing time by 13 percent between 1985 and 1987 (see Table 19), while their filings per felony judge increased by 52 percent, from 274 to 416. Thus, case processing time was reduced in New Orleans and Detroit despite increases in filings per judge in recent years.

Why could Detroit and New Orleans maintain or reduce their pace of litigation while Portland and Phoenix increased their processing times? It should be noted that, despite their significant increases in filings per judge from 1985 to 1987, New Orleans had only the 11th and Detroit the 17th largest number of filings per FTE felony judge among the 26 courts in 1987 (see Table 12). On the other hand, Portland had the fifth largest and Phoenix the fourth largest number of filings per FTE judge in 1987. Portland and Phoenix had considerably larger caseloads per judge in 1985 than Detroit and New Orleans, whose caseloads per judge were smaller than the average (425 filings per judge) in 1985. Thus, Portland and Phoenix may have reached a caseload saturation point after which they were unable to manage the rapid increase in filings per judge without a substantial increase in overall case processing times. Courts that are already relatively fast, and have higher than average caseload per judge, probably cannot absorb a rapid rise in filings per judge without some increase in case processing time. The number of filings per judge might not be related to court delay in any particular year. But when courts reach a caseload/case processing saturation point, case processing times can be expected to rise, and more judges may be necessary to handle the caseload effectively.

In summary, 8 of 17 courts reduced their upper court processing times between 1976 and 1987, though 9 courts increased their disposition times. Some progress, therefore, has been made in reducing delay in felony trial courts. The reasons for significant changes in case processing time, however, are not entirely clear. More in-depth information on changes in staff, caseload, and procedures in these courts over time is required. Yet, the comparable caseload data that are available on these courts provide some basis for encouragement. For example, New Orleans, which ranked in the upper half of the 26 courts in 1987 on caseload per judge, reduced its case processing time over the years despite a significant increase in case filings. Portland and Phoenix experienced the most significant increases in case processing times in the 1985-1987 period, and both had relatively fast case processing times and larger than average caseloads per judge in earlier years; they also experienced a rapid increase in felony filings per judge over a short period. The data, therefore, suggest that caseload per judge is related to case processing time when relatively fast courts with a large caseload per judge reach a caseload/case processing saturation point. A substantial increase in caseload in such courts could justify additional judges to maintain expeditious case processing.

Fluctuations in felony case processing time are likely to occur given changes in crime rates, agency and court leadership, and available resources. The long-term trends suggest that significant reductions in court delay are achievable. Almost half the courts in the study have reduced their overall processing times since 1976. The data provide reasons for optimism, but also indicate that much work remains to be done in many urban trial courts to reduce delay.

Trends in Drug-Related Cases and the Pace of Litigation

Recent research and reports from local police and courts confirm that drug-related cases have increased dramatically in many urban jurisdictions while the crime rate generally has been declining. (Bureau of Justice Statistics (1989); Bennett (1989)). According to one state court administrator, in many of the urban courts that have been hit hardest by the influx of cocaine-related crimes, case backlogs have increased so substantially that the credibility of the judicial system is being undermined (Lipscher 1989). In addition, as observed earlier, there was a substantial correlation between the percentage of drug cases in the caseload and felony case processing times in 1987 among the courts in this study. In order to examine more closely the relationship between the increase in drug cases and court delay, changes in drug-related caseloads and their potential impact on case processing time will be examined in this section.

Table 21 indicates changes in median upper court case processing time and changes in the percentage of drug-related cases in the caseload between 1983 and 1987 in 17 jurisdictions. The percentage of drug-related cases in the caseload increased by an average of 56 percent among the 17 courts during this period. Three courts (Boston, Jersey City, and Bronx) experienced more than a 100 percent increase in the percentage of drug-related cases, while four courts (Dayton, Newark, Phoenix, and Detroit) saw less than a 10 percent increase.

Table 21 also provides some indication of the impact that the influx of drug cases had on case processing times. The courts are ranked from fast to slow on median upper court case processing time in 1983. The three fastest courts in 1983 (San Diego, Detroit, and Phoenix) had an average of 20 percent drug-related cases in 1983. The three slowest courts (Boston, Jersey City, and Bronx, excluding Newark which had an unusually high percentage of drug-related cases in 1983) also averaged 20 percent drug-related cases in their caseload. The average among the 17 courts was 18

Table 21

Percentage of Drug-Related Cases
and Case Processing Times, 1983-1987[a]

	Upper Court Median Case Processing Time			Percent Drug-related Cases		
	1983[b]	1987	Percent Change	1983[b]	1987	Percent Change
San Diego	36[c]	50	39	18	28	56
Detroit	43	38	-12	20	20	0
Phoenix	44	85	93	23	24	4
New Orleans	49	42	-14	20	32	60
Portland	52	94	81	10	18	80
Dayton	64	42	-34	11	12	9
Oakland	*	65	*	19	37	95
Minneapolis	84	84	0	9	10	11
Cleveland	88	82	-7	12	17	42
Pittsburgh	90	97	8	7	13	86
Miami	92	112	22	19	33	74
Wichita	108	133	23	12	17	42
Providence	*	111	*	20	30	50
Jersey City	121	150	24	21	45	114
Newark	146	125	-14	40	42	5
Bronx	161[c]	114	-29	22	46	109
Boston	307	233	-24	16	44	175
Mean	99	97	-2.0%	17.6%	27.5%	+56.2%

a   Case types determined by the most serious charge in the indictment or information. Does not count as "drug-cases" those in which drug-related charges were included but which were not the most serious (e.g., murder, rape, robbery, kidnapping).
b   1983 data obtained through research conducted by the NCSC in a study funded by the National Institute of Justice. Case processing times reported in Mahoney et al. (1985).
c   Median CPT based on estimates. Mahoney et al. (1985) did not include guilty pleas to felony charges entered in the lower court, upon waiver of indictment, in calculating time from indictment or information to disposition. Lower court guilty pleas were included in felony CPTs for 1987. In 1987, median felony CPT excluding lower court guilty pleas was 30 percent longer in Bronx and 17 percent longer in San Diego than median CPT including lower court guilty pleas. These proportions were used with the case processing times reported by Mahoney et al. (1985) to estimate 1983 median CPT.
*   Data unavailable or not comparable.

percent. Correlation analysis confirms that in 1983 the association between drug caseload and median upper court processing time was not significant (r = .17, p = .27).

Interestingly, the courts that were among the slowest in 1983 (Boston, Jersey City, and Bronx) were the ones that experienced the largest increase in drug-related cases between 1983 and 1987. The correlation observed earlier (see also Appendix H) between the percentage of drug-related cases in the caseload and court delay in 1987 is probably due to this coincidence. Trend data, then, suggest that a higher percentage of drug cases in the caseload were not a cause of court delay in 1987.

Another noteworthy trend in Table 21 is that some of the courts that had the greatest increase in drug-related cases *reduced* their median upper court case processing times between 1983 and 1987; Boston's was down 74 days and Bronx's was down 47 days. They had among the smallest caseloads per judge, however, and so probably had the capacity to reduce their pace of litigation despite the influx of drug cases. But it is clear from discussions with judges and court administrators that the increase in caseload caused by the influx of drug cases had a detrimental impact on the pace of litigation in Jersey City, Portland, and Miami. Miami and Portland had among the largest caseloads per judge in both 1985 and 1987 (see Table 20). The increase in the drug-related caseload in these two courts could have led to a caseload/case processing saturation point.

In conclusion, data on trends in drug caseloads support the argument that a higher percentage of drug cases in the caseload were not a cause of longer case processing times in 1987. Rather, courts that were already slow in earlier years experienced the greatest increase in drug-related cases between 1983 and 1987. This led to the correlation between the percentage of drug cases in the caseload and 1987 case processing times observed earlier. However, the increase in caseload per judge caused by the influx of drug cases had a deterimental impact on the pace of litigation in some jurisdictions, especially those that already had a large caseload per judge.

The Relationship Between Civil and Felony Caseflow Management

Examination of civil and felony case processing times as separate phenomena contributes to a greater understanding of the nature of court delay. But the picture remains incomplete if the relationship between civil and felony case processing is not examined. In 10 of the 26 courts, judges handled both civil and felony cases (see Tables 3 and 14). Even where there are separate civil and criminal divisions, decisions must be made regarding the allocation of resources to process various cases within the court's jurisdiction. Management theory and the concept of local legal culture suggest that there are patterns in the pace at which civil and criminal cases are processed within a jurisdiction.

A cursory examination of the preceding tables shows that some jurisdictions are among the fastest in both civil and felony litigation, while some courts are slow in both. **Table 22** below shows how each jurisdiction in the study ranked compared to the other courts on median civil and felony case processing times. The table indicates that 9 of the 25 courts[128] ranked approximately the same on civil and felony case processing times: 2 courts were fast on both, 4 fell in the middle range on both, and 3 were slow on both. These courts performed in a manner predicted by the hypothesis that the pace of litigation in a jurisdiction will be consistent for civil and criminal cases within a jurisdiction. Six courts performed in a manner that clearly contradicted the hypothesis. Three courts were fast on felonies but slow on civil cases. Of these courts, San Diego is probably somewhat faster on civil cases than shown here because its civil case disposition times include only cases in which a trial readiness document was filed. Wichita, one court that was fast on civil cases and slow on criminal, was slow on median felony disposition time but had all but 5 percent of its cases completed within the one-year ABA disposition time standard. Therefore, it was not among the slowest on the 90th percentile disposition time.[129] In

Table 22

Rankings on Civil and Felony Case Processing Times–1987

All Felony Cases* (Median CPT)	All Civil Cases* (Median CPT)		
	Fastest 8	Middle 9	Slowest 8
Fastest 8	Dayton Fairfax	Salinas New Orleans Atlanta	San Diego † Detroit D.C.
Middle 9	Minneapolis Norfolk St. Paul	Colo Springs Portland Phoenix Cleveland	Pittsburgh †† Oakland
Slowest 8	Wichita Denver Miami	Jersey City Tucson	Boston Newark Providence

* Median disposition time (upper court time for felonies).
† Civil cases include only those in which a trial readiness document was filed.
†† Does not include civil cases disposed by mandatory arbitration.

general, there was a moderate to strong association between median civil and felony case processing times.[130]

A moderate to strong correlation between civil and felony case processing times suggests that the effectiveness of case and resource management is relatively consistent within jurisdictions. It also provides some support for the concept of a local legal culture. Within local legal communities there are probably shared values and expectations regarding the role of the court in controlling the processing of cases, whether civil or criminal. Through assertive court leadership and cooperation with the public and private bar, however, resistance to court control over the caseflow can be overcome and delay can be reduced.[131]

Finally, the relationship between civil and felony case processing times suggests that courts should carefully consider the impact within the jurisdiction of changes in case or resource management in felony cases. If improvements in one area cause increased delay in another area, no real improvement is achieved. On the other hand, measures that improve the efficiency of case processing in one area (e.g., felonies) could release resources to be used in another area (civil or domestic relations). A holistic approach to improvements in case processing would consider these possible consequences.

Summary: The Pace of Felony Case Litigation, 1987

There is some reason for optimism based on the findings in this report. Seven of the 26 courts in the study exceeded by 5 percent or less the ABA disposition time standard that all felony cases be concluded within one year. Only 9 courts exceeded this standard by more than 10 percent. But none of the courts were close (within 5 percent) to meeting the standard that 98 percent of all felony cases be concluded within 180 days. Clearly, considerable improvement must occur in most courts before they achieve compliance with the ABA standards.

One primary purpose of this report is to help judges and court administrators understand more clearly the factors related to court delay. Furthermore, in order to be useful for those who are interested in delay reduction, the findings should identify a few factors that are subject to the control of judges and administrators, factors they can change and manage. The best interpretation of the data after the multivariate analysis, suggests that court size, calendar type, charging procedure, jury trial rate, and caseload per judge were not important predictors of case processing time. The most important predictor of faster case processing times was a firm trial date policy (a high percentage of trial cases starting on the first scheduled trial date) (see Figure 27). Firm trial dates were most likely to be found in courts that achieved early resolution of pretrial motions. Together, these factors indicate that early and continuous control over the caseflow, especially an insistence that trials take place when scheduled, are related to faster case processing times. Of course, implementing and maintaining early control and a firm trial date policy can be difficult. They require considerable commitment by judges and effective case and court management to achieve more certainty in scheduled events. They also require effective scheduling and management of court resources. But through cooperation with relevant justice system agencies, it is within the capacity of the courts to achieve early resolution of pretrial motions and firm trial dates.

After firm trial dates, the percentage of bench warrant cases have the greatest impact on felony case processing time. A higher percentage of bench warrant cases were associated with longer median upper court processing times and longer 90th percentile total and upper court processing time for all felonies. It was also related to longer median upper court time for drug sale cases. As noted earlier, a high percentage of bench warrant cases were related to a higher percentage of cases over the ABA disposition time goals. However, a high percentage of bench warrant cases were also related to a higher percentage of nonbench warrant cases over the ABA disposition time standards. Courts with slower case processing times in nonbench warrant cases tended to be in jurisdictions that had difficulty screening and monitoring defendants released on bail or recognizance. This evidence suggests that there is a relationship between the effectiveness of caseflow management and the effectiveness of management in the pretrial release programs within the jurisdictions. Thus, unlike case mix, the bench warrant "problem" is not beyond the control of the local jurisdiction.

Case mix also retained an important role in explaining felony case processing time. As Figure 27 indicates, a higher percentage of drug sale cases were associated with longer median total case processing time for all felony cases. A higher percentage of most serious cases were related to longer median upper court processing times for all felonies. These findings support the conventional wisdom that the characteristics of the caseload affect the pace of litigation. But a relatively large percentage of drug sale cases do not necessarily cause court delay.[132] Data on trends in the percentage of drug-related cases in the caseload among 17 courts indicate that the greatest increase in drug cases during recent years tended to occur in jurisdictions that were already among the slowest courts in previous years. This fact probably explains the relationship between a larger percentage of drug sale cases and longer processing times in 1987.

Trends among 17 of the courts in the study also indicate that 8 reduced their median felony case processing times between 1976 and 1987. While it is encouraging that some courts made significant strides in reducing delay, at least an equal number of courts in the study lost ground in the past decade.

In addition, analysis of trend data suggests that although caseload per judge was not a significant predictor of delay during 1987, caseload per judge affects the pace of litigation in courts that are already operating at a relatively high level of efficiency. For instance, Phoenix and Portland had relatively fast case processing times in 1985 despite having considerably larger than average caseloads per judge. Their caseloads per judge rose significantly between 1985 and 1987, and their case processing times increased dramatically. One hypothesis that explains this pattern is that Phoenix and Portland reached a caseload/case processing saturation point. Where courts move cases relatively quickly and a have large caseload per judge, a substantial increase in filings could justify the addition of new judges to maintain the efficient processing of cases.

Finally, jail crowding was reported to be a serious problem in almost all the jurisdictions, with some jails operating at twice their intended capacity. Despite the seriousness of jail crowding, it was only related to longer drug sale case processing time. This could be because almost every site had the same problem, so the effects were generally the same everywhere. However, courts that received information weekly or monthly regarding the number of defendants in jail awaiting trial were more likely to be in jurisdictions with a less serious jail-crowding problem. Information may be associated with greater cooperation between courts and sheriff's departments. This relationship deserves further investigation.

Implications for Court Management and Future Research

Implications for Court Management

The clearest policy implication of the findings presented here is that courts that take early control of their cases and insist that events take place when scheduled are likely to provide a faster pace of litigation in civil and felony cases. Unlike court size, caseload per judge, and case mix, early control over case events (e.g., early resolution of pretrial motions) and firm trial dates are within the control of the court.

A second finding with significant policy implications is that caseload per judge was not related to either civil or felony case processing times after the influence of other factors was controlled. In both civil and felony courts, however, higher percentages of certain case types (torts in civil, most serious in felony) were related to smaller caseloads per judge. Larger caseloads per judge were also found among larger courts (those with a larger number of filings) in both civil and felony courts. The relationship between jurisdiction size, case mix, and case processing times is, therefore, quite complex; but in general, a larger caseload per judge was not linked to court delay. This finding generally has been confirmed by several other studies of the pace of litigation in trial and appellate courts.[133] One policy implication of this finding is that adding more judges probably should not be the first policy option for courts concerned about reducing delay, *particularly* those with relatively slow case processing times. Adding more judges could simply add to the court's inefficiency. The best interpretation of the data suggests that many or most courts could better manage their resources to process their cases more quickly. Slower courts would benefit greatly by learning the resource and caseflow management techniques used by the faster courts. It is important to remember that the judges in the slower courts are not entirely responsible for slower case processing. Rather, case mix, nonjudicial staff resources, resources among other judicial system agencies, interagency cooperation, organization and resource management, and leadership also play important roles in determining the extent of court delay.

Furthermore, this analysis of case processing time trends supports the argument that a larger caseload per judge does at some point lead to longer case processing times and, under certain conditions, could justify the addition of new judges to a court. According to the saturation point hypothesis presented here, a court might have a larger than average judicial caseload and process its cases relatively expeditiously. If a court then experiences a rapid and substantial increase in filings, there will likely be a noticeable increase in overall case processing times. Given this combination of circumstances, a court could justify additional judges to maintain its pace of litigation. Slower courts that experience a considerable increase in caseload must improve resource and case management procedures and, perhaps, add administrative or support staff, as means for handling increased caseload per judge before adding more judges.

Besides early and continuous control over case events, case mix had some impact on felony case processing times. A larger percentage of most serious and drug sale cases in a caseload were associated with longer case processing times for all felony cases. The relationship between a high percentage of violent crime and drug sale cases and longer case processing times for other felony cases raises the issue of resource allocation. Should the violent or drug cases receive special attention to expedite them through the courts? Prosecutors and judges in many jurisdictions could concentrate on specific case types (e.g., drug cases) in response to public pressure. Such a policy should be pursued with great caution. Concentration on special case types could delay the processing of other felony cases, especially in courts that already exhibit long case processing times for all case types.

Courts that were relatively fast in disposing other types of cases also disposed of the most serious cases rather quickly; courts that were slow in processing other cases tended to be slow in disposing the most serious cases. A better strategy for handling violent crime or drug cases more quickly would probably be to manage better the resources and caseflow of the court as a whole, especially in courts where the pace of litigation is currently slow for all case types.

However, the fact that a higher percentage of certain case types in the caseload were found to be related to longer case processing across the 26 courts provides some empirical basis for subjecting specific case types to differentiated case management (DCM). Through a DCM policy, cases are placed on different "tracks," depending on the nature of the case, which provide different deadlines for the pleadings, discovery time, motions, and trial readiness. The goal is to get cases to disposition in time periods that more closely reflect the complexity of the cases and demands on court resources. Again, there is a danger that concentration of resources on specific case types could result in other cases taking longer than they do now. In theory, however, a DCM program should incorporate and enforce case processing time goals for *all* cases, not just for particular case types (e.g., drug sale or medical malpractice cases). If it is a comprehensive approach to case management, DCM could overcome the dangers inherent in concentrating court resources on specific case types. In fact, some courts have begun systematic, evaluated DCM experiments, and some early reports are promising.[134]

In general, the urban jurisdictions in this study have made more progress in reducing delay in criminal cases than in civil cases. More courts are close to meeting the ABA disposition time standards for felony cases than are close to meeting the standards for civil cases. More courts have reduced their felony case processing times since the late 1970s than have reduced their civil case processing times. This suggests that courts have emphasized felony rather than civil case processing. The focus on felony case processing is understandable. The media and public are more aware of what is happening in the local criminal courts, and the public wants the courts to get tough on criminals. There also has been more money available through federal and state agencies for improvements in local criminal justice systems. But the size of the civil caseload in every general jurisdiction court far exceeds the size of the felony caseload. When there is court delay in civil cases, many people are affected. Furthermore, civil and felony case processing obviously are interrelated problems. As noted earlier, fast felony case processing times tended to be associated with relatively fast civil case processing times. Thus, fast case processing times in one area were generally not due to sacrifices made in another area. The effectiveness of caseflow and resource management tended to be relatively consistent within jurisdictions. The most effective approach for reducing court delay would be to emphasize efficient case and resource management procedures throughout the local court system.

Finally, one of the most salient factors related to effective caseflow management is court leadership. There is a long-standing recognition in the literature on court administration[135] and in the popular and academic literature[136] that effective leadership is essential to successful organizational performance. Even though court leadership was not examined in this study, it should be an important concern for policymakers and court managers. Some courts might be fortunate that skilled leaders emerge through the usual process of advancement in the local court system. However, courts probably would be well served if policies and procedures could be developed to identify potential court leaders (judges and administrators) before their selection; prepare them for leadership roles; select them in ways and for terms of office that facilitate rather than retard effective management; continue their education and development as leaders after their selection; and plan for their succession. Courts should examine factors that facilitate or inhibit the development and effectiveness of leaders and leadership teams. Effective identification, preparation, selection, education, and succession policies and practices could have a profound impact on the pace of litigation and the quality of justice.

Implications for Future Research

Significant differences in the pace of litigation appear to be explained by differences in caseflow management, especially early court control over the caseflow and insistence that case events take place when scheduled. This finding supports the new conventional wisdom in the literature and the tenets of court management taught by the National Center for State Courts, the Institute for Court Management, the National Judicial College, and others. But the lack of association between caseload per judge and case processing times suggests that resource management is also an important factor. Why do courts with a similar number of judges and similiar case management procedures perform at substantially different levels of efficiency? Is there an optimal ratio of administrative and support staff to judicial staff? How do prosecutor, public defender, and probation department caseloads affect the pace of felony litigation? How do fast and slow courts differ in the way they allocate resources to various caseloads (civil, felony, domestic relations, probate, traffic, juvenile, etc.)? What about courts that perform substantially better in one area than others? Is there a concentration of resources in one area at the expense of the other? In-depth case studies would be required to address these issues. Such research would contribute significantly to the transfer of more effective caseflow and resource management procedures from successful courts to those interested in attacking court delay.

Related to the issue of resource management, researchers should concentrate on obtaining better measures of court resources. The number of judges and caseload per judge are only part of the court resource picture. It could be that slower courts with relatively small caseloads per judge lack the support staff found in faster courts with the same number of judges. Identifying the numbers of administrative and support staff per judge in each court would be an important contribution to the measurement of resources, if problems regarding whom and how much time to count can be adequately resolved.[137] If total staff resources can be adequately determined, an assessment of how staff are organized and how their time is allocated to various court functions would provide a more complete picture of resource allocation and management.

Third, case mix was identified as an important factor related to caseload per judge. Researchers could examine the extent to which the concept of "weighted caseload" is used in determining the optimum number of judges and staff in trial courts. How could the idea of weighted caseload be refined and made more useful?

Fourth, correlations found in this study among the percentages of various case types and case processing times suggest that there may be an empirical basis for establishing criteria for tracking cases in a DCM program. As noted earlier, some DCM programs have already been established. Researchers should evaluate these programs. Such research would be valuable for assessing the effectiveness of these programs in reducing court delay and possibly provide information that could help court managers refine their DCM procedures.

Finally, research needs to be done in court leadership and leadership development. The importance of effective leadership is repeatedly cited as a major correlate of successful organizational performance. Yet, there is almost no empirical research about court leadership and its impact on the pace of litigation or quality of justice.[138] What are the characteristics of successful trial court leaders and leadership teams? What do they do that is different from leadership teams in less successful courts? Are there characteristics of leaders and leadership teams that are transferable to other court leaders through education programs? Are there patterns in the ways successful courts identify, prepare, select, and educate their leaders for their positions? There is virtually no empirical research in trial courts to answer any of these questions. If leadership is such an important factor in organizational performance, research in this area is required to help improve the pace of litigation and quality of justice.

This study of the pace of litigation in 26 large urban trial courts is one in a series performed by the National Center for State Courts. The motivation for these studies is the conviction that court delay is a serious threat to the quality of justice and public trust and confidence in our court system. The analysis presented here advances our knowledge and understanding of the factors related to the pace of litigation. Although it is difficult to achieve, delay reduction can be achieved through commitment and long-term effort. Researchers can play a role in reducing court delay by monitoring the pace of litigation around the country and providing useful information to court leaders and policymakers.

Notes

71. In unified trial courts, including Minneapolis, St. Paul, Wichita, and Colorado Springs, which do not use a lower court and do not usually use a grand jury indictment, the date of the first appearance of the defendant was used as the date the information was filed (as the start of upper court time). Also, San Diego and the Bronx allow guilty pleas to felony charges to be entered upon an information filed by the prosecutor in the lower court. Lower court judges sit as general jurisdiction court judges to accept these guilty pleas. These cases are included in the calculation of upper court time. Mahoney et al. (1985, 1988) did not include these cases in upper court time.

72. As was true of the figures related to civil case processing time, the numbers shown on the bar charts for each court indicate only the median and 90th percentile processing times. The 75th percentile time can be determined approximately by comparing the bar to the scale at the bottom of the chart.

73. The COSCA/CCJ standard is not clear whether all cases or the average case should be completed in 180 days.

74. The percentage of cases over the ABA disposition time standards could not be determined for Boston, Portland, and Tucson because original arrest dates were not obtained.

75. The District of Columbia shows 5 percent most serious cases, but case types in D.C. were determined by the most serious charge at conviction, not the most serious charge in the indictment/information, as it was determined for the other courts.

76. Median upper court time for all felony cases ($r = .50$); less serious cases ($r = .46$); most serious ($r = .44$); and drug sale cases ($r = .43$), $p < .03$ for all correlations. See Appendix H.

77. $r > .10$ more than the correlation established by the percentage of drug sale cases alone.

78. $r = .57$, $p = .002$. See Appendix J1.

79. $r = -.56$, $p = .003$. See Appendix J1.

80. Upper court median: $r = -.33$, $p = .05$; upper court 90th: $r = -.44$, $p = < .02$. See Appendix H.

81. The percentage of bench warrant cases exhibited a moderate relationship with the following: all felonies: total median ($r = .42$), upper court median ($r = .56$), most serious total median ($r = .57$), less serious total median ($r = .46$), less serious upper court median ($r = .59$), drug sale upper court median ($r = .46$), and trial case upper court median ($r = .43$). All values of $p < .04$. The percentage of bench warrant cases exhibited a strong relationship with all felonies: total 90th ($r = .69$), upper court 90th ($r = .79$), and median upper court time for most serious ($r = .64$) For the latter two correlations, $p < .001$. See Appendix H.

82. Percent all cases over: 180 days ($r = .61$); percent over one year ($r = .66$). See Appendix J1.

83. Percent bench warrant cases and percent nonbench warrant cases over: 180 days ($r = .60$, $p = .003$) and one year ($r = .68$, $p = .001$). See Appendix J1.

84. Courts vary in how they count felony cases. Most courts in this study begin to count cases when an indictment/information is filed. The state of Ohio, however, counts cases that reach arraignment. Thus, Cleveland and Dayton figures for cases filed might understate their filings compared to other courts. Also, most courts count all the charges against one defendant arising from a single incident as a case. But the number of incidents included in one indictment/information varies in Phoenix, Tucson, Denver, Colorado Springs, Boston, Providence, Bronx, and New Orleans. Thus, the number of cases filed in these courts as reported in Table 12 probably understates to some extent the size of their caseloads compared

to other courts in the study. For more information on how courts count cases, see *State Court Caseload Statistics: Annual Report, 1987*, Williamsburg, VA: National Center for State Courts, 1989.

85. The number of judges who spent at least part of their time handling felony case matters multiplied by the estimated average proportion of time the judges spent on felony case matters in 1987. Estimates were obtained from court administrators. See also the next section.

86. Total (r = .49), upper court (r = .49), p < .02 (see Appendix I).

87. See National Center for State Courts, *State Court Caseload Statistics, 1987* (1989), which identifies how each state counts criminal cases.

88. The number of pending cases on January 1, 1987 for each court is listed in Appendix K. Pending cases are used to calculate the backlog index in Table 16.

89. See Flanders (1977); Church et al. (1978a); Friesen et al. (1978); Neubauer et al. (1981); Weller et al. (1982); Mahoney et al. (1988).

90. For an example of the complexity of measuring nonjudicial staff resources, see Cassidy and Stoever (1974); Kuban et al. (1984).

91. See Church et al. (1978a) p.47; Mahoney et al. (1988) p. 58.

92. See Church et al. (1978a) p. 39; Mahoney et al. (1985, 1988).

93. Median total time in drug possession cases (r = -.38, p = .05). See Appendix I.

94. Median upper court time (r = .46, p < .02) and total time (r = .42, p < .03). See Appendix I.

95. Median for all felonies (r = .47), most serious (r = .63), less serious (r = .52), drug sale (r = .38), and trial cases (r = .51). 90th percentile for all felonies (r = .46). Judicial assignment was also weakly or moderately related to five measures of total disposition time. See Appendix I. All statistically significant, p < .05.

96. r = .52, p = .003 (see Appendix J2).

97. The finding that specialized assignments could be related to longer case processing times might raise concerns about the creation of special courts to handle drug cases.

98. See Mahoney et al. (1988) pp. 197-204.

99. Data presented at pp. 90-92 ("Perceived Causes of Felony Case Delay") provide some support for this interpretation.

100. See Mahoney et al. (1988) pp. 197-204. They identify the following characteristics as being generally found among courts with expeditious case processing times: strong leadership; commitment to expeditious case processing; goals; an information system designed and used to monitor achievement of goals; interagency and intracourt communication; early and continuous control by the court over caseflow; and staff training.

101. Median upper court time for all felonies (r = .53), most serious (r = .54), less serious (r = .56), drug sale (r = .44), jury trials (r = .56); less serious (r = .44), jury trials (r = .51); 90th percentile upper court time for all felonies (r = .53); and 90th percentile total time for all felonies (r = .50). All statistically significant (p < .05). See Appendix I.

102. Correlations ranged from r = .62 to .78 for seven measures of felony case processing time. See Appendix I.

103. Median FSTD to trial start related to: percentage over 180 days (r = .63), percentage over one year (r = .81). Both had p < .02. See Appendix J3.

104. r = .65, p < .02. See Appendix J2.

105. r = -.46, p < .05. See Appendix J3.

106. Early resolution of pretrial motions and median first scheduled trial date to start of jury trial: r = .61, p = .01. See Appendix J2.

107. Correlations ranged from r = -.50 to -.70. See Appendix I. Note in Table 15 that 6 of the 14 courts with relevant data were the 6 fastest courts. Only 1 of the slowest 7 courts had

relevant data. Correlations should be interpreted to apply only to the courts with relevant data.

108. Percentage over 180 days (r = -.72, p = .004); percentage over one year (r = -.69, p = .007). Nonbench warrant cases: percentage over 180 days (r = -.69, p = .007); percentage over one year (r = -.69, p = .006). See Appendix J3.

109. r = -.46, p = .05. See Appendix J3.

110. See Church et al. (1978a) p. 29; Mahoney et al. (1985) p. 18; (1988) pp. 55-56.

111. Percentage bench warrants (r = .59, p = .004). See Appendix J3.

112. r = -.44, p < .02. See Appendix J3.

113. See pp. 90-92, "Perceived Causes of Felony Case Delay"; see also Bureau of Justice Statistics (1988).

114. In most courts, the court administrator contacted the sheriff to obtain the jail population and capacity information.

115. r = .45, p = .04. See Appendix I.

116. r = -.50, p = .007.

117. r = .43, p = .02. See Appendix J3.

118. Percentage bench warrant cases is arguably not a case management factor. But the range of percentage bench warrant cases among the courts suggests that it is at least partly a management issue.

119. See Appendix A for a discussion of the regression analysis used in this study.

120. Because the percentage of jury trial cases that started on the first scheduled trial date were obtained from only 14 courts, the regression analysis on firm trial dates should be viewed as tentative. A larger number of courts are necessary to improve the reliability of the results reported here.

121. None were statistically significant at the .05 level as determined by Fisher's Exact Test, a form of chi square.

122. If guilty pleas entered on an information in the lower court are not included in the calculation of median upper court time (indictment/information to disposition), the Bronx would show 163 days for its median time in 1987, rather than the 114 days shown in Table 19.

123. For brief case studies on changes in caseflow management procedures during the 1980s in Dayton, Detroit, Wichita, and Jersey City, see Mahoney et al. (1988) Chapters six and seven.

124. See Table 12.

125. For 1983 filings per judge, see Mahoney et al. (1985) p. 13.

126. For 1983 data, see Mahoney et al. (1985) p. 13.

127. See Mahoney et al. (1985) p. 13.

128. The Bronx is not included in this table because its civil case data were not included in this study.

129. See Figures 17- 18.

130. Median all civil case disposition time displayed an (r) of .62 or higher with total and upper court median and 90th percentile times for all felonies. All were statistically significant at the .001 level or better. (See Appendix M.)

131. See Mahoney et al. (1988) Chapters six and seven.

132. Although Fairfax (20 percent) and Oakland (26 percent) had relatively large drug sale caseloads, they were among the faster half of the courts in this study (see Figure 21).

133. See Flanders (1977); Church et al. (1978a); Friesen et al. (1978); Neubauer et al. (1981); Martin and Prescott (1981); Weller et al. (1982); Mahoney et al. (1985, 1988).

134. See Guynes and Miller (1988), which describes the nature and progress of differentiated case management in two New Jersey courts. The Bureau of Justice Assistance (BJA) is

currently funding four experiments in differentiated case management in urban trial courts. A description and evaluation of these programs will be provided by the National Center for State Courts during 1989. BJA is also sponsoring experiments in expediting the processing of drug cases through its Comprehensive Adjudication of Drug Arrestees (CADA) Project. A description and evaluation of these programs will also be provided by NCSC in 1989.

135. See, e.g., Mahoney et al. (1988); Gallas (1987); Zaffarano (1985); Church et al. (1978a); Friesen, Gallas and Gallas (1971).

136. See, e.g., Bennis (1959); Fiedler (1974); Sayles (1979); Selznick (1957); Peters and Waterman (1982).

137. Court, court clerk, sheriff, and corrections staff might all contribute time to the management of court cases. Determining what percentage of time each spends in handling court cases can be very difficult and can create a lack of comparability across courts.

138. See Zaffarano (1985); Gallas (1987).

Appendices

Appendix A:
Methods and Statistics

Defining a Case

Defining a case was a problem, especially in felony cases. Some courts count defendants and include all charges arising from multiple incidents. Others count defendants, but count each incident (e.g., burglary) and all related charges (e.g., weapons possession, drug possession) as one case. It could also be possible to include multiple defendants in a case. In general, the courts in this study counted defendants, but varied in whether they included multiple or single incidents within a case against a defendant. Differences in how the courts counted cases are noted in Table 12. It is difficult to determine the impact of these differences in comparing the courts on "cases filed" and "filings per judge." At best, findings related to caseload should be interpreted with caution.

Sources and Coding of Data

Data were obtained in a manner that would yield the most reliable information while imposing the least burden on the court or clerk's office. Some courts sent docket sheets generated from an automated system. Some sites required coding on site from manual files. A few courts generated just the necessary data items for each case by means of a computer program that searched automated court or clerk records. Coding of data was supervised by the project director or, if coded on site, by a knowledgeable court or clerk staff member.

In New Orleans, civil case samples were not obtained from 2 of the 12 judges. The court administrator, however, believed that the cases handled by the two judges were similar in type and processing time compared to the other judges in the court. Newark and Jersey City could sample only civil cases in which an answer was filed, so their case processing times will be somewhat longer than other courts. Civil case data from San Diego included only cases handled by the city branch of the Superior Court for San Diego County. However, the number of filings, judges, and population in Table 2 are for the whole county. The city branch had 17 civil judges and 14,575 civil case filings in 1987. The city branch civil caseload per FTE judge was 902, 7 percent higher than the 843 case per FTE judge reported in Table 2. This discrepancy was noted too late to make changes in the report.

Statistics

Pearson's correlation coefficient measures the relationship between two variables. That is, to what extent is an increase in (or presence of) one factor (e.g., percent tort cases) related to an increase or decrease in case processing time. Causation should not be inferred from a correlation. Both factors may, in fact, be caused by a third or multiple other factors. A correlation merely measures association. Causation involves a certain logical and temporal order or relationship among the factors. Furthermore, more sophisticated statistical analysis is required to identify the relative influence of other factors that might affect the relationship between two variables (e.g., percent torts and case processing time).

Twenty to 26 courts constitutes a small sample for purposes of correlation analysis. When just two or three courts are dropped from the analysis, substantial fluctuations in the correlations could occur. Thus, correlations based on fewer than 20 courts should be viewed as tentative. Correlations based on small sample sizes are not necessarily the best evidence of a relationship between variables. Tables or scatter plots might be the best method of presentation under these circumstances. Correlations are reported here for purposes of expediency and uniformity of presentation and interpretation.

It should be noted that if courts did not have data that were comparable to the other courts, their data were not included in the correlations analysis. For example, Pittsburgh's civil data were not included in most correlation analyses because their data did not include cases disposed by arbitration. San Diego's civil case data were excluded from most correlations because they included only trial list cases. Some courts could not distinguish drug sale and drug possession cases, so their percentages of these case types and drug case processing times were excluded from the correlations. The District of Columbia could identify only the most serious charge at conviction; all others provided the charges in the indictment (or information). Thus, the District of Columbia's percentages of case types and case processing times for case types were excluded from the correlation analyses. Furthermore, there had to be at least 20 cases of a particular case type (e.g., jury trial cases) before a court's case processing time was included in a correlation analysis. Boston, for example, had only 13 felony jury trials in its sample, so it was not included in median jury trial times. All the appendices that include correlations also provide (in parentheses) the number of courts included in the particular correlation. Correlations are reported only if there was a minimum of 12 courts with comparable data. Again, the reader should be cautious about interpreting correlations involving fewer than 18 or 20 courts.

A form of regression analysis was used to identify the most important predictors of case processing time. It allows the researcher to determine which of the factors that appear to explain (or be related to) case processing time actually affect case processing time when the relationships among the other factors are controlled.

A stepwise regression analysis was used. Two explanatory variables (e.g., percentage drug sale cases and caseload per FTE judge) were entered simultaneously into the equation to determine their relative impact on case processing time. Several outcomes are possible when both variables are present: (1) both variables could retain a significant relationship to case processing time; (2) either one of the variables could remain significant but not the other; or (3) both variables could be statistically insignificant. Each variable in Figures 14 and 26 was entered into a series of stepwise regressions (two explanatory variables per regression) so that each variable was examined with each of the other variables to determine their relative impact on case processing times. If a variable (e.g., firm trial dates) displayed a statistically significant relationship with case processing time after controlling for *all* of the other variables, it was displayed in Figures 15 and 27 with a bold line leading to the appropriate case processing time. If a variable retained significance after analysis with *all but one* other variable, it was displayed in Figures 15 and 27 with a narrow line leading to the appropriate case processing time. If an explanatory variable failed to retain a statistically significant association with the measure of case processing time in more than one regression analysis, it was not deemed to be among the most important predictors of case processing time. With a larger sample of courts (e.g., 100) all explanatory variables could be entered into one equation simultaneously to determine their relative impact on case processing time. Due to the small sample size (14 to 26 courts, depending on the variables), only two variables could be examined simultaneously without violating statistical rules. A more common technique for examining the relative importance of multiple explanatory variables is partial correlation analysis (see, e.g., Blalock (1979) pp. 451-506). However, regression analysis and partial correlations generally rank variables in the same order of importance (Blalock (1979) p. 480).

For more information on multiple regression analysis, see Kerlinger and Pedhazer (1973). For information on the stepwise regression procedure used in this study, see Norusis (1986) pp. 127-31.

Sample Sizes

Determining what sample size is needed to obtain a sampling error of plus or minus 5 percent depends on several factors. (See, e.g., Arkin and Colton, 1963.) The following statements greatly simplify what is involved in determining sample sizes. If the number of dispositions in 1987 was approximately 10,000, a sample of 566 cases would provide us a sampling error of plus or minus 4 percent. If there were 10,000 dispositions, a sample of 370 would provide a sampling error of plus or minus 5 percent. (Tables 2 and 12 show the number of civil and felony filings in each court.) Thus, the sampling error is smaller for case processing times that are based on larger samples. Median times for all civil and total and upper court times for all felony cases are the most accurate. The case processing times for particular case types will have somewhat larger sampling errors because they are based on smaller sample sizes.

Because of the problems posed by small sample sizes, case processing times were reported only if there were at least 20 cases in the sample. Some courts were dropped from the analysis of jury trial or drug sale cases because they did not have 20 cases in the sample.

Appendix B

Civil Case Processing Times and Percentages of Case Types–1987
Pearson's (r) Correlations

	All Civil Cases Median	All Civil Cases 90th Per.	Tort Cases Median	Tort Cases 90th Per.	Contract Cases Median	Contract Cases 90th Per.	Trial List Cases Median	Trial List Cases 90th Per.	Jury Trial Median	Percent Tort Cases	Percent Contract Cases	Percent Jury Trials	Percent Over 1 Year	Percent Over 2 Years
All Civil Cases Median	----	.7919 (23) P=.000	.9203 (23) P=.000	.7573 (23) P=.000	.9647 (23) P=.000	.8285 (23) P=.000	.8772 (14) P=.000	.7065 (14) P=.002	.7950 (16) P=.000	.4165 (23) P=.024	−.3738 (23) P=.039	.1100 (23) P=.309	.8540 (23) P=.000	.9211 (23) P=.000
All Civil Cases 90th Per.		----	.7684 (23) P=.000	.9791 (23) P=.000	.7786 (23) P=.000	.9425 (23) P=.000	.7055 (14) P=.002	.8213 (14) P=.000	.8923 (16) P=.000	.3741 (23) P=.039	−.2760 (23) P=.101	−.1664 (23) P=.224	.6789 (23) P=.000	.8938 (23) P=.000
Tort Cases Median			----	.7852 (23) P=.000	.8797 (23) P=.000	.7686 (23) P=.000	.8353 (14) P=.000	.5997 (14) P=.012	.8252 (16) P=.000	.2472 (23) P=.128	−.1767 (23) P=.210	.0901 (23) P=.341	.8332 (23) P=.000	.8960 (23) P=.000
Tort Cases 90th Per.				----	.7536 (23) P=.000	.9017 (23) P=.000	.6794 (14) P=.004	.7993 (14) P=.000	.8126 (16) P=.000	.2527 (23) P=.122	−.1694 (23) P=.220	−.2295 (23) P=.146	.6433 (23) P=.000	.8565 (23) P=.000
Contract Cases Median					----	.8284 (23) P=.000	.8957 (14) P=.000	.6702 (14) P=.004	.8764 (16) P=.000	.3523 (23) P=.050	−.3560 (23) P=.048	−.0008 (23) P=.499	.7529 (23) P=.000	.8812 (23) P=.000
Contract Cases 90th Per.						----	.7514 (14) P=.001	.7797 (14) P=.001	.8564 (16) P=.000	.3869 (23) P=.034	−.3038 (23) P=.079	−.1133 (23) P=.303	.6909 (23) P=.000	.8970 (23) P=.000
Trial List Cases Median							----	.7662 (16) P=.000	†††	.4145 (14) P=.070	−.3073 (14) P=.143	.0988 (14) P=.368	.8338 (14) P=.000	.8536 (14) P=.000
Trial List Cases 90th Per.								----	†††	.7099 (14) P=.002	−.5521 (14) P=.020	−.1105 (14) P=.353	.8478 (14) P=.000	.7921 (14) P=.000
Jury Trial Cases Median									----	.3688 (16) P=.080	−.2836 (16) P=.144	−.0522 (16) P=.424	.6620 (16) P=.003	.8812 (16) P=.000
Percent Tort Cases										----	−.8381 (23) P=.000	.2973 (23) P=.084	.5655 (23) P=.002	.4655 (23) P=.013
Percent Contract Cases											----	−.1301 (23) P=.277	−.4466 (23) P=.016	−.3722 (23) P=.040
Percent Jury Trial Cases												----	.2414 (23) P=.134	.0306 (23) P=.445
Percent All Civil Cases Over 1 Year													----	.8282 (23) P=.000

††† Less than 12 courts.

120 / Examining Court Delay

Appendix C

Measures of Court Size, Caseload, Backlog, and Civil Case Processing Times–1987
Pearson's (r) Correlations

	All Civil Cases Median	All Civil Cases 90th Per.	Tort Cases Median	Tort Cases 90th Per.	Contract Cases Median	Contract Cases 90th Per.	Trial List Cases Median	Trial List Cases 90th Per.	Jury Trial Median	Percent Tort Cases	Percent Contract Cases	Percent Jury Trials	Percent Over 1 Year	Percent Over 2 Years
Population 1986	−.0112 (23) P=.480	−.1062 (23) P=.315	.0448 (23) P=.420	−.0676 (23) P=.380	.0042 (23) P=.492	−.0500 (23) P=.410	.1667 (16) P=.269	.2568 (16) P=.169	.3009 (18) P=.112	−.1224 (23) P=.289	−.0173 (23) P=.469	−.1891 (23) P=.194	.1348 (23) P=.270	−.0051 (23) P=.491
Civil Cases Filed	−.2273 (22) P=.155	−.2483 (22) P=.133	−.1539 (22) P=.247	−.1880 (22) P=.201	−.2337 (22) P=.148	−.2728 (22) P=.110	−.1263 (15) P=.327	−.1523 (15) P=.294	−.0012 (17) P=.498	−.3952 (22) P=.034	.3475 (22) P=.057	−.2495 (22) P=.131	−.1620 (22) P=.236	−.2118 (22) P=.172
FTE Civil Judges	−.1087 (23) P=.311	−.1584 (23) P=.235	−.0242 (23) P=.456	−.1152 (23) P=.300	−.1042 (23) P=.318	−.1342 (23) P=.271	.0007 (16) P=.499	.0725 (16) P=.395	.2847 (18) P=.126	−.2517 (23) P=.123	.1252 (23) P=.285	−.2839 (23) P=.095	.0407 (23) P=.427	−.0698 (23) P=.376
Filings per FTE Judge	−.3085 (22) P=.081	−.3048 (22) P=.084	−.2839 (22) P=.100	−.2542 (22) P=.127	−.3233 (22) P=.071	−.3790 (22) P=.041	−.3317 (15) P=.114	−.4311 (15) P=.054	−.3239 (17) P=.102	−.3835 (22) P=.039	.4398 (22) P=.020	−.0299 (22) P=.448	−.3979 (22) P=.033	−.3397 (22) P=.061
Civil Backlog Index	.6119 (17) P=.005	.6725 (17) P=.002	.5097 (17) P=.018	.5987 (17) P=.006	.6077 (17) P=.005	.6898 (17) P=.001	†††	†††	−.2990 (14) P=.150	.3362 (17) P=.093	−.2602 (17) P=.157	.3093 (17) P=.114	.4632 (17) P=.031	.6769 (17) P=.001
Calendar Type	−.4157 (23) P=.024	−.4272 (23) P=.021	−.3827 (23) P=.036	−.3821 (23) P=.036	−.3820 (23) P=.036	−.4258 (23) P=.021	−.2468 (16) P=.178	−.1658 (16) P=.270	−.4817 (18) P=.021	−.5129 (23) P=.006	.3951 (23) P=.031	−.3326 (23) P=.061	−.3496 (23) P=.051	−.4879 (23) P=.009
Judicial Assignment	.1193 (23) P=.294	−.0003 (23) P=.500	.1775 (23) P=.209	.0394 (23) P=.429	.0793 (23) P=.360	.0138 (23) P=.475	.1942 (16) P=.236	.1273 (16) P=.319	.3716 (18) P=.064	.0729 (23) P=.370	.1503 (23) P=.247	.0046 (23) P=.492	.1844 (23) P=.200	.1204 (23) P=.292
Point of Court Control	.4334 (22) P=.022	.5030 (22) P=.009	.4129 (22) P=.028	.4892 (22) P=.010	.3669 (22) P=.047	.4547 (22) P=.017	.5085 (16) P=.022	.7475 (16) P=.000	.2291 (17) P=.188	.5250 (22) P=.006	−.1920 (22) P=.196	.1260 (22) P=.288	.5097 (22) P=.008	.5020 (22) P=.009
Trial Backup System	−.2790 (23) P=.099	−.3993 (23) P=.030	−.3335 (23) P=.060	−.3992 (23) P=.030	−.1983 (23) P=.182	−.2344 (23) P=.141	.2105 (16) P=.217	.0465 (16) P=.432	−.1192 (18) P=.319	−.3326 (23) P=.060	.2467 (23) P=.128	.0973 (23) P=.329	−.4413 (23) P=.018	−.3758 (23) P=.039
Dispo. Time Goals	−.2522 (23) P=.257	−.4970 (23) P=.008	−.0757 (23) P=.366	−.4104 (23) P=.026	−.2206 (23) P=.156	−.5024 (23) P=.007	−.1963 (16) P=.233	−.5263 (16) P=.018	−.0744 (18) P=.385	−.4700 (23) P=.012	.4109 (23) P=.026	.0246 (23) P=.456	−.2466 (23) P=.128	−.3757 (23) P=.039

††† Less than 12 courts.

Appendix D

Court Size, Caseload, Backlog, and Civil Caseflow Management Procedures
Pearson's (r) Correlations

	Population 1986	Civil Cases Filed	FTE Civil Judges	Filings per FTE Judge	Civil Backlog Index	Calendar Type	Judicial Assignment	Point of Court Control	Trial Backup System	Dispo. Time Goals
Population 1986	-----	.7348 (24) P= .000	.9340 (25) P= .000	-.0577 (24) P= .394	-.1223 (18) P= .314	.1629 (25) P= .218	.1816 (25) P= .192	.0110 (24) P= .480	.2065 (25) P= .161	.0172 (25) P= .467
Civil Cases Filed		-----	.8149 (24) P= .000	.5367 (24) P= .003	-.1686 (18) P= .252	.3727 (24) P= .036	.3313 (24) P= .057	-.1425 (23) P= .258	.2573 (24) P= .112	.1576 (24) P= .231
FTE Civil Judges			-----	.0188 (24) P= .465	-.2237 (18) P= .186	.2424 (25) P= .122	.2267 (25) P= .138	-.1200 (24) P= .288	.0965 (25) P= .323	.0908 (25) P= .333
Filings per FTE Judge				-----	-.0980 (18) P= .349	.2144 (24) P= .157	.2788 (24) P= .094	-.1359 (23) P= .268	.3158 (24) P= .066	.1615 (24) P= .225
Civil Backlog Index					-----	-.2740 (18) P= .136	-.3401 (18) P= .084	.4095 (17) P= .051	-.3618 (18) P= .070	-.7081 (18) P= .001
Calendar Type						-----	-.0797 (25) P= .352	-.3174 (24) P= .065	.2717 (25) P= .094	.3159 (25) P= .062
Judicial Assignment							-----	.1630 (24) P= .223	.2215 (25) P= .144	.3165 (25) P= .062
Point of Court Control								-----	-.3154 (24) P= .067	-.4818 (24) P= .009
Trial Backup System									-----	.2381 (25) P= .126

Appendix E

Civil Court Caseloads–1987
Ranked by Median Tort Case Processing Time (Days)

	Torts Median	Pending Civil Cases 1-1-87	Civil Dispositions in 1987	Pending Civil Cases 1-1-88	Dispositions per FTE Civil Judge†
Wichita	215	6935	19549	4508	2413
Dayton	276	2658	4602	2511	639
Fairfax	297	15787	10039	17017	1521
Norfolk	342	6513	4852	7149	1078
Cleveland	363	17623	23204	17551	1254
Minneapolis	371	9627	*	8138	*
Phoenix	376	26098	35350	36319	1360
Atlanta	385	4037	4434	3556	739
Colo Springs	392	3734	7905	2983	1976
Denver	398	13198	28532	11085	2536
New Orleans	405	*	*	*	*
Jersey City	441	3947	5760	4901	1069
Salinas	461	*	1895	*	820
Portland	463	5459	8730	4327	1559
Tucson	474	8552	9775	8822	1131
St Paul	477	2316	6179	3032	736
Miami	482	34201	33931	33792	2121
Oakland	504	*	*	*	*
Detroit	532	31807	36059	25546	1281
Dist of Col	619	*	*	*	*
Newark	710	9756	8546	9892	855
San Diego	742	2871	23512	2372	904
Providence	818	*	4358	*	872
Pittsburgh	825	*	*	*	*
Boston	953	18166	10581	15246	*

† Number of civil cases disposed in 1987 divided by "full-time equivalent (FTE) civil judges" (see Table 2).
* Information not available or comparable.

Appendix F

Civil Case Information Collected by the Court†–1987

	Torts Median	# Cases Pending	# Cases Filed	# Cases Disposed	Age of Pending Cases	Age of Disposed Cases	# Cases Over Goals	# Trial Conts. Grant	# Other Conts. Grant	# Pend W/Next Action
Wichita	215	WEEKLY	*	*	WEEKLY	QUARTER	WEEKLY	*	*	*
Dayton	276	MONTHLY	MONTHLY	MONTHLY	MONTHLY	MONTHLY	MONTHLY	*	*	MONTHLY
Fairfax	297	YEARLY	QUARTER	QUARTER	*	*	*	*	*	*
Norfolk	342	YEARLY	YEARLY	YEARLY	ON REQ	ON REQ	*	ON REQ	ON REQ	ON REQ
Cleveland	363	MONTHLY	MONTHLY	MONTHLY	MONTHLY	MONTHLY	MONTHLY	*	*	*
Minneapolis	371	WEEKLY	ON REQ	ON REQ	ON REQ	ON REQ	ON REQ	*	*	ON REQ
Phoenix	376	MONTHLY	MONTHLY	MONTHLY	MONTHLY	QUARTER	MONTHLY	*	*	*
Atlanta	385	MONTHLY	YEARLY	YEARLY	MONTHLY	YEARLY	YEARLY	*	*	*
Colo Springs	392	MONTHLY	*	MONTHLY	*	*	*	MONTHLY	MONTHLY	MONTHLY
Denver	398	MONTHLY	MONTHLY	MONTHLY	*	*	*	*	*	*
New Orleans	405	*	MONTHLY	*	*	*	*	*	*	*
Jersey City	441	MONTHLY	MONTHLY	MONTHLY	MONTHLY	MONTHLY	MONTHLY	*	*	*
Salinas	461	MONTHLY	MONTHLY	MONTHLY	*	MONTHLY	*	*	*	*
Portland	463	MONTHLY	MONTHLY	MONTHLY	MONTHLY	MONTHLY	MONTHLY	MONTHLY	MONTHLY	*
Tucson	474	YEARLY	YEARLY	YEARLY	*	*	*	*	*	WEEKLY
St Paul	477	MONTHLY	MONTHLY	MONTHLY	QUARTER	*	YEARLY	MONTHLY	MONTHLY	*
Miami	482	MONTHLY	YEARLY	YEARLY	MONTHLY	MONTHLY	MONTHLY	*	*	*
Oakland	504	YEARLY	*	*	*	*	*	*	*	*
Detroit	532	MONTHLY	MONTHLY	QUARTER	MONTHLY	*	*	*	*	MONTHLY
Dist of Col	619	MONTHLY	MONTHLY	MONTHLY	MONTHLY	MONTHLY	*	MONTHLY	MONTHLY	*
Newark	710	MONTHLY	MONTHLY	MONTHLY	MONTHLY	MONTHLY	*	*	*	*
San Diego	742	*	WEEKLY	WEEKLY	*	MONTHLY	MONTHLY	*	*	*
Providence	818	*	*	*	*	*	*	*	*	*
Pittsburgh	825	MONTHLY	MONTHLY	MONTHLY	MONTHLY	MONTHLY	*	MONTHLY	MONTHLY	*
Boston	953	MONTHLY	MONTHLY	MONTHLY	MONTHLY	MONTHLY	*	*	*	*

† Data from survey of court administrators.
* Information not collected/desseminated on a regular basis.
ON REQ = On request

Appendix G

Felony Case Processing Time Measures–1987
Pearson's (r) Correlations

	All Total Median	All Total 90th Per.	All Upper Ct Median	All Upper Ct 90th Per.	Most Ser. Total Median	Most Ser. Upper Ct Median	Less Ser. Total Median	Less Ser. Upper Ct Median	Drug Sale Total Median	Drug Sale Upper Ct Median	Drug Poss. Total Median	Drug Poss. Upper Ct Median	Jury Trial Total Median	Jury Trial Upper Ct Median
All Cases Total Median	----	.7984 (23) P=.000	.7296 (23) P=.000	.8205 (23) P=.000	.7622 (22) P=.000	.6277 (22) P=.001	.9739 (22) P=.000	.7655 (22) P=.000	.9207 (18) P=.000	.4094 (18) P=.046	.8697 (19) P=.000	.6403 (20) P=.001	.7815 (21) P=.000	.6313 (21) P=.001
All Cases Total 90th Per.		----	.7003 (23) P=.000	.9144 (23) P=.000	.7588 (22) P=.000	.7028 (22) P=.000	.7769 (22) P=.000	.7512 (22) P=.000	.7299 (18) P=.000	.4189 (18) P=.042	.6859 (19) P=.001	.5481 (20) P=.006	.7979 (21) P=.000	.7327 (21) P=.000
All Cases Upper Ct Median			----	.7572 (26) P=.000	.6525 (22) P=.000	.8487 (25) P=.000	.7303 (22) P=.000	.9934 (25) P=.000	.5845 (18) P=.005	.8992 (21) P=.000	.5909 (19) P=.004	.9156 (22) P=.000	.6741 (21) P=.000	.7334 (23) P=.000
All Cases Upper Ct 90th Per.				----	.7770 (22) P=.000	.7607 (25) P=.000	.8288 (22) P=.000	.8078 (25) P=.000	.6751 (18) P=.001	.5105 (21) P=.009	.6582 (19) P=.001	.5108 (22) P=.008	.8164 (21) P=.000	.7299 (23) P=.000
Most Serious Total Median					----	.9135 (22) P=.000	.7612 (22) P=.000	.6864 (24) P=.000	.5736 (18) P=.006	.2898 (18) P=.122	.6255 (19) P=.002	.4856 (20) P=.015	.8837 (20) P=.000	.8160 (20) P=.000
Most Serious Upper Ct Median						----	.6601 (22) P=.000	.8565 (25) P=.000	.4144 (18) P=.044	.6924 (21) P=.000	.4795 (19) P=.019	.5908 (22) P=.002	.8373 (20) P=.000	.8920 (22) P=.000
Less Serious Total Median							----	.7799 (22) P=.000	.8385 (18) P=.000	.3742 (18) P=.063	.8216 (19) P=.000	.6415 (20) P=.001	.8731 (20) P=.000	.7351 (20) P=.000
Less Serious Upper Ct Median								----	.6148 (18) P=.003	.8572 (21) P=.000	.6289 (19) P=.002	.8876 (22) P=.000	.7405 (20) P=.000	.7774 (22) P=.000
Drug Sale Total Median									----	.4422 (18) P=.033	.7959 (17) P=.000	.5262 (18) P=.012	.5428 (17) P=.012	.3591 (17) P=.078
Drug Sale Upper Ct Median										----	.3030 (17) P=.119	.8131 (20) P=.000	.2761 (17) P=.142	.3895 (19) P=.050
Drug Poss. Total Median											----	.6143 (19) P=.003	.6281 (18) P=.003	.4692 (18) P=.025
Drug Poss. Upper Ct Median												----	.5534 (19) P=.007	.5732 (21) P=.003
Jury Trial Total Median													----	.9412 (21) P=.000

Appendix H

Felony Case Processing Time and Percentages of Case Types–1987
Pearson's (r) Correlations

	All Total Median	All Total 90th per.	All Upper Ct Median	All Upper Ct 90th per.	Most Ser. Total Median	Most Ser. Upper Ct Median	Less Ser. Total Median	Less Ser. Upper Ct Median	Drug Sale Total Median	Drug Sale Upper Ct Median	Drug Poss. Total Median	Drug Poss. Upper Ct Median	Jury Trial Total Median	Jury Trial Upper Ct Median
Percent Most Serious	.1512 (22) P=.251	.0303 (22) P=.447	.5022 (25) P=.005	.1686 (25) P=.210	.1373 (22) P=.271	.4385 (25) P=.014	.1239 (22) P=.291	.4646 (25) P=.010	.1137 (18) P=.327	.4281 (21) P=.026	.2248 (19) P=.177	.2248 (19) P=.177	.213 (20) P=.184	.2810 (22) P=.103
Percent All Drug Cases	.4708 (22) P=.014	.4374 (22) P=.021	.3788 (25) P=.031	.5237 (25) P=.004	.5678 (22) P=.003	.5096 (25) P=.005	.4903 (22) P=.010	.4250 (25) P=.017	.4564 (18) P=.028	.1343 (21) P=.281	.3975 (19) P=.046	.3975 (19) P=.046	.5551 (20) P=.006	.4506 (22) P=.018
Percent Drug Sale Cases	.5115 (20) P=.011	.3404 (20) P=.071	.5135 (23) P=.006	.4544 (23) P=.015	.4898 (20) P=.014	.5358 (23) P=.004	.5384 (20) P=.007	.5391 (23) P=.004	.4370 (18) P=.035	.2783 (21) P=.111	.4255 (19) P=.035	.4255 (19) P=.035	.5936 (19) P=.004	.5464 (21) P=.005
Percent Drug Poss. Cases	.0522 (20) P=.414	.1457 (20) P=.270	-.2538 (23) P=.121	.0851 (23) P=.350	.2225 (20) P=.173	-.0713 (23) P=.373	.0186 (20) P=.469	-.2290 (23) P=.147	.1133 (18) P=.327	-.3211 (21) P=.078	-.0412 (19) P=.434	-.0412 (19) P=.434	.0027 (19) P=.496	-.1183 (21) P=.305
Percent Most Serious & Drug Sale	.4885 (20) P=.014	.2925 (20) P=.105	.5740 (23) P=.002	.4041 (23) P=.028	.4635 (20) P=.020	.5696 (23) P=.002	.5015 (20) P=.012	.5805 (23) P=.002	.4041 (18) P=.048	.3586 (21) P=.055	.4328 (19) P=.032	.4328 (19) P=.032	.5756 (19) P=.005	.5480 (21) P=.005
Percent Most Serious & All Drug	.4931 (22) P=.010	.4194 (22) P=.026	.5068 (25) P=.005	.4962 (25) P=.006	.5789 (22) P=.002	.5896 (25) P=.001	.5018 (22) P=.009	.5302 (25) P=.003	.4551 (18) P=.029	.2696 (21) P=.119	.4531 (19) P=.026	.4531 (19) P=.026	.5838 (20) P=.003	.5021 (22) P=.009
Percent Jury Trials	-.0725 (23) P=.371	-.3422 (23) P=.055	-.3262 (26) P=.052	-.4379 (26) P=.013	-.0457 (22) P=.420	-.2484 (25) P=.116	-.0628 (22) P=.391	-.3196 (25) P=.060	.0586 (18) P=.409	-.3394 (21) P=.066	.0363 (19) P=.441	.1383 (22) P=.270	-.1298 (21) P=.288	-.2073 (23) P=.171
Percent Bench Warrants	.4208 (19) P=.036	.6856 (19) P=.001	.5564 (22) P=.004	.7907 (22) P=.000	.5651 (19) P=.006	.6355 (22) P=.001	.4582 (19) P=.024	.5865 (22) P=.002	.2933 (16) P=.135	.4603 (19) P=.024	.3494 (17) P=.085	.3246 (20) P=.081	.3671 (18) P=.067	.4328 (20) P=.028
Percent Guilty Pleas	-.2228 (23) P=.153	-.1148 (23) P=.301	.0260 (26) P=.450	-.1118 (26) P=.293	-.0208 (22) P=.463	.1391 (25) P=.254	-.2053 (22) P=.180	.0013 (25) P=.498	-.2039 (18) P=.209	.0858 (21) P=.356	.0047 (19) P=.492	-.0345 (22) P=.439	-.2059 (21) P=.185	-.1186 (23) P=.295
% All Cases Over 180 Days	.9406 (23) P=.000	.8756 (23) P=.000	.7543 (23) P=.000	.8746 (23) P=.000	.7917 (22) P=.000	.7011 (22) P=.000	.9309 (22) P=.000	.7999 (22) P=.000	.8632 (18) P=.000	.4270 (18) P=.000	.8032 (19) P=.000	.6397 (20) P=.001	.8650 (21) P=.000	.7668 (21) P=.000
% All Cases Over 1 Year	.8702 (23) P=.000	.9545 (23) P=.000	.6871 (23) P=.000	.9179 (23) P=.000	.7608 (22) P=.000	.6857 (22) P=.000	.8797 (22) P=.000	.7479 (22) P=.000	.7702 (18) P=.000	.3555 (18) P=.074	.7574 (19) P=.000	.5465 (20) P=.006	.8539 (21) P=.000	.7507 (21) P=.000
Non-BW Cases Over 180 Days	.8732 (19) P=.000	.8032 (19) P=.000	.7342 (19) P=.000	.7607 (19) P=.000	.8701 (19) P=.000	.8362 (20) P=.000	.8855 (19) P=.000	.7506 (19) P=.000	.5822 (16) P=.009	.3518 (16) P=.091	.6397 (17) P=.003	.6668 (18) P=.007	.8280 (18) P=.000	.7715 (18) P=.000
Non-BW Cases Over 1 Year	.7048 (19) P=.000	.9241 (19) P=.000	.5706 (19) P=.005	.8099 (19) P=.000	.8016 (19) P=.000	.7615 (19) P=.000	.7487 (19) P=.000	.6224 (19) P=.002	.4664 (16) P=.034	.2478 (16) P=.177	.5743 (17) P=.008	.3892 (18) P=.055	.8114 (18) P=.000	.7897 (18) P=.000

126 / Examining Court Delay

Appendix I

Court Size, Backlog, Charging, Calendar, Judicial Assignment, Elements of Control, and Felony Case Processing Times–1987
Pearson's (r) Correlations

	All Total Median	All Total 90th Per.	All Upper Ct Median	All Upper Ct 90th Per.	Most Ser. Total Median	Most Ser. Upper Ct Median	Less Ser. Total Median	Less Ser. Upper Ct Median	Drug Sale Total Median	Drug Sale Upper Ct Median	Drug Poss. Total Median	Drug Poss. Upper Ct Median	Jury Trial Total Median	Jury Trial Upper Ct Median
Population 1986	.0409 (23) P=.427	-.0239 (23) P=.457	-.0375 (26) P=.428	.0116 (26) P=.478	.0025 (22) P=.496	-.0141 (25) P=.473	.0296 (22) P=.448	-.0479 (25) P=.410	.0065 (18) P=.490	-.1578 (21) P=.247	-.0768 (19) P=.377	-.0989 (22) P=.331	.0959 (21) P=.340	.0579 (23) P=.397
Felonies Filed in 1987	-.0732 (23) P=.370	-.0410 (23) P=.426	-.1290 (26) P=.265	.1030 (26) P=.308	.0796 (22) P=.362	-.0144 (25) P=.473	-.0203 (22) P=.464	-.0846 (25) P=.344	-.1887 (18) P=.227	-.2452 (21) P=.142	-.2046 (19) P=.200	-.1102 (22) P=.313	.1724 (21) P=.227	.1171 (23) P=.297
FTE Felony Judges	.0900 (23) P=.342	.0615 (23) P=.390	.0133 (26) P=.474	.1588 (26) P=.219	.3141 (22) P=.077	.2513 (25) P=.113	.2181 (22) P=.165	.0679 (25) P=.374	-.1169 (18) P=.322	-.2401 (21) P=.147	-.0710 (19) P=.386	-.0322 (22) P=.443	.4909 (21) P=.012	.4879 (23) P=.009
Filings/ FTE Felony Judge	-.2410 (23) P=.134	-.1964 (23) P=.185	-.3739 (26) P=.030	-.1826 (26) P=.186	-.1752 (22) P=.218	-.3764 (25) P=.032	-.3166 (22) P=.076	-.3828 (25) P=.029	-.2001 (18) P=.213	-.2550 (21) P=.132	-.2412 (19) P=.160	-.2356 (22) P=.146	-.2678 (21) P=.120	-.3676 (23) P=.042
Backlog Index	.5268 (20) P=.009	.6056 (20) P=.002	.7334 (23) P=.000	.6750 (23) P=.000	.5047 (19) P=.014	.6793 (22) P=.000	.5462 (19) P=.008	.7220 (22) P=.000	.4679 (17) P=.029	.7640 (20) P=.000	.3420 (17) P=.090	.5152 (20) P=.010	.5374 (18) P=.011	.4955 (20) P=.013
Charging Procedure	-.1901 (23) P=.192	-.0126 (23) P=.477	-.1693 (26) P=.204	-.1424 (26) P=.244	-.1249 (22) P=.290	-.1084 (25) P=.303	-.2947 (22) P=.092	-.2151 (25) P=.151	-.1732 (18) P=.246	-.1555 (21) P=.250	-.3799 (19) P=.054	-.1809 (22) P=.210	-.3582 (21) P=.055	-.2670 (23) P=.109
Calendar Type	.0212 (23) P=.462	-.0595 (23) P=.394	-.0110 (26) P=.479	.0730 (26) P=.362	.1680 (22) P=.227	.1483 (25) P=.240	.1163 (22) P=.303	.0253 (25) P=.452	-.1594 (18) P=.264	.0015 (21) P=.497	-.0533 (19) P=.414	.0696 (22) P=.379	.4232 (21) P=.028	.4620 (23) P=.013
Judicial Assignment	.3973 (23) P=.030	.3836 (23) P=.035	.4704 (26) P=.008	.4646 (26) P=.008	.5333 (22) P=.005	.6263 (25) P=.000	.4667 (22) P=.014	.5198 (25) P=.004	.3402 (18) P=.084	.3850 (21) P=.042	.2282 (19) P=.174	.3273 (22) P=.069	.5194 (21) P=.008	.5070 (23) P=.007
When Pretrial Motions Decided	.3388 (23) P=.057	.5011 (23) P=.007	.4997 (26) P=.005	.5296 (26) P=.003	.3776 (22) P=.042	.5444 (25) P=.002	.4419 (22) P=.020	.5588 (25) P=.002	.2627 (18) P=.146	.4403 (21) P=.023	.2239 (19) P=.178	.3321 (22) P=.066	.5109 (21) P=.009	.5569 (23) P=.003
Trial Backup System	.0615 (23) P=.390	.1520 (23) P=.244	-.1861 (26) P=.181	-.0639 (26) P=.378	.0600 (22) P=.395	-.1266 (25) P=.273	.0844 (22) P=.354	-.1552 (25) P=.229	-.0233 (18) P=.463	-.3514 (21) P=.059	.1880 (19) P=.220	.1871 (22) P=.202	.0947 (21) P=.342	.0537 (23) P=.404
Median 1st Sched Trial Trial Start	.4740 (12) P=.060	.7664 (12) P=.002	.6570 (14) P=.005	.7011 (14) P=.003	.4876 (12) P=.054	.6967 (14) P=.003	.5038 (12) P=.047	.6185 (14) P=.009	†††	†††	†††	.4580 (13) P=.058	.7743 (12) P=.002	.7766 (14) P=.001
% Jury Trials on 1st Tr Date	-.5173 (12) P=.042	-.6993 (12) P=.006	-.6482 (14) P=.006	-.6455 (14) P=.006	-.4183 (12) P=.088	-.5459 (14) P=.022	-.4966 (12) P=.050	-.5996 (14) P=.012	†††	†††	†††	-.5356 (13) P=.030	-.5253 (12) P=.040	-.5475 (14) P=.021
Avg Pop/ Intended Capacity	.2009 (20) P=.198	.0323 (20) P=.446	-.1845 (23) P=.200	-.1141 (23) P=.302	.0619 (19) P=.401	-.1784 (22) P=.214	-.0057 (19) P=.491	-.2350 (22) P=.146	.4455 (16) P=.042	-.1683 (19) P=.246	.0956 (16) P=.362	-.2776 (19) P=.125	-.0752 (19) P=.380	-.1163 (21) P=.308

††† Less than 12 courts.

Appendix J1

Felony Case Mix, Percent Jury Trials, Bench Warrants, and Percent Over ABA Standards
Pearson's (r) Correlations

	Percent Most Serious	Percent All Drug Cases	Percent Drug Sale Cases	Percent Drug Poss. Cases	Percent Jury Trials	Percent Bench Warrants	Percent Guilty Pleas	Percent Over 180 Days	Percent Over 1 Year	Non-BW Cases over 180 Days	Non-BW Cases over 1 Year
Percent Most Serious	--	.2697 (25) P=.096	.5658 (23) P=.002	-.5557 (23) P=.003	.1692 (25) P=.209	.1630 (22) P=.234	.1161 (25) P=.290	.2379 (22) P=.143	.0528 (22) P=.408	.4484 (19) P=.027	.2004 (19) P=.205
Percent All Drug Cases		--	.8444 (23) P=.000	.1799 (23) P=.206	.0392 (25) P=.426	.2611 (22) P=.120	.1438 (25) P=.246	.5513 (22) P=.004	.5305 (22) P=.006	.4131 (19) P=.039	.4383 (19) P=.030
Percent Drug Sale Cases			--	-.3748 (23) P=.039	.0344 (23) P=.438	.1376 (21) P=.276	.0124 (23) P=.478	.5434 (20) P=.007	.4532 (20) P=.022	.3664 (18) P=.067	.3655 (18) P=.068
Percent Drug Poss. Cases				--	-.1317 (23) P=.275	.1197 (21) P=.303	.0399 (23) P=.428	.0501 (20) P=.417	.1133 (20) P=.317	.1036 (18) P=.341	.1174 (18) P=.321
Percent Jury Trials					--	-.5060 (22) P=.008	-.0914 (26) P=.328	-.1506 (23) P=.246	-.3038 (23) P=.079	-.0684 (19) P=.390	-.2825 (19) P=.121
Percent Bench Warrants						--	.2404 (22) P=.141	.6101 (19) P=.003	.6555 (19) P=.001	.5982 (19) P=.003	.6763 (19) P=.001
Percent Guilty Pleas							--	-.2081 (23) P=.170	-.1484 (23) P=.250	.0489 (19) P=.421	.0977 (19) P=.345
% All Cases Over 180 Days								--	.9338 (23) P=.000	.9814 (19) P=.000	.8494 (19) P=.000
% All Cases Over 1 Year									--	.8438 (19) P=.000	.9547 (19) P=.000
Non-BW Cases Over 180 Days										--	.8539 (19) P=.000

Appendix J2

Court Size, Caseload, Backlog, and Felony Caseflow Management Procedures
Pearson's (r) Correlations

	Population 1986	Felony Cases Filed	FTE Felony Judges	Filings per FTE Judge	Felony Backlog Index	Charging Procedure	Calendar Type	Judicial Assignment	When Pretrial Motions	Trial Backup System	Median 1st Sched. Tr. to Tr. Start	% on 1st Sched. Trial Date	Avg. Pop./ Intended Capacity
Population 1986	----	.6569 (26) P=.000	.5522 (26) P=.002	.1610 (26) P=.216	−.2210 (23) P=.155	.2089 (26) P=.153	.1618 (26) P=.215	.3177 (26) P=.057	.0029 (26) P=.494	.3727 (26) P=.030	.1313 (14) P=.327	−.3269 (14) P=.127	.1843 (23) P=.200
Felony Cases Filed		----	.7375 (26) P=.000	.4067 (26) P=.020	−.2389 (23) P=.136	.0840 (26) P=.342	.3874 (26) P=.025	.3642 (26) P=.034	−.0051 (26) P=.490	.3004 (26) P=.068	.0095 (14) P=.487	−.0290 (14) P=.461	−.0606 (23) P=.392
FTE Felony Judges			----	−.1607 (26) P=.216	−.1390 (23) P=.264	−.0420 (26) P=.419	.3274 (26) P=.051	.5254 (26) P=.003	.1802 (26) P=.189	.2536 (26) P=.106	−.1830 (14) P=.266	.1254 (14) P=.335	−.1264 (23) P=.283
Filings per FTE Judge				----	−.0762 (23) P=.365	−.0110 (26) P=.479	.1769 (26) P=.194	−.3641 (26) P=.034	−.2518 (26) P=.107	.1780 (26) P=.192	.2856 (14) P=.161	−.2307 (14) P=.213	.1133 (23) P=.303
Felony Backlog Index					----	−.2387 (23) P=.136	.0485 (23) P=.413	.3438 (23) P=.054	.5396 (25) P=.004	−.0552 (23) P=.401	.6499 (12) P=.011	†††	−.1676 (20) P=.240
Charging Procedure						----	−.2503 (26) P=.109	.0852 (26) P=.340	−.0588 (26) P=.388	.2031 (26) P=.160	.3114 (14) P=.139	−.2319 (14) P=.213	.2128 (23) P=.165
Calendar Type							----	.2373 (26) P=.122	.1072 (26) P=.301	.1538 (26) P=.227	.4130 (14) P=.071	−.0770 (14) P=.397	−.2546 (23) P=.121
Judicial Assignment								----	.4095 (26) P=.019	.1238 (26) P=.273	.4573 (14) P=.050	−.3427 (14) P=.115	−.0833 (23) P=.353
When Pretrial Motions Decided									----	−.0055 (26) P=.489	.6075 (14) P=.011	−.6058 (14) P=.011	−.0194 (23) P=.465
Trial Backup System										----	.2926 (14) P=.155	−.2257 (14) P=.219	−.3969 (23) P=.030
Median: 1st Sched. Trial to Trial Start											----	−.7002 (14) P=.003	−.0060 (13) P=.492
% on 1st Scheduled Trial Date												----	−.3720 (13) P=.105

††† Less than 12 courts.

Appendix J3

Felony Case Mix, Caseflow Management Procedures, and Percent Over ABA Standards
Pearson's (r) Correlations

	Population 1986	Felony Cases Filed	FTE Felony Judges	Filings per FTE Judge	Felony Backlog Index	Charging Procedure	Calendar Type	Judicial Assignment	When Pretrial Motions	Trial Backup System	Median 1st Sched. Tr. to Tr. Start	% on 1st Sched. Trial Date	Avg. Pop./ Intended Capacity
Percent Most Serious	.0580 (25) P= .392	-.2670 (25) P= .098	.0968 (25) P= .323	-.5222 (25) P= .004	.2379 (22) P= .143	-.0225 (25) P= .457	-.3548 (25) P= .041	.183 (25) P= .189	.2836 (25) P= .085	-.1801 (25) P= .195	.1115 (14) P= .352	-.2118 (14) P= .234	.2562 (22) P= .125
Percent All Drug Cases	.1389 (25) P= .254	.1149 (25) P= .292	.3398 (25) P= .048	-.3452 (25) P= .046	.0478 (22) P= .416	-.2226 (25) P= .142	.0015 (25) P= .497	.3515 (25) P= .042	.3333 (25) P= .052	-.3475 (25) P= .044	-.2362 (14) P= .208	.1170 (14) P= .345	.2120 (22) P= .172
Percent Drug Sale Cases	.1338 (23) P= .271	-.0522 (23) P= .406	.3023 (23) P= .080	-.3925 (23) P= .032	.2202 (21) P= .169	-.4160 (23) P= .024	-.0951 (23) P= .333	.2455 (23) P= .129	.4257 (23) P= .021	-.3562 (23) P= .048	-.3179 (13) P= .145	.1779 (13) P= .281	.1843 (20) P= .218
Percent Drug Poss. Cases	-.0072 (23) P= .487	.2743 (23) P= .103	-.0263 (23) P= .453	.2976 (23) P= .084	-.2803 (21) P= .109	.3176 (23) P= .070	.1566 (23) P= .238	.1113 (23) P= .307	-.1975 (23) P= .183	-.2259 (23) P= .150	.0565 (13) P= .427	-.0365 (13) P= .453	.3035 (20) P= .097
Percent Jury Trial Cases	.0059 (26) P= .489	-.0722 (26) P= .363	.1178 (26) P= .283	-.2583 (26) P= .101	-.4444 (23) P= .017	-.0253 (26) P= .451	-.1352 (26) P= .255	.0388 (26) P= .425	-.3217 (26) P= .054	.1543 (26) P= .226	-.4646 (14) P= .047	.4208 (14) P= .067	-.0160 (23) P= .471
Percent Bench Warrants	.0371 (22) P= .435	.1221 (22) P= .294	.1304 (22) P= .281	-.1539 (22) P= .247	.5874 (19) P= .004	-.0957 (22) P= .336	.0366 (22) P= .436	.3562 (22) P= .052	.3549 (22) P= .053	-.1061 (22) P= .319	-.0156 (14) P= .479	-.4586 (14) P= .050	-.0303 (20) P= .450
Percent Guilty Pleas	.0233 (26) P= .455	-.1696 (26) P= .204	-.0498 (26) P= .404	-.2171 (26) P= .143	-.0552 (23) P= .401	-.0741 (26) P= .360	.0164 (26) P= .468	.1802 (26) P= .189	.1333 (26) P= .258	.0521 (26) P= .400	.0560 (14) P= .425	-.2340 (14) P= .210	-.0105 (23) P= .481
% All Cases Over 180 Days	.0643 (23) P= .385	.0205 (23) P= .463	.2109 (23) P= .167	-.2665 (23) P= .110	.5525 (20) P= .006	-.1705 (23) P= .218	.0647 (23) P= .385	.4556 (23) P= .014	.4575 (23) P= .014	.0878 (23) P= .345	.6328 (12) P= .014	-.7167 (12) P= .004	.2632 (20) P= .131
% All Cases Over 1 Year	-.0122 (23) P= .478	-.0329 (23) P= .441	.1337 (23) P= .272	-.2483 (23) P= .127	.6023 (20) P= .002	-.1072 (23) P= .313	.1312 (23) P= .444	.3644 (23) P= .044	.5265 (23) P= .005	.1497 (23) P= .248	.8092 (12) P= .001	-.6887 (12) P= .007	.0368 (20) P= .439
% Non-BW Cases Over 180 Days	.2356 (19) P= .166	.1198 (19) P= .313	.2879 (19) P= .116	-.1709 (19) P= .242	.3699 (16) P= .079	.1769 (19) P= .234	-.0245 (19) P= .460	.5264 (19) P= .010	.3114 (19) P= .097	.3365 (19) P= .079	.6407 (12) P= .012	-.6888 (12) P= .007	.1997 (17) P= .221
% Non-BW Cases Over 1 Year	.0723 (19) P= .384	.0091 (19) P= .485	.1595 (19) P= .257	-.1236 (19) P= .307	.4464 (16) P= .042	.0986 (10) P= .344	-.1536 (10) P= .265	.3144 (19) P= .095	.4334 (19) P= .032	.2586 (19) P= .142	.7773 (12) P= .001	-.6952 (12) P= .006	.0158 (17) P= .476

Appendix K

Felony Court Caseloads–1987
Ranked by Median Upper Court Case Processing Time (Days)

	Upper Court Median	Pending Felony Cases 1-1-87	Felonies Disposed 1987	Pending Felony Cases 1-1-88	Dispositions per FTE Felony Judge†
Salinas	22	42	1274	120	364
Fairfax	29	524	2721	635	618
Detroit Rec	38	2583	15222	4094	448
New Orleans	42	650	6243	650	595
Dayton	42	359	2120	460	530
San Diego	50	778	8912	593	469
Atlanta	50	1454	7968	1872	1035
Dist of Col	62	2445	11120	2455	674
Oakland	65	424	4856	416	690
Norfolk	69	2044	4306	2268	957
St Paul	70	523	2081	917	416
Colo Springs	76	2510	3390	2521	848
Cleveland	82	2094	9639	1927	584
Minneapolis	84	877	3179	1318	408
Phoenix	85	5571	11545	6436	853
Portland	94	2549	5613	3274	802
Pittsburgh	97	*	*	6863	980
Tucson	103	2209	3114	2317	410
Denver	109	3915	3074	3751	455
Providence	111	1988	3102	1643	574
Miami	112	*	*	*	*
Bronx	114	2781	8377	2927	226
Newark	125	4410	6810	4740	368
Wichita	133	330	1057	967	189
Jersey City	150	916	2323	978	350
Boston	233	1524	1738	1432	217

† Number of felonies disposed in 1987 divided by "full-time equivalent (FTE) felony judges" (see table 12).

* Information not available or comparable.

Appendix L

Felony Case Information Collected by the Court†–1987

	Upper Court Median	Total Median	Number Felonies Pending	Number Felonies Filed	Number Felonies Disposed	Age of Pending Cases	Age of Disposed Cases	# Cases Over Goals	# Trial Conts. Granted	# Other Conts. Granted
Salinas	22	62	MONTHLY	MONTHLY	MONTHLY	*	MONTHLY	*	*	*
Fairfax	29	102	YEARLY	QUARTER	QUARTER	*	*	*	*	*
Detroit Rec	38	71	WEEKLY	WEEKLY	WEEKLY	MONTHLY	MONTHLY	MONTHLY	MONTHLY	QUARTER
New Orleans	42	89	*	*	*	*	*	*	*	*
Dayton	42	56	MONTHLY	QUARTER	QUARTER	*	*	MONTHLY	*	MONTHLY
San Diego	50	121	MONTHLY	MONTHLY	MONTHLY	*	*	*	*	*
Atlanta	50	108	WEEKLY	YEARLY	YEARLY	WEEKLY	WEEKLY	WEEKLY	*	*
Dist of Col	62	100	MONTHLY	MONTHLY	MONTHLY	MONTHLY	*	MONTHLY	*	*
Oakland	65	144	MONTHLY	MONTHLY	MONTHLY	MONTHLY	MONTHLY	MONTHLY	*	*
Norfolk	69	127	YEARLY	YEARLY	YEARLY	*	*	*	*	*
St Paul	70	77	MONTHLY	MONTHLY	MONTHLY	QUARTER	QUARTER	QUARTER	MONTHLY	MONTHLY
Colo Springs	76	85	MONTHLY	YEARLY	MONTHLY	YEARLY	*	*	MONTHLY	MONTHLY
Cleveland	82	135	WEEKLY	WEEKLY	MONTHLY	*	*	*	*	*
Minneapolis	84	107	*	*	*	*	*	*	*	*
Phoenix	85	98	MONTHLY	MONTHLY	MONTHLY	*	QUARTER	MONTHLY	*	*
Portland	94	*	MONTHLY	MONTHLY	MONTHLY	MONTHLY	MONTHLY	MONTHLY	MONTHLY	MONTHLY
Pittsburgh	97	153	MONTHLY	MONTHLY	MONTHLY	*	*	*	*	*
Tucson	103	*	MONTHLY	MONTHLY	MONTHLY	MONTHLY	MONTHLY	MONTHLY	*	*
Denver	109	156	MONTHLY	MONTHLY	MONTHLY	*	*	*	*	*
Providence	111	192	*	*	*	*	*	*	*	*
Miami	112	119	WEEKLY	MONTHLY	MONTHLY	WEEKLY	MONTHLY	WEEKLY	MONTHLY	MONTHLY
Bronx	114	145	WEEKLY	MONTHLY	MONTHLY	MONTHLY	MONTHLY	MONTHLY	*	*
Newark	125	308	MONTHLY	MONTHLY	*	MONTHLY	*	MONTHLY	QUARTER	QUARTER
Wichita	133	149	WEEKLY	*	*	WEEKLY	QUARTER	WEEKLY	*	*
Jersey City	150	198	WEEKLY	MONTHLY	MONTHLY	MONTHLY	WEEKLY	WEEKLY	WEEKLY	MONTHLY
Boston	233	*	MONTHLY	MONTHLY	MONTHLY	MONTHLY	MONTHLY	MONTHLY	*	*

† Data from survey of court administrators; information collected and disseminated to judges.
* Information not collected/disseminated on a regular basis.

Appendix M

Felony and Civil Case Processing Times–1987
Pearson's (r) Correlations

	All Civil Cases Median	All Civil Cases 90th Per.	Tort Cases Median	Tort Cases 90th Per.	Contract Cases Median	Contract Cases 90th Per.	Trial List Cases Median	Trial List Cases 90th Per.	Jury Trial Median
All Cases Total Median	.6503 (19) P=.001	.0314 (19) P=.449	.5330 (19) P=.009	-.0027 (19) P=.496	.5129 (19) P=.012	.1548 (19) P=.263	.5436 (13) P=.027	.1826 (13) P=.275	.3541 (15) P=.098
All Cases Total 90th Per.	.7616 (19) P=.000	.2123 (19) P=.191	.7693 (19) P=.000	.2276 (19) P=.174	.7481 (19) P=.000	.3226 (19) P=.089	.6672 (13) P=.006	.1750 (13) P=.284	.5472 (15) P=.017
All Cases Upper Ct Median	.6222 (22) P=.001	.2297 (22) P=.152	.5763 (22) P=.002	.2598 (22) P=.121	.6191 (22) P=.001	.3112 (22) P=.079	.3655 (16) P=.082	-.0838 (16) P=.379	.1884 (17) P=.234
All Cases Upper Ct 90th Per.	.6903 (22) P=.000	.2851 (22) P=.099	.7319 (22) P=.000	.3070 (22) P=.082	.6620 (22) P=.000	.3442 (22) P=.058	.6484 (16) P=.003	.1830 (16) P=.249	.3947 (17) P=.058
Most Serious Total Median	.7589 (18) P=.000	.3324 (18) P=.089	.7179 (18) P=.000	.3159 (18) P=.101	.7115 (18) P=.000	.4235 (18) P=.040	.6455 (12) P=.012	.3304 (12) P=.147	.5613 (14) P=.018
Most Serious Upper Ct Median	.7537 (21) P=.000	.4581 (21) P=.018	.7524 (21) P=.000	.4873 (21) P=.013	.7601 (21) P=.000	.5062 (21) P=.010	.6111 (15) P=.008	.1883 (15) P=.251	.5065 (16) P=.023
Less Serious Total Median	.6169 (18) P=.003	.0073 (18) P=.489	.5890 (18) P=.005	-.0134 (18) P=.479	.4590 (18) P=.028	.0813 (18) P=.374	.5211 (12) P=.041	0224 (12) P=.472	.3255 (14) P=.128
Less Serious Upper Ct Median	.6420 (21) P=.001	.2520 (21) P=.135	.6530 (21) P=.001	.2940 (21) P=.098	.6328 (21) P=.001	.3219 (21) P=.077	.3779 (15) P=.082	-.1060 (15) P=.353	.2398 (16) P=.186
Drug Sale Total Median	.6817 (15) P=.003	.0849 (15) P=.382	.5700 (15) P=.013	.0180 (15) P=.475	.5375 (15) P=.019	.1953 (15) P=.243	†††	†††	.4765 (12) P=.059
Drug Sale Upper Ct Median	.4800 (18) P=.022	.2040 (18) P=.208	.4354 (18) P=.035	.2136 (18) P=.197	.4868 (18) P=.020	.2499 (18) P=.159	.1906 (12) P=.276	-.2606 (12) P=.207	.1536 (14) P=.300
Drug Poss. Total Median	.5538 (16) P=.013	.0342 (16) P=.450	.4452 (16) P=.042	-.0201 (16) P=.470	.4732 (16) P=.032	.2451 (16) P=.180	†††	†††	.2889 (12) P=.181
Drug Poss. Upper Ct Median	.0141 (19) P=.477	-.4370 (19) P=.031	.0644 (19) P=.397	-.3954 (19) P=.047	-.0127 (19) P=.479	-.3276 (19) P=.085	-.3724 (12) P=.117	-.7988 (12) P=.001	.0003 (15) P=.500
Jury Trial Total Median	.6467 (17) P=.003	-.0194 (17) P=.471	.6912 (17) P=.001	.0102 (17) P=.485	.5144 (17) P=.017	.0461 (17) P=.430	†††	†††	.2081 (14) P=.238
Jury Trial Upper Ct Median	.4334 (19) P=.032	-.1725 (19) P=.240	.5152 (19) P=.012	-.0966 (19) P=.347	.3769 (19) P=.056	-.1250 (19) P=.305	-.1557 (13) P=.306	-.4347 (13) P=.069	.0862 (16) P=.375

††† Less than 12 courts.

Appendix N

Regression Analysis Results Related to Civil Case Processing Times†

Dependent Variables

Explanatory Variables	All Civil Cases Median	All Civil Cases 90th	Tort Cases Median	Tort Cases 90th	Trial List Cases Median	Trial List Cases 90th
% Torts and Filings	*	*	*	*	*	Torts
% Torts and Filings per Judge	*	*	*	*	*	Torts
% Torts and Calendar	Torts	Calendar	*	*	*	Torts
% Torts and Control ††	Control	Control	*	Control	*	Control & Torts
% Torts and Goals	Torts	Goals	*	*	*	Torts
Filings per Judge and Filings	*	*	*	*	*	*
Filings per Judge and Calendar	*	Calendar	*	*	*	*
Filings per Judge and Control	*	Control	Control	Control	*	Control
Filings per Judge and Goals	*	Goals	*	Goals	*	*
Filings per Judge and Judicial Assignment	*	*	*	*	*	*
Control and Calendar	Control	Control	*	Control	Control	Control
Control and Goals	Control	Control	*	Control	Control	Control
Calendar and Goals	Calendar	Goals	*	*	*	Goals

† Stepwise regression procedure used. Both explanatory factors listed in the left column were entered simultaneously. Explanatory factors listed under the dependent variable columns are the ones that retained a statistically sigificant (F≤.05) correlation with the dependent variable when the explanatory factors were entered in a stepwise regression analysis (see Appendix A).

†† "Control" means early court control over case events.

* No significant association.

134 / EXAMINING COURT DELAY

Appendix O

Regression Analysis Results Related to Felony Case Processing Times†

Dependent Variables

Expanatory Variables	All Felonies: Upper Court Median	All Felonies: Upper Court 90th	All Felonies: Upper Court Median	All Felonies: Upper Court 90th	Drug Sale CPT: Median Total	Drug Sale CPT: Median Upper Court
Population & Filings	*	*	*	*	*	*
& % Drug Sale	DS	*	DS	DS	*	*
& % Most Serious	*	*	MS	*	*	*
& Early Pretrial Motions	*	EPTM	EPTM	EPTM	*	EPTM
& % Firm Trial Dates	*	PFTD	PFTD	PFTD	*	PFTD
& % Bench Warrants	*	BW	BW	BW	*	BW
& Judical Assignments	*	*	JA	JA	*	*
Filings & % Drug Sale	DS	*	DS	DS	*	*
& % Most Serious	*	*	MS	*	*	*
& Early Pretrial Motions	*	EPTM	EPTM	EPTM	*	EPTM
& % Firm Trial Dates	*	PFTD	PFTD	PFTD	*	PFTD
& % Bench Warrants	*	BW	BW	BW	*	BW
& Judicial Assignment	*	*	JA	JA	*	*
FTE Judges & % Drug Sale	DS	*	DS	DS	*	*
& % Most Serious	*	*	MS	*	*	*
& % Firm Trial Dates	*	PFTD	PFTD	PFTD	*	PFTD
& % Bench Warrants	*	BW	BW	BW	*	BW
& Judicial Assignment	*	*	JA	JA	*	*
FILS/Judge & % Drug Sale	DS	*	DS	DS	*	*
& % Most Serious	*	*	MS	*	*	*
& Early Pretrial Motions	*	EPTM	EPTM	EPTM	*	EPTM
& Judicial Assignment	*	*	JA	JA	*	*
% B. Warrants & % Drug Sale	BW	BW	BW	BW	*	BW
& % Most Serious	*	BW	MS & BW	BW	*	BW
& Early Pretrial Motions	*	BW	BW	BW	*	BW
& % Firm Trial Dates	*	PFTD	PFTD	PFTD	*	PFTD
& Judicial Assignment	*	BW	BW	BW	*	BW
Early PTM & % Drug Sale	DS	EPTM	EPTM	EPTM	*	EPTM
& % Most Serious	*	EPTM	EPTM & MS	EPTM	*	EPTM
& % Firm Trial Dates	*	PFTD	PFTD	PFTD	*	PFTD
% Firm T.D. & % Drug Sale	*	PFTD	PFTD	PFTD & DS	*	PFTD
& % Most Serious	*	PFTD	PFTD	PFTD	MS	PFTD
& Judicial Assignment	*	PFTD	PFTD	PFTD	*	PFTD
& Jury Trial Rate	*	PFTD	PFTD	PFTD	*	PFTD
Jud. Assign. & % Drug Sale	DS	*	DS & JA	JA	*	*
& % Most Serious	JA	*	JA & MS	JA	*	*
& Early Pretrial Motions	*	EPTM	EPTM	EPTM	*	EPTM
% Most Serious & % Drug Sale	DS	*	MS	DS	*	*

Dependent Variables

Explanatory Variables	% Firm Trial Dates	% Bench Warrants	Filings per FTE Judge	% Most Serious	% Drug Sale
% Most Serious & % Drug Sale	*	*	MS	—	—
FTE Judges & % Most Serious	*	*	*	—	MS
& % Drug Sale	*	*	*	DS	—
& % Bench Warrants	*	*	*	*	*
& Judicial Assignment	*	*	*	*	*
& Early Pretrial Motions	EPTM	*	*	*	*
& Jury Trail Rate	*	JTRATE	*	*	*
& Firm Trial Dates	*	*	*	*	*
Filings & FTE Judges	*	*	*	*	*
& % Most Serious	*	*	MS	—	MS
& % Drug Sale	*	*	FILINGS	DS	—
Population & Filings	*	*	*	*	*
& FTE Judges	*	*	*	*	*
& % Drug Sale	*	*	*	DS	—
& % Most Serious	*	*	*	—	MS

† Stepwise regression procedure used. Both explanatory factors listed in the left column were entered simultaneously. Explanatory factors listed under the dependent variable columns are the ones that retained a statistically significant (F≤.05) correlation with the dependent variable when the explanatory factors were entered in a stepwise regression analysis (see Appendix A).

* No significant association.

— Regression analysis not performed; not appropriate.

DS= % drug sale; MS= % most serious; EPTM= early pretrial motions; PFTD= percent jury trials on first scheduled trial date; BW= percent bench warrants; JA= judicial assignment; JTRATE= jury trial rate.

Appendix P

Numbers of Valid Civil Cases–1987

	All Civil	Torts	Contracts	Trial List	Jury Trial	FSTD To TSD[d]
Atlanta	510	338	122	—	83[a]	—
Boston	481	224	135	20	2[b]	—
Cleveland	446	215	66	—	87[a]	—
Colo Springs	414	119	262	—	36[a]	36[a]
Dayton	476	202	147	—	57[a]	—
Denver	481	103	319	—	28[a]	28[a]
Detroit	502	289	89	—	82[a]	—
Dist of Col	545	193	330	313	42[a]	—
Fairfax	476	279	165	—	44[b]	23[b]
Jersey City	471	409	57	—	101[a]	99[a]
Miami	549	149	244	132	23[a]	—
Minneapolis	501	171	220	205	38[a]	—
New Orleans	385	274	62	162	5[b]	—
Newark	550	451	82	—	98[a]	81[a]
Norfolk	404	236	149	170	18[b]	—
Oakland	573	460	100	236	8[b]	—
Phoenix	455	142	302	93	9[b]	—
Pittsburgh	454	182	127	228	69[a]	—
Portland	538	263	151	279	75[a]	71[a]
Providence	481	353	108	325	81[a]	—
St Paul	509	225	207	245	50[c]	—
Salinas	331	230	74	121	15[a]	—
San Diego	496	303	51	495	32[b]	32[b]
Tucson	595	183	284	286	47[a]	44[a]
Wichita	405	174	135	415	—	—

a Jury trial cases obtained from separate sample of 100 or more trial cases.
b Jury trial cases obtained from original sample of 500 cases.
c Includes all jury trial cases obtained from both the original sample and the additional trial sample.
d FSTD to TSD = first scheduled trial date to trial start date.

136 / Examining Court Delay

Appendix Q

Number of Valid Felony Cases–1987

Court	All Cases — Arrest to Disposition	All Cases — Indictment to Disposition	Most Serious — Arrest to Disposition	Most Serious — Indictment to Disposition	Less Serious — Arrest to Disposition	Less Serious — Indictment to Disposition
Atlanta	446	562	33	37	287	365
Boston[a]	—	449	—	132	—	117
Bronx	551	549	109	109	185	183
Cleveland	331	474	51	74	218	319
Colo Springs	387	418	62	63	279	307
Dayton	496	494	64	65	369	366
Denver	261	372	48	69	164	231
Detroit[b]	465	463	64	63	311	311
Dist of Col[b]	593	594	38	38	356	357
Fairfax	371	421	54	55	244	253
Jersey City	437	514	58	73	174	212
Miami	457	494	39	39	255	289
Minneapolis[c,d]	530	531	89	89	372	372
Newark	424	511	47	60	173	235
New Orleans	511	563	30	31	318	353
Norfolk	476	481	75	76	346	350
Oakland	530	510	114	108	219	211
Phoenix[b]	348	470	26	46	248	310
Pittsburgh	400	427	47	42	293	324
Portland[a]	—	417	—	39	—	303
Providence	403	455	42	51	236	274
Salinas	359	436	43	55	187	238
San Diego	528	646	98	120	263	345
St Paul[c,d]	492	492	54	54	343	343
Tucson	—	584	—	59	—	446
Wichita[c,d]	482	483	83	83	318	319

a Arrest date and date complaint filed unavailable.
b Arrest date unavailable; used date lower court complaint filed.
c Arrest date unavailable; used date complaint filed in clerk's office; (no lower court).
d Indictment/information date unavailable; used date of first appearance in upper court.
e Could not distinguish drug sale from drug possession cases; represents all drug-related felony cases.
f FSTD to TSD = first scheduled trial date to trial start.
g Jury trial cases obtained from separate sample of 100 trial cases.
h Jury trial cases obtained from original sample of 500 cases.

Appendix Q (Continued)

Number of Valid Felony Cases–1987

Court	Drug Sale Arrest to Disposition	Drug Sale Indictment to Disposition	Drug Possession Arrest to Disposition	Drug Possession Indictment to Disposition	Jury Trial Arrest to Disposition	Jury Trial Indictment to Disposition	FSTD to TSD[f]
Atlanta	79	103	47	57	55[g]	73[g]	—
Boston[a]	—	197	—	3	—	13[h]	—
Bronx	224	224	27	27	121[g]	120[g]	—
Cleveland	40	51	22	30	84[g]	110[g]	78[g]
Colo Springs	24	25	22	23	30[g]	34[g]	34[g]
Dayton	31	31	30	30	77[g]	76[g]	77[g]
Denver	7	8	42	64	46[g]	48[g]	48[g]
Detroit[b]	58	58	29	28	37[h]	37[h]	35[h]
Dist of Col[b]	67	67	132	132	78[g]	79[g]	—
Fairfax	54	86	18	26	58[h]	66[h]	65[h]
Jersey City	175	195	30	34	74[g]	103[g]	—
Miami	49	50	113	115	73[g]	66[g]	—
Minneapolis[c,d]	33	33	20	20	61[g]	60[g]	—
Newark	138	150	66	66	76[g]	90[g]	—
New Orleans	16	16	147	163	35[h]	44[h]	43[h]
Norfolk	55[e]	55[e]	—	—	17[g]	17[g]	—
Oakland	137	134	59	57	43[h]	41[h]	—
Phoenix[b]	32	65	42	49	59[g]	88[g]	87[g]
Pittsburgh	60[e]	61[e]	—	—	25[g]	26[g]	26[g]
Portland[a]	—	31	—	44	—	47[g]	43[g]
Providence	55	54	70	76	10[h]	12[h]	—
Salinas	61	70	68	73	27[g]	37[g]	37[g]
San Diego	109	118	56	56	53[g]	66[g]	60[g]
St Paul[c,d]	32	32	55	55	22[h]	23[h]	—
Tucson	—	41	—	37	—	94[g]	94[g]
Wichita[a,d]	51	51	30	30	110[g]	109[g]	47[h]

a Arrest date and date complaint filed unavailable.
b Arrest date unavailable; used date lower court complaint filed.
c Arrest date unavailable; used date complaint filed in clerk's office; (no lower court).
d Indictment/information date unavailable; used date of first appearance in upper court.
e Could not distinguish drug sale from drug possession cases; represents all drug-related felony cases.
f FSTD to TSD = first scheduled trial date to trial start.
g Jury trial cases obtained from separate sample of 100 trial cases.
h Jury trial cases obtained from original sample of 500 cases.

Bibliography

Bibliography

ARKIN, Herbert, and Raymond COLTON (1963), *Tables for Statisticians*. New York: Barnes and Noble.

BANFIELD, Laura, and C.D. ANDERSON (1968), "Continuances in Cook County Courts," 35 *University of Chicago Law Review* 256.

BENNETT, G., (1989), *Crime Warps: The Future of Crime in America*. New York: Anchor Books.

BENNIS, Warren (1959), "Leadership Theory and Administrative Behavior," 4 *Administrative Science Quarterly* 259.

BLALOCK, Hubert M. (1979), *Social Statistics*. New York: McGraw-Hill.

BOYUM, Keith (1979), "A Perspective on Civil Delay in Trial Courts," 5 *The Justice System Journal* 170.

BUREAU OF JUSTICE STATISTICS (1988) "Jail Inmates, 1987," *Bureau of Justice Statistics Bulletin* (December). Washington, DC: U.S. Department of Justice.

BUREAU OF JUSTICE STATISTICS (1989), *BJS Data Report, 1988*. Washington, DC: U.S. Department of Justice.

CASSIDY, Robert C., and William A. STOEVER (1974), *A Survey of Court-Related Personnel in Four New Jersey Courts*. Washington, DC: Law Enforcement Assistance Administration.

CHAPPER, Joy, Kathy SHUART, Lynae OLSON, Michael PLANET, Paul CONNOLLY and Saundra SMITH (1984), *Attacking Litigation Costs and Delay*. Chicago, IL: American Bar Association.

CHURCH, Thomas W., Jr., Alan CARLSON, Jo-Lynne LEE, and Teresa TAN (1978a), *Justice Delayed: The Pace of Litigation in Urban Trial Courts*. Williamsburg, VA: National Center for State Courts.
(1978b) *Pretrial Delay: A Review and Bibliography*. Williamsburg, VA: National Center for State Courts.
(1982) "The 'Old and the New' Conventional Wisdom of Court Delay," 7 *The Justice System Journal* 395.
(1986) "Examining Local Legal Culture," 1985 *The American Bar Association Research Journal* 449.

CONNOLLY, Paul, and Michael PLANET (1982), "Controlling the Caseflow—Kentucky Style," 21 *Judges' Journal* 8.
FIEDLER, Fred (1974), *A Theory of Leadership*. New York: McGraw-Hill.
FLANDERS, Steven (1977), *Case Management and Court Management in U.S. District Courts*. Washington, DC: Federal Judicial Center.
FLEMMING, Roy B., Peter F. NARDULLI, and James EISENSTEIN (1987), "The Timing of Justice in Felony Trial Courts," 9 *Law and Policy* 179.
FRANK, John P. (1969), *American Law: The Case for Radical Reform*. New York: Macmillan.
FRIESEN, Ernest C., Jr., Edward C. GALLAS, and Nesta M. GALLAS (1971), *Managing the Courts*. Indianapolis: Bobbs-Merrill.
FRIESEN, Ernest C., Jr., Joseph JORDAN, and Alfred SULMONETTI (1978), *Arrest to Trial in Forty-five Days*. Los Angeles: Whittier College School of Law.
FRIESEN, Ernest C., Jr. (1984), "Cures for Court Congestion," 23 *Judges Journal* 4.
GALLAS, Geoff (1987), "Judicial Leadership Excellence: A Research Prospectus," 12 *Justice System Journal* 39.
GOERDT, John, and John MARTIN (1989), "The Impact of Drug Cases on Felony Case Processing," 13 *State Court Journal* (Fall 1989) (Forthcoming).
GILLESPIE, Robert W. (1977), *Judicial Productivity and Court Delay: An Exploratory Analysis of Federal District Courts*. Washington, DC: National Institute of Law Enforcement and Criminal Justice.
GROSSMAN, Joel, Herbert M. KERTZER, Kristin BUMILLER, and Stephen MCDOUGAL (1981), "Measuring the Pace of Litigation in Federal and State Trial Courts," 65 *Judicature* 86.
GUYNES, Randall, and Neal MILLER (1988), "Improving Court Productivity: Two New Jersey Experiments," 208 *NIJ Reports* 1.
HALL, Charles W., "Delay Frees Suspect in Murder Plot." (December 17, 1986) *Washington Post* A1.
KATZ, L.R., L.P. LITWIN, and R.H. BAMBERGER (1972), *Justice is the Crime: Pretrial Delay in Felony Cases*. Cleveland: Case Western Reserve University Press.
KERLINGER, Fred N., and Elazar J. PEDHAZUR (1973), *Multiple Regression in Behavioral Research*. New York: Holt, Rinehart and Winston.
KUBAN, Gerald B., Samuel D. CONTI, James G. GAINEY, David C. STEELMAN, and Douglas C. DODGE (1984), *New Jersey In-Court Personnel Survey*. Williamsburg, VA: National Center for State Courts.
LIPSCHER, Robert D. (1989), "Judiciary Response to the Drug Crisis: A Report of an Executive Symposium Involving Judicial Leaders of the Nation's Nine Most Populous States." 13 *State Court Journal* (Fall 1989) (Forthcoming).
LUSKIN, Mary Lee, and Robert C. LUSKIN (1987), "Case Processing Times in Three Courts," 9 *Law and Policy* 207.
(1986) "Why So Fast, Why So Slow?: Explaining Case Processing Time," 77 *The Journal of Criminal Law and Criminology* 190.

MAHONEY, Barry, Alexander AIKMAN, Pamela CASEY, Gene FLANGO, Geoff GALLAS, Thomas HENDERSON, Jeanne ITO, David STEELMAN, and David WELLER (1988), *Changing Times in Urban Trial Courts*. Williamsburg, VA: National Center for State Courts.

MAHONEY, Barry, and Dale Anne SIPES (1988), "Toward Better Management of Criminal Litigation," 72 *Judicature* 29.

MAHONEY, Barry, Larry L. SIPES, and Jeanne A. ITO (1985), *Implementing Delay Reduction and Delay Prevention Programs in Urban Trial Courts: Preliminary Findings From Current Research*. Williamsburg, VA: National Center for State Courts.

MAHONEY, Barry, and Larry SIPES (1985), "Zeroing in on Court Delay: The Powerful Tools of Times Standards and Management Information," *Court Management Journal* 8.

MARTIN, John A., and Elizabeth A. PRESCOTT (1981), *Appellate Court Delay: Structural Responses to the Problems of Volume and Delay*. Williamsburg, VA: National Center for State Courts.

MURRAY, Philip (1984), "Nine Steps to an Information System," 23 *Judges' Journal* 19.

MYERS, Robert D. (1984), "We Know What's in It for Judges, but What's in It for Lawyers?" 23 *Judges' Journal* 26.

NATIONAL ADVISORY COMMISSION ON CRIMINAL JUSTICE STANDARDS AND GOALS (1973), *The Courts*. Washington, DC: Government Printing Office.

NATIONAL CENTER FOR STATE COURTS, (1989), *State Court Caseload Statistics: Annual Report, 1987*. Williamsburg, VA: National Center for State Courts.

NEUBAUER, David W., Marcia J. LIPETZ, Mary Lee LUSKIN, and John Paul RYAN (1981), *Managing the Pace of Justice: An Evaluation of LEAA's Court Delay Reduction Programs*. Washington, DC: Government Printing Office.

(1983) "Improving the Analysis and Presentation of Case Processing Time Data," 74 *Journal of Criminal Law and Criminology* 1589.

NIMMER, Raymond (1976), "A Slightly Moveable Object: A Case Study in Judicial Reform in the Criminal Justice Process: The Omnibus Hearing," 48 *Denver Law Journal* 206.

NORUSIS, Marija (1986), *SPSS PC+ for Personal Computers*. Chicago, IL: SPSS Inc.

OTTO, STEVE (1985), "Court Delay: A Bibliography," *Court Management Journal* 20.

PETERS, Thomas, and Robert H. WATERMAN (1982), *In Search of Excellence*. New York: Harper & Row.

POUND, Roscoe (1906 lecture), "The Causes of Popular Dissatisfaction with the Administration of Justice," in (1979) *The Pound Conference: Perspectives on Justice in the Future*, A. Leo Levin and Russell R. Wheeler, eds. St. Paul, MN: West Publishing.

RESNICK, Judith (1984), "Managerial Judges and Court Delay: Unproven Assumptions," 23 *Judges' Journal* 8.

ROSENBERG, Maurice (1965), "Court Congestion: Status, Causes, and Proposed Remedies," in American Assembly, *The Courts, the Public and the Law Explosion*, Harry Jones, ed. Englewood Cliffs, NJ: Prentice Hall.

SARAT, Austin (1978), "Understanding Trial Courts: A Critique of Social Science Approaches," 61 *Judicature* 324.

SAYLES, Leonard (1979), *Leadership: What Effective Managers Do and How They Do It*. New York: McGraw-Hill.

SCHWARTZ, Howard, and Robert BROOMFIELD (1984), "Delay: How Kansas and Phoenix Are Making It Disappear," 23 *Judges' Journal* 22.

SELZNICK, Philip (1957), *Leadership in Administration*. Evanston, IL: Row-Peterson.

SOLOMON, Maureen (1973), *Caseflow Management in the Trial Court*. Chicago, IL: American Bar Association.

SOLOMON, Maureen, and Douglas SOMERLOT (1987), *Caseflow Management in the Trial Court: Now and for the Future*. Chicago, IL: American Bar Association.

SOLOMON, Maureen, and Barry MAHONEY (1989), *Caseflow Management Improvement in Wayne County Circuit Court*. Williamsburg, VA: National Center for State Courts (unpublished report).

U.S. Bureau of the Census (1988), *County and City Data Book, 1988*. Washington, DC: U.S. Government Printing Office.

WELLER, Steven, John A. MARTIN, and J. RUHNKA (1982), "American Experiments for Reducing Civil Trial Costs and Delays," 1 *Civil Justice Quarterly* 151.

YANKELOVICH, SKELLY and WHITE, INC. (1978), *The Public Image of Courts: Highlights of a National Survey of the General Public, Judges, Lawyers and Community Leaders*. Williamsburg, VA: National Center for State Courts

ZAFFARANO, Mark (1985), "Understanding Leadership in State Trial Courts: A Review Essay," 10 *Justice System Journal* 229.

ZEISEL, Hans, Harry KALVEN, and Bernard BUCHHOLZ (1959), *Delay in the Court*. Boston: Little, Brown.